X-MEN
FIRST CLASS

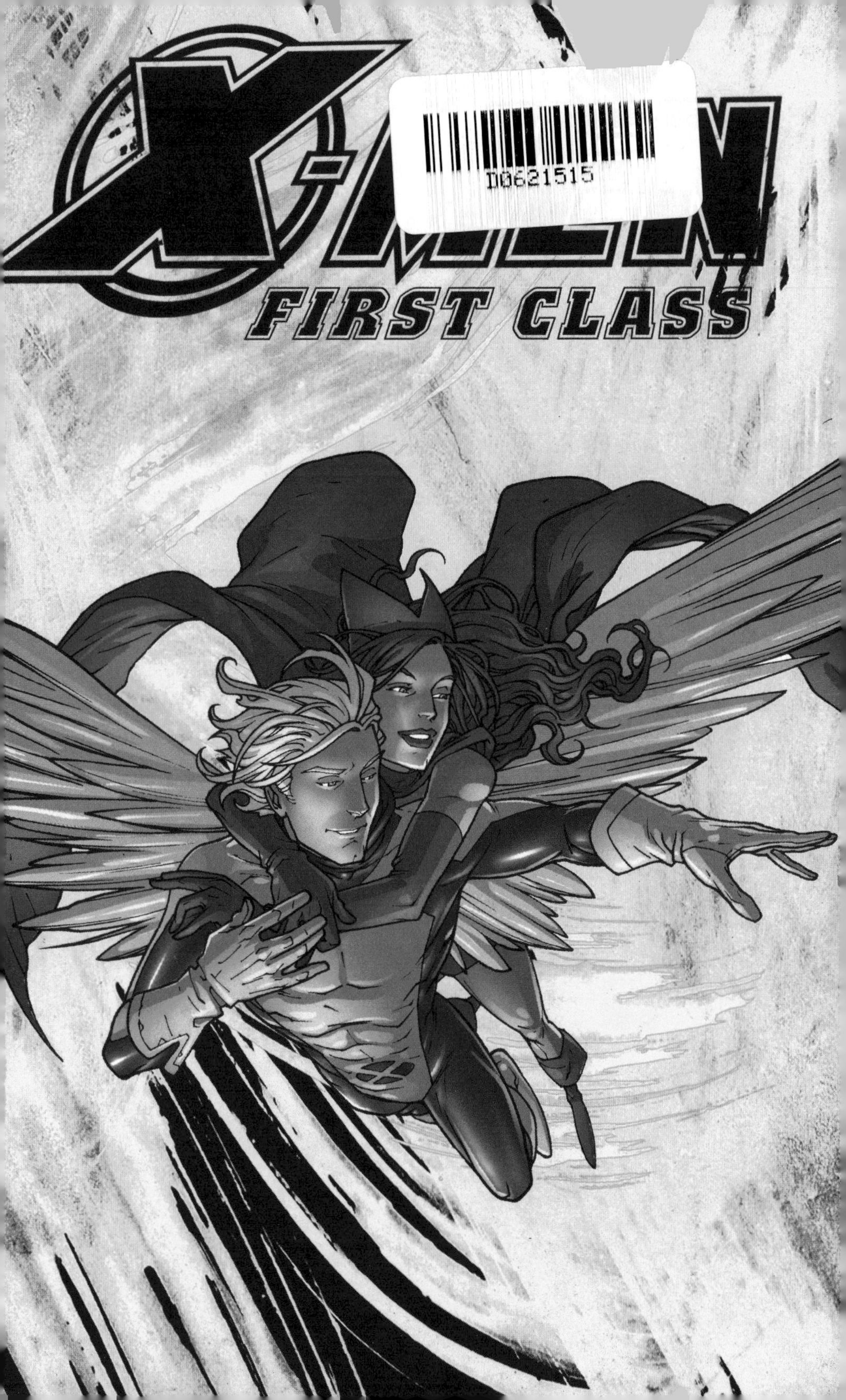

X-MEN FIRST CLASS

Writer: **JEFF PARKER**
Penciler: **ROGER CRUZ**
Inkers: **VICTOR OLAZABA** & **ROGER CRUZ**
Colorist: **VAL STAPLES**
Letterer: **BLAMBOT'S NATE PIEKOS**

"The Museum of Oddities" from *X-Men: First Class Special*
Writer: **JEFF PARKER**
Artist & Letterer: **KEVIN NOWLAN**

Cover Artists: **MARKO DJURDJEVIC** & **KEVIN NOWLAN**
Assistant Editor: **NATHAN COSBY**
Editor: **MARK PANICCIA**

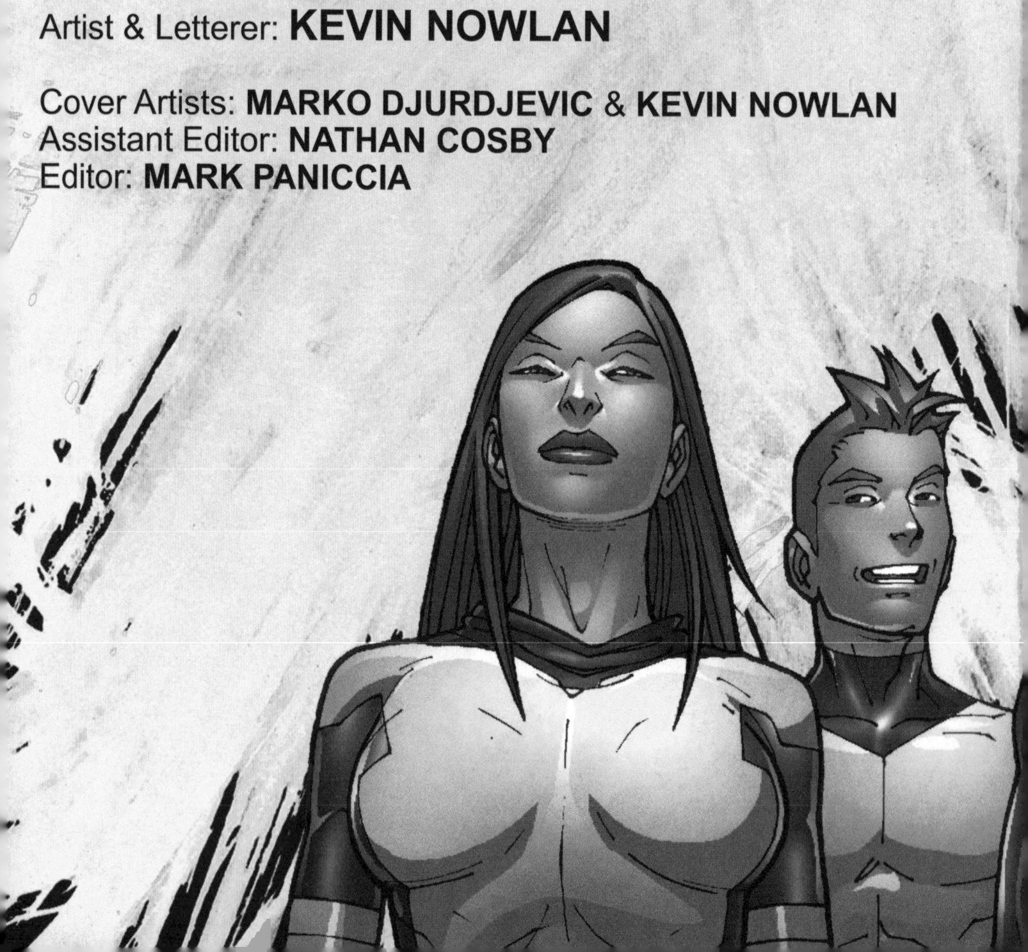

Collection Editor & Design: **CORY LEVINE**
Editorial Assistants: **JAMES EMMETT** & **JOE HOCHSTEIN**
Assistant Editors: **MATT MASDEU**, **ALEX STARBUCK** & **NELSON RIBEIRO**
Editors, Special Projects: **JENNIFER GRÜNWALD** & **MARK D. BEAZLEY**
Senior Editor, Special Projects: **JEFF YOUNGQUIST**
Senior Vice President of Sales: **DAVID GABRIEL**

Editor In Chief: **AXEL ALONSO**
Chief Creative Officer: **JOE QUESADA**
Publisher: **DAN BUCKLEY**
Executive Producer: **ALAN FINE**

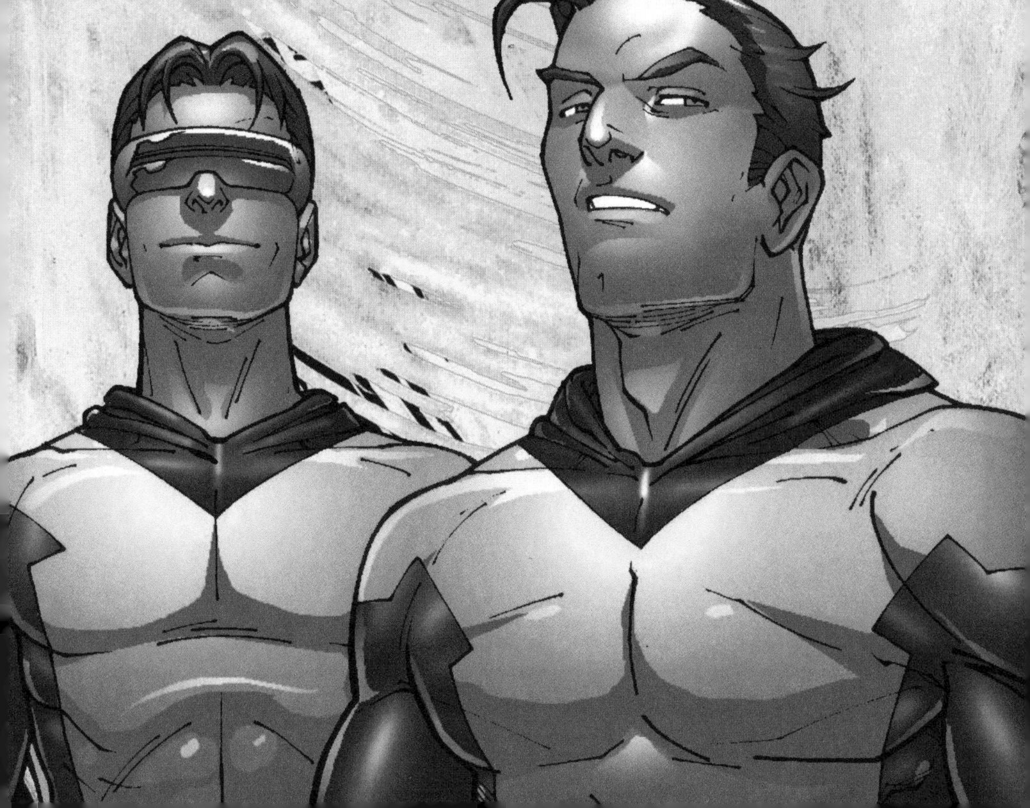

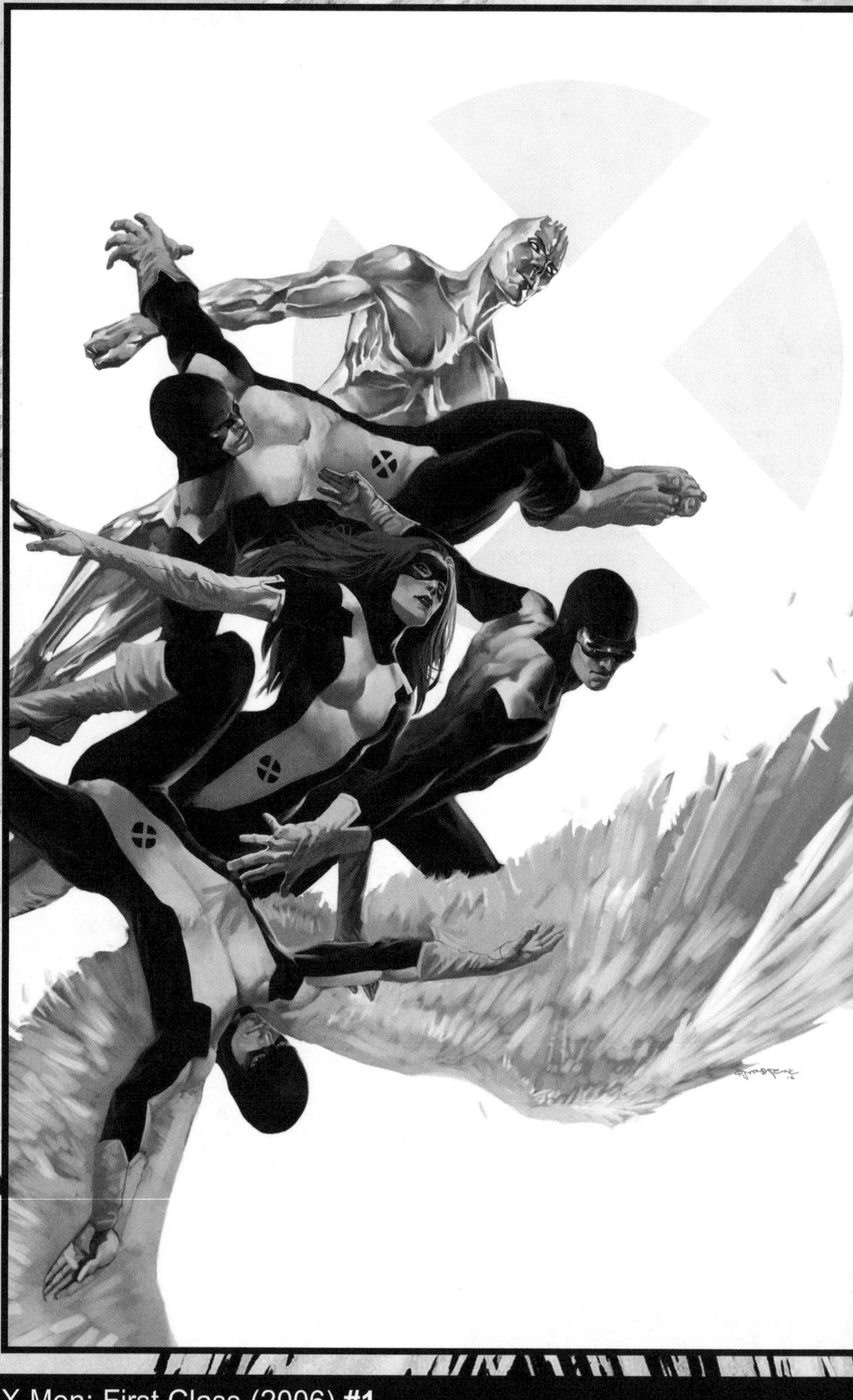

X-Men: First Class (2006) **#1**

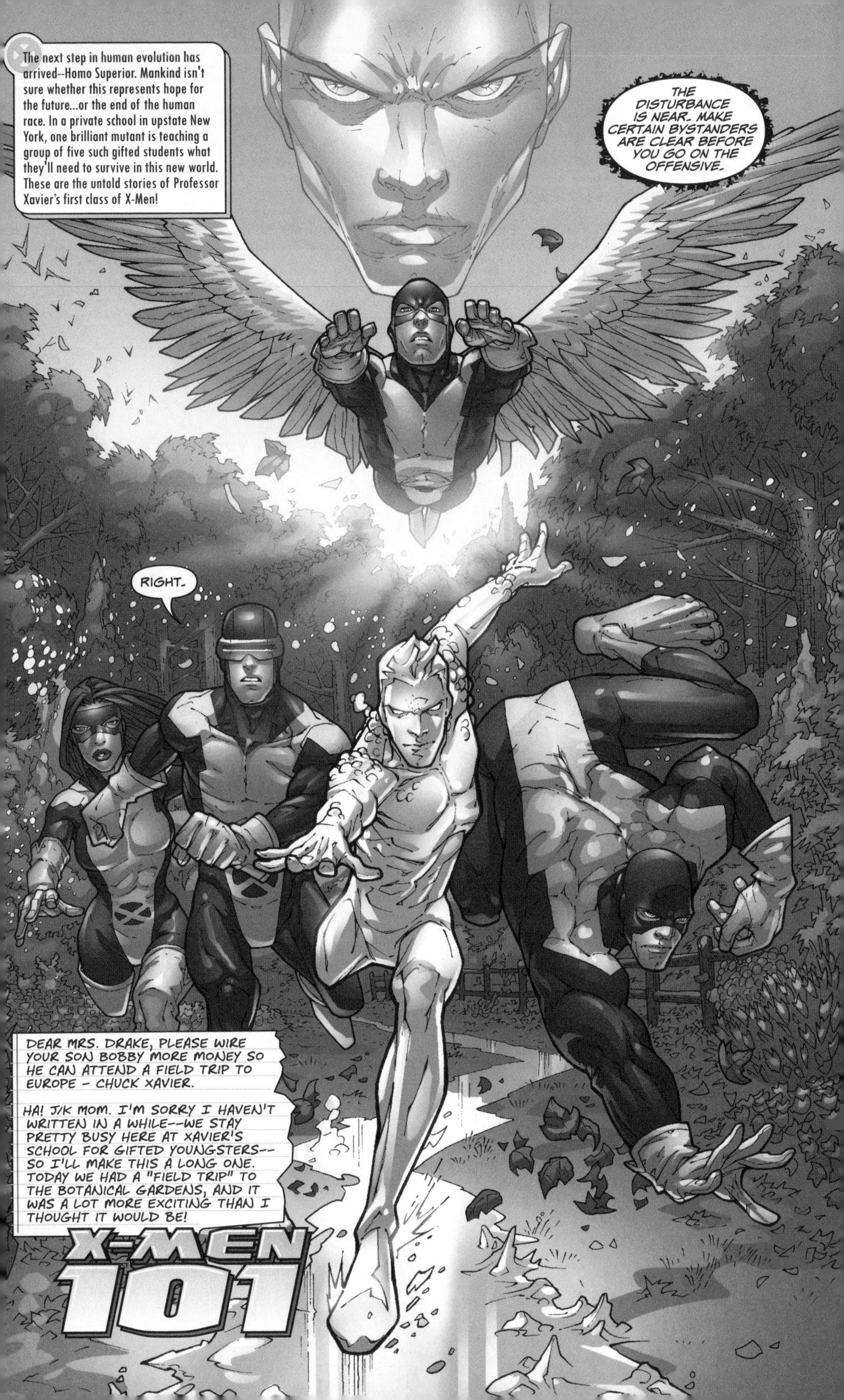

The next step in human evolution has arrived--Homo Superior. Mankind isn't sure whether this represents hope for the future...or the end of the human race. In a private school in upstate New York, one brilliant mutant is teaching a group of five such gifted students what they'll need to survive in this new world. These are the untold stories of Professor Xavier's first class of X-Men!
THE DISTURBANCE IS NEAR. MAKE CERTAIN BYSTANDERS ARE CLEAR BEFORE YOU GO ON THE OFFENSIVE.
RIGHT.
DEAR MRS. DRAKE, PLEASE WIRE YOUR SON BOBBY MORE MONEY SO HE CAN ATTEND A FIELD TRIP TO EUROPE - CHUCK XAVIER.
HA! J/K MOM. I'M SORRY I HAVEN'T WRITTEN IN A WHILE--WE STAY PRETTY BUSY HERE AT XAVIER'S SCHOOL FOR GIFTED YOUNGSTERS--SO I'LL MAKE THIS A LONG ONE. TODAY WE HAD A "FIELD TRIP" TO THE BOTANICAL GARDENS, AND IT WAS A LOT MORE EXCITING THAN I THOUGHT IT WOULD BE!
X-MEN 101

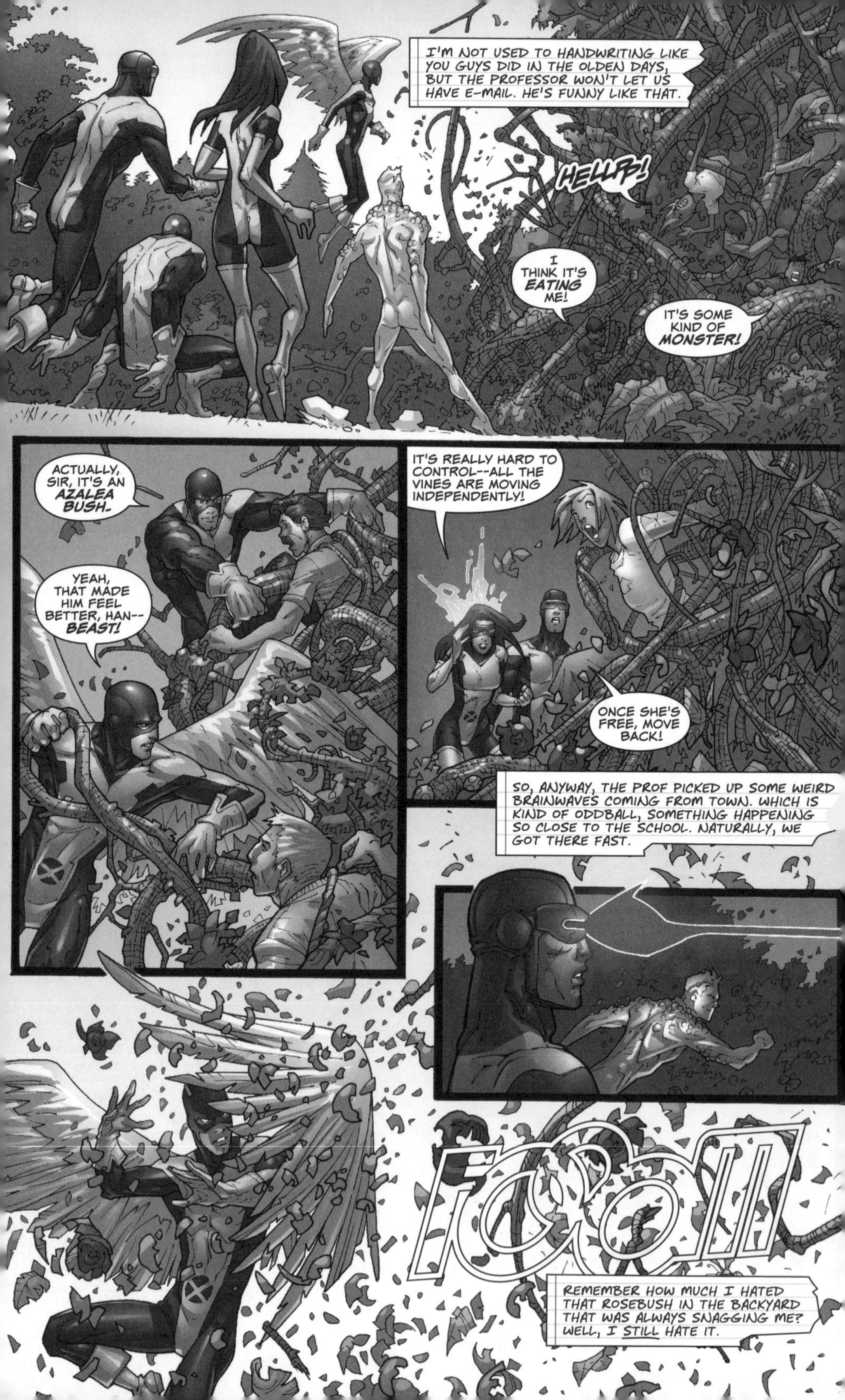
I'M NOT USED TO HANDWRITING LIKE YOU GUYS DID IN THE OLDEN DAYS, BUT THE PROFESSOR WON'T LET US HAVE E-MAIL. HE'S FUNNY LIKE THAT.
HELLLP!
I THINK IT'S EATING ME!
IT'S SOME KIND OF MONSTER!
ACTUALLY, SIR, IT'S AN AZALEA BUSH.
YEAH, THAT MADE HIM FEEL BETTER, HAN-- BEAST!
IT'S REALLY HARD TO CONTROL--ALL THE VINES ARE MOVING INDEPENDENTLY!
ONCE SHE'S FREE, MOVE BACK!
SO, ANYWAY, THE PROF PICKED UP SOME WEIRD BRAINWAVES COMING FROM TOWN. WHICH IS KIND OF ODDBALL, SOMETHING HAPPENING SO CLOSE TO THE SCHOOL. NATURALLY, WE GOT THERE FAST.
REMEMBER HOW MUCH I HATED THAT ROSEBUSH IN THE BACKYARD THAT WAS ALWAYS SNAGGING ME? WELL, I STILL HATE IT.

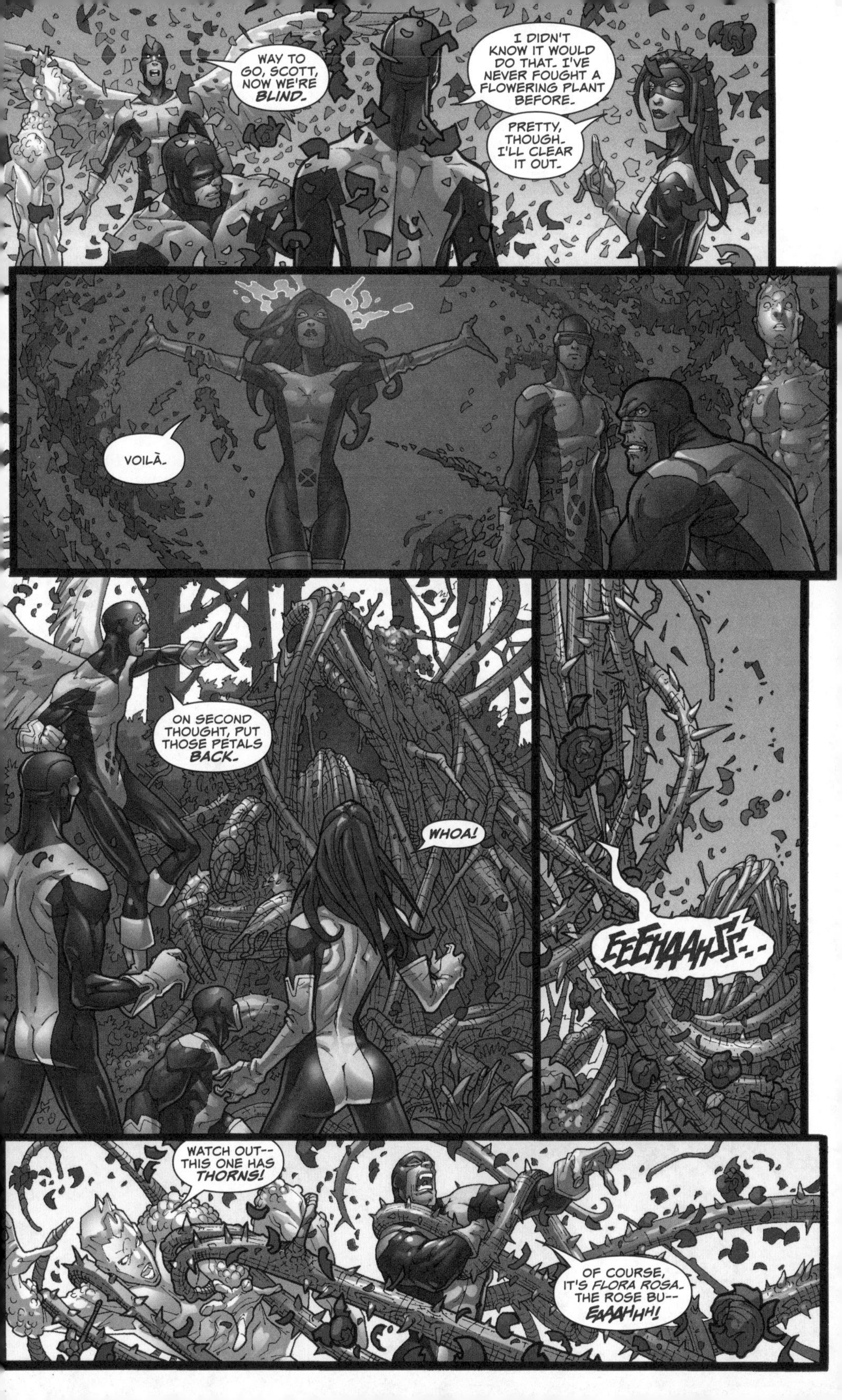
WAY TO GO, SCOTT, NOW WE'RE BLIND.
I DIDN'T KNOW IT WOULD DO THAT. I'VE NEVER FOUGHT A FLOWERING PLANT BEFORE.
PRETTY, THOUGH. I'LL CLEAR IT OUT.
VOILÀ.
ON SECOND THOUGHT, PUT THOSE PETALS BACK.
WHOA!
EEEHAAAHSS...
WATCH OUT-- THIS ONE HAS THORNS!
OF COURSE, IT'S FLORA ROSA. THE ROSE BU-- EAAAHHH!

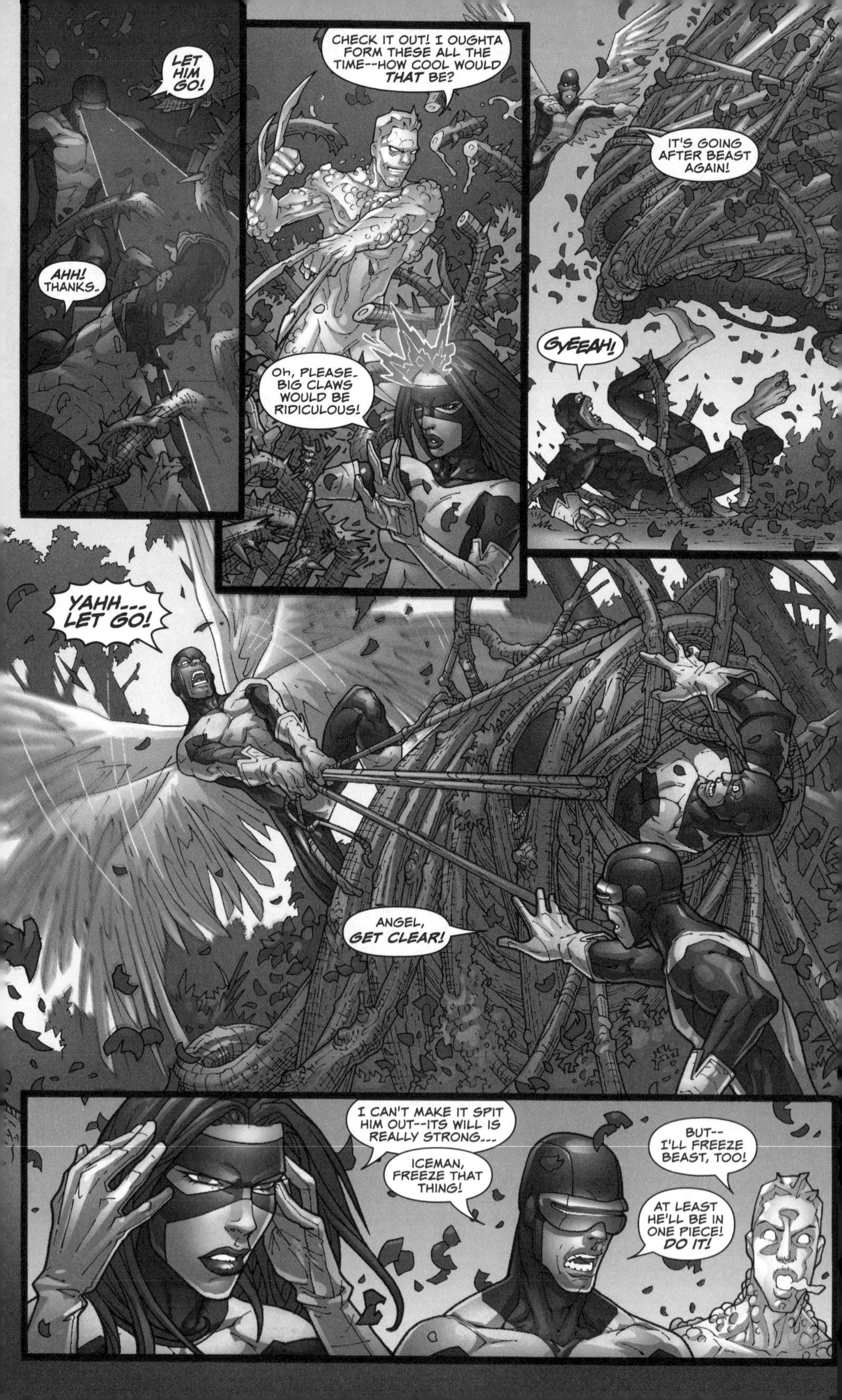
LET HIM GO!
AHH! THANKS.
CHECK IT OUT! I OUGHTA FORM THESE ALL THE TIME--HOW COOL WOULD THAT BE?
Oh, PLEASE. BIG CLAWS WOULD BE RIDICULOUS!
IT'S GOING AFTER BEAST AGAIN!
GYEEAH!
YAHH... LET GO!
ANGEL, GET CLEAR!
I CAN'T MAKE IT SPIT HIM OUT--ITS WILL IS REALLY STRONG...
ICEMAN, FREEZE THAT THING!
BUT-- I'LL FREEZE BEAST, TOO!
AT LEAST HE'LL BE IN ONE PIECE! DO IT!

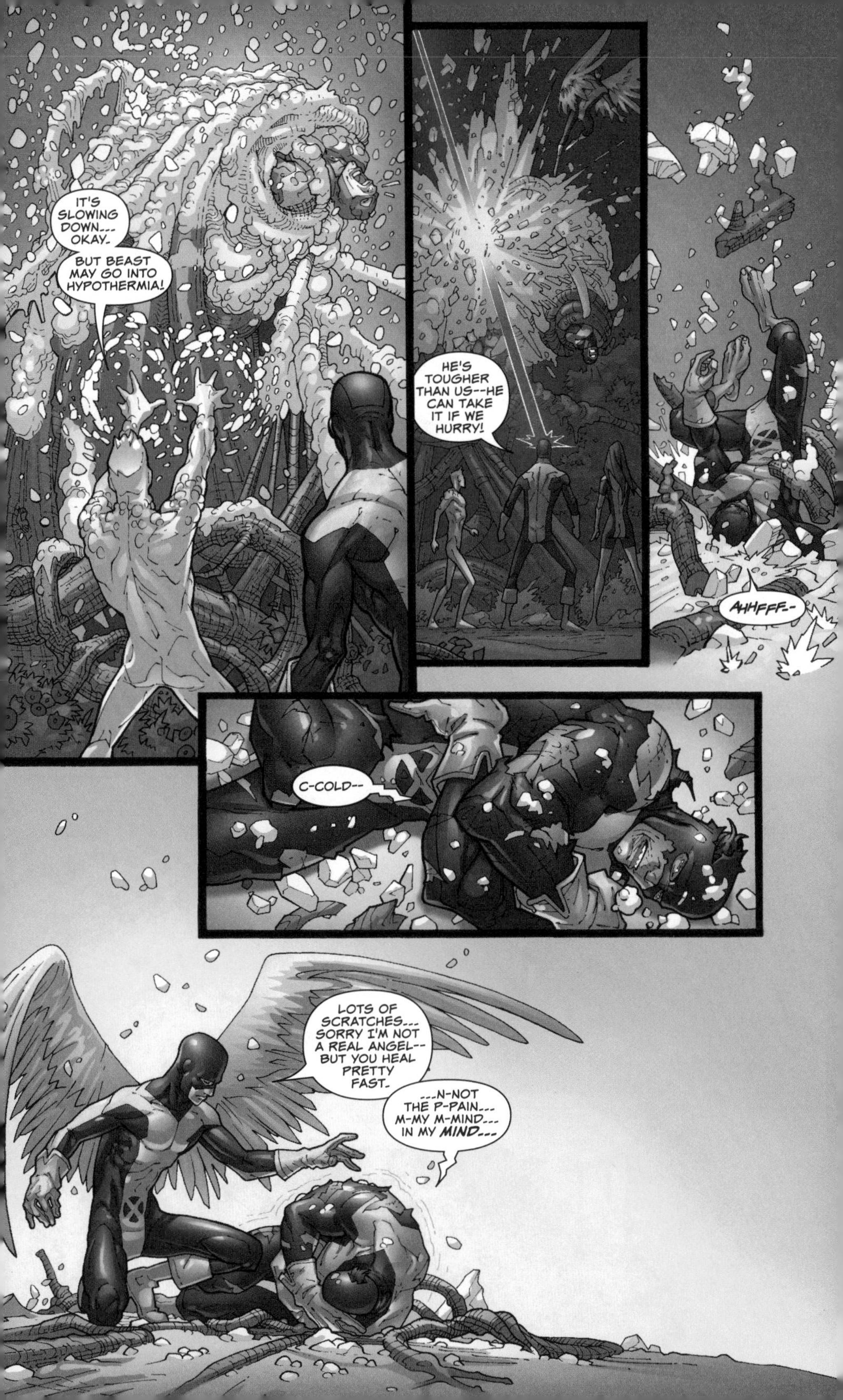
IT'S SLOWING DOWN... OKAY.
BUT BEAST MAY GO INTO HYPOTHERMIA!
HE'S TOUGHER THAN US--HE CAN TAKE IT IF WE HURRY!
AHHFFF--
C-COLD--
LOTS OF SCRATCHES... SORRY I'M NOT A REAL ANGEL--BUT YOU HEAL PRETTY FAST.
...N-NOT THE P-PAIN... M-MY M-MIND... IN MY MIND...

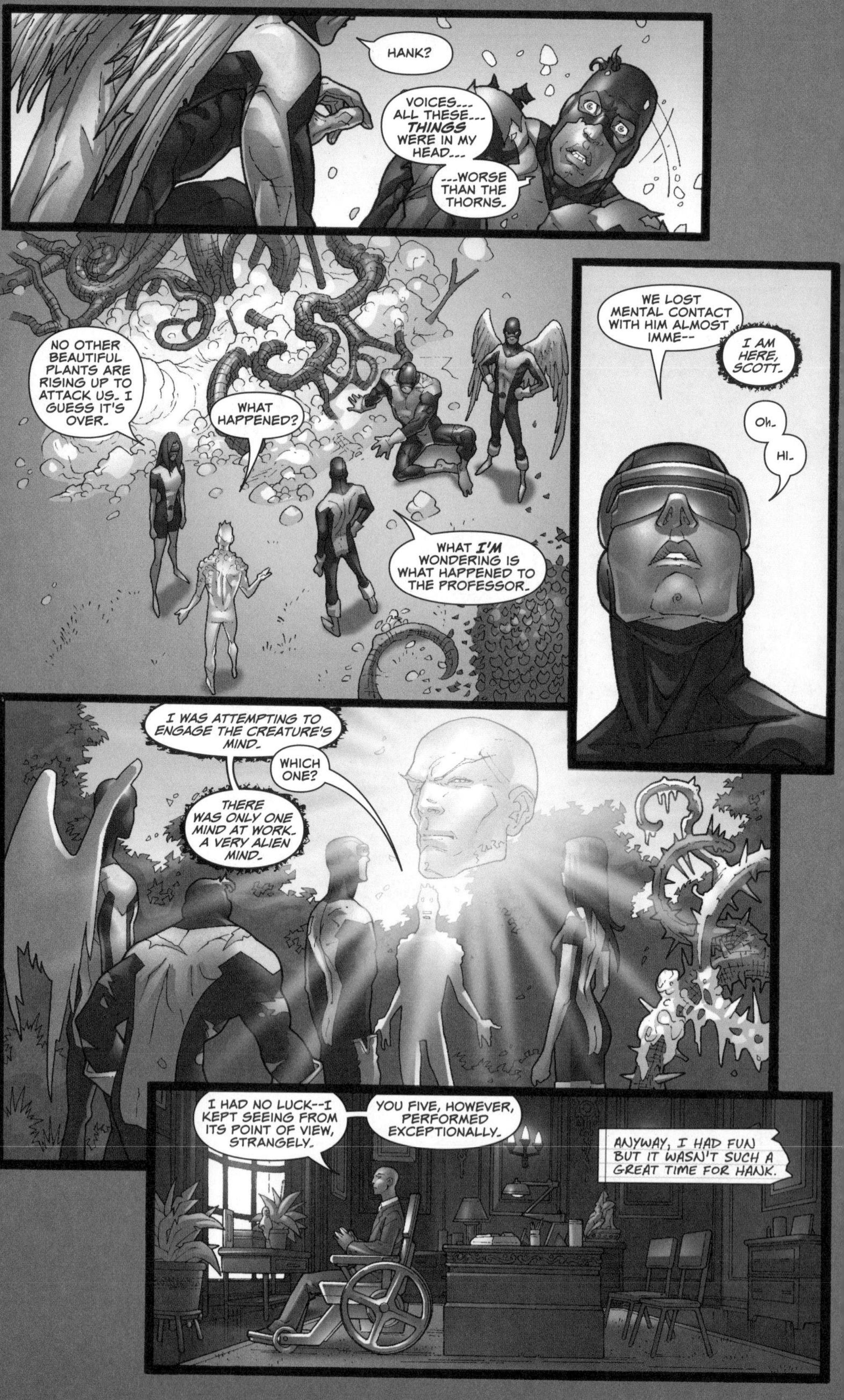
HANK?
VOICES... ALL THESE... THINGS WERE IN MY HEAD...
...WORSE THAN THE THORNS.
NO OTHER BEAUTIFUL PLANTS ARE RISING UP TO ATTACK US. I GUESS IT'S OVER.
WHAT HAPPENED?
WHAT I'M WONDERING IS WHAT HAPPENED TO THE PROFESSOR.
WE LOST MENTAL CONTACT WITH HIM ALMOST IMME--
I AM HERE, SCOTT.
Oh.
Hi.
I WAS ATTEMPTING TO ENGAGE THE CREATURE'S MIND.
WHICH ONE?
THERE WAS ONLY ONE MIND AT WORK. A VERY ALIEN MIND.
I HAD NO LUCK--I KEPT SEEING FROM ITS POINT OF VIEW, STRANGELY.
YOU FIVE, HOWEVER, PERFORMED EXCEPTIONALLY.
ANYWAY, I HAD FUN BUT IT WASN'T SUCH A GREAT TIME FOR HANK.

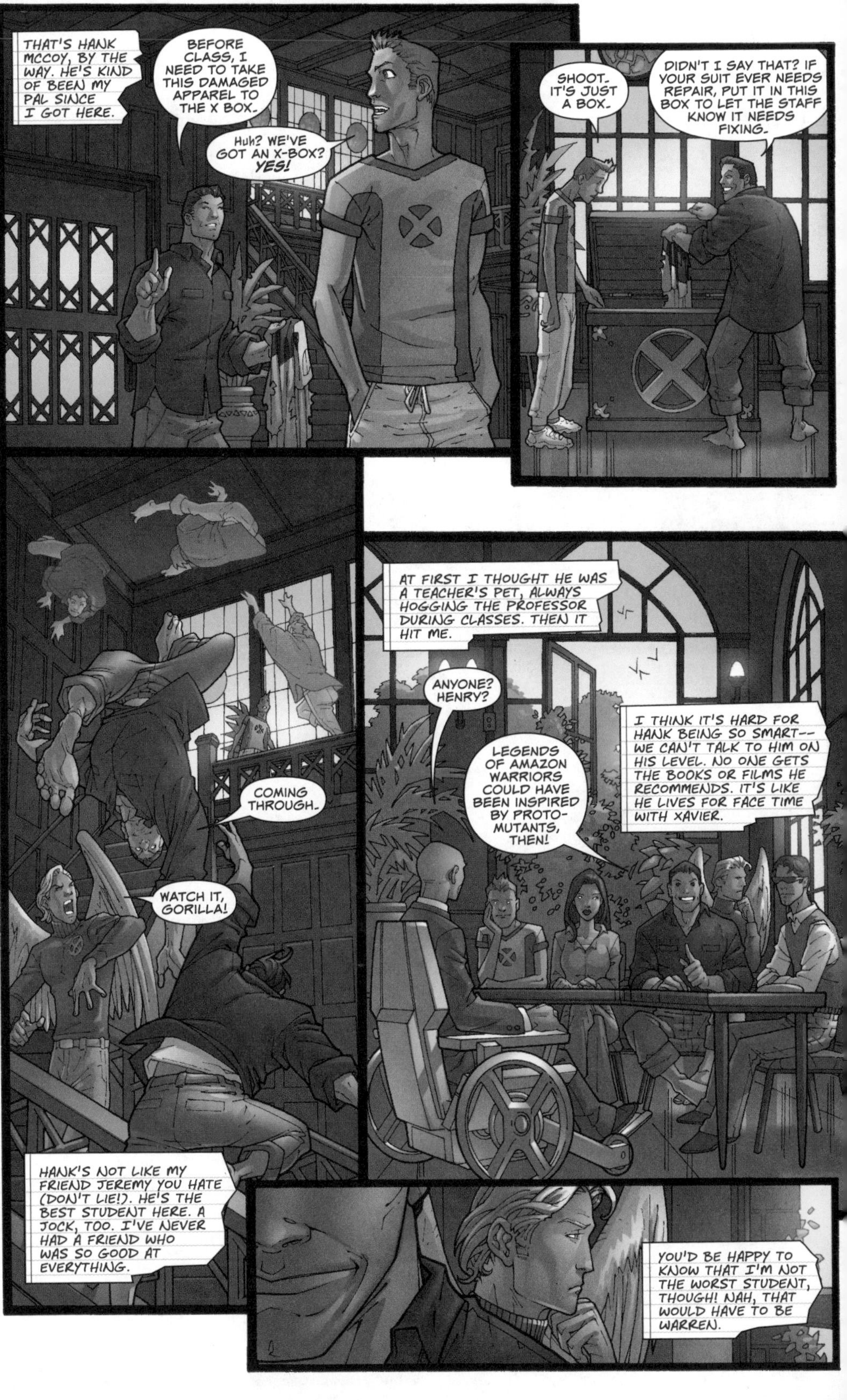
THAT'S HANK McCOY, BY THE WAY. HE'S KIND OF BEEN MY PAL SINCE I GOT HERE.
BEFORE CLASS, I NEED TO TAKE THIS DAMAGED APPAREL TO THE X BOX.
Huh? WE'VE GOT AN X-BOX? YES!
SHOOT. IT'S JUST A BOX.
DIDN'T I SAY THAT? IF YOUR SUIT EVER NEEDS REPAIR, PUT IT IN THIS BOX TO LET THE STAFF KNOW IT NEEDS FIXING.
COMING THROUGH.
WATCH IT, GORILLA!
HANK'S NOT LIKE MY FRIEND JEREMY YOU HATE (DON'T LIE!). HE'S THE BEST STUDENT HERE. A JOCK, TOO. I'VE NEVER HAD A FRIEND WHO WAS SO GOOD AT EVERYTHING.
AT FIRST I THOUGHT HE WAS A TEACHER'S PET, ALWAYS HOGGING THE PROFESSOR DURING CLASSES. THEN IT HIT ME.
ANYONE? HENRY?
LEGENDS OF AMAZON WARRIORS COULD HAVE BEEN INSPIRED BY PROTO-MUTANTS, THEN!
I THINK IT'S HARD FOR HANK BEING SO SMART-- WE CAN'T TALK TO HIM ON HIS LEVEL. NO ONE GETS THE BOOKS OR FILMS HE RECOMMENDS. IT'S LIKE HE LIVES FOR FACE TIME WITH XAVIER.
YOU'D BE HAPPY TO KNOW THAT I'M NOT THE WORST STUDENT, THOUGH! NAH, THAT WOULD HAVE TO BE WARREN.

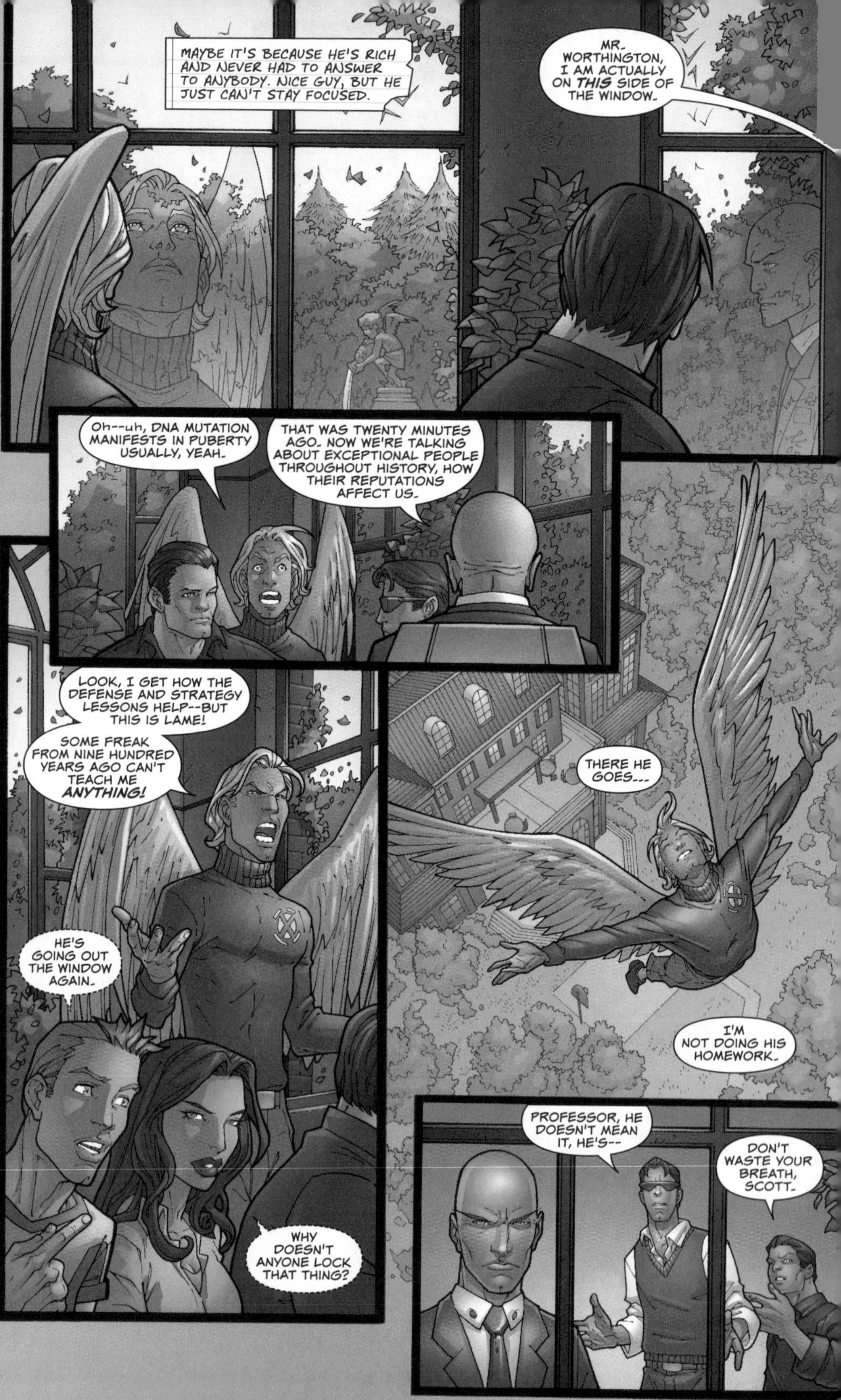
MAYBE IT'S BECAUSE HE'S RICH AND NEVER HAD TO ANSWER TO ANYBODY. NICE GUY, BUT HE JUST CAN'T STAY FOCUSED.
MR. WORTHINGTON, I AM ACTUALLY ON *THIS* SIDE OF THE WINDOW.
Oh--uh, DNA MUTATION MANIFESTS IN PUBERTY USUALLY, YEAH.
THAT WAS TWENTY MINUTES AGO. NOW WE'RE TALKING ABOUT EXCEPTIONAL PEOPLE THROUGHOUT HISTORY, HOW THEIR REPUTATIONS AFFECT US.
LOOK, I GET HOW THE DEFENSE AND STRATEGY LESSONS HELP--BUT THIS IS LAME!
SOME FREAK FROM NINE HUNDRED YEARS AGO CAN'T TEACH ME *ANYTHING!*
HE'S GOING OUT THE WINDOW AGAIN.
WHY DOESN'T ANYONE LOCK THAT THING?
THERE HE GOES...
I'M NOT DOING HIS HOMEWORK.
PROFESSOR, HE DOESN'T MEAN IT, HE'S--
DON'T WASTE YOUR BREATH, SCOTT.

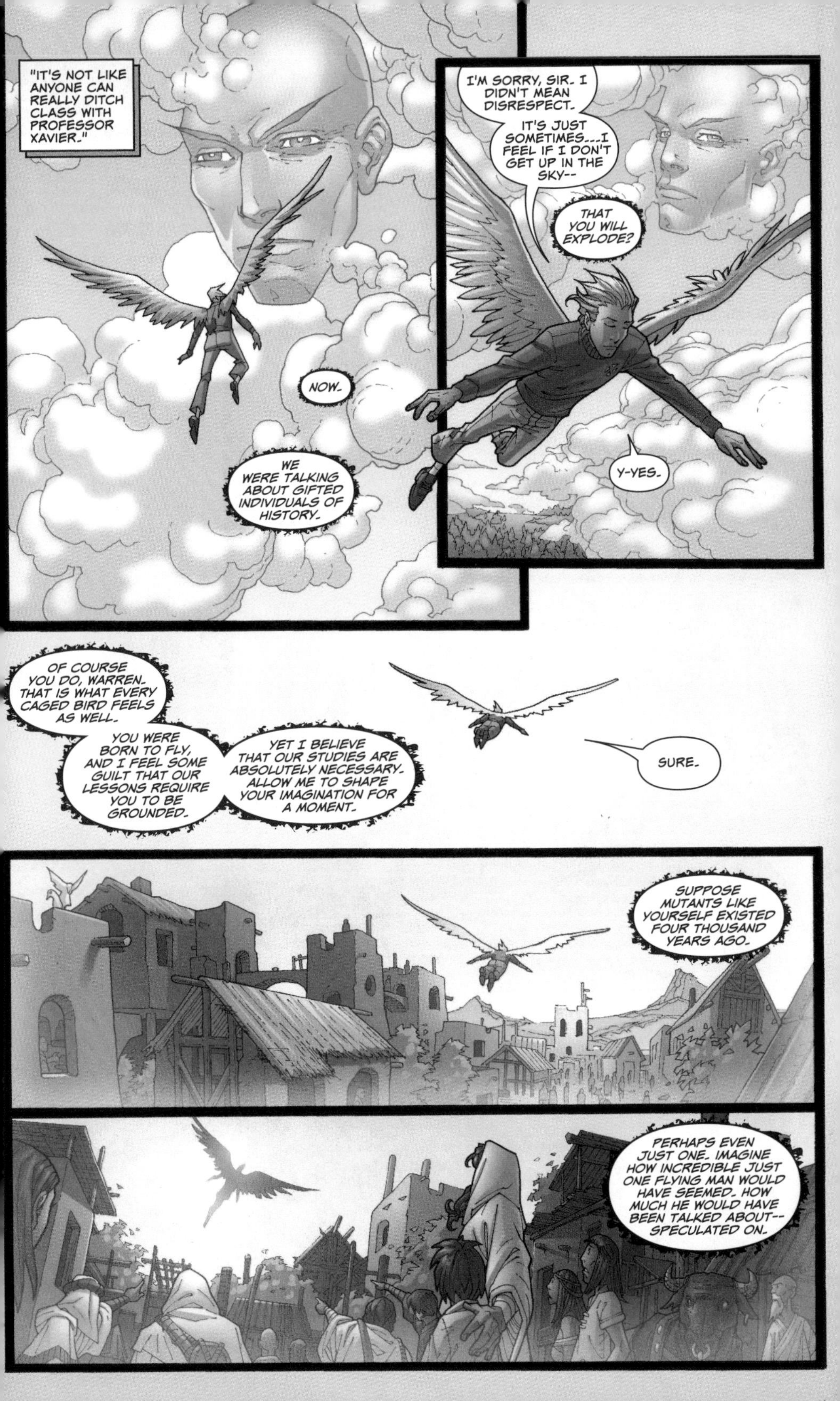
"IT'S NOT LIKE ANYONE CAN REALLY DITCH CLASS WITH PROFESSOR XAVIER."
NOW.
WE WERE TALKING ABOUT GIFTED INDIVIDUALS OF HISTORY.
I'M SORRY, SIR. I DIDN'T MEAN DISRESPECT.
IT'S JUST SOMETIMES... I FEEL IF I DON'T GET UP IN THE SKY--
THAT YOU WILL EXPLODE?
Y-YES.
OF COURSE YOU DO, WARREN. THAT IS WHAT EVERY CAGED BIRD FEELS AS WELL.
YOU WERE BORN TO FLY, AND I FEEL SOME GUILT THAT OUR LESSONS REQUIRE YOU TO BE GROUNDED.
YET I BELIEVE THAT OUR STUDIES ARE ABSOLUTELY NECESSARY. ALLOW ME TO SHAPE YOUR IMAGINATION FOR A MOMENT.
SURE.
SUPPOSE MUTANTS LIKE YOURSELF EXISTED FOUR THOUSAND YEARS AGO.
PERHAPS EVEN JUST ONE. IMAGINE HOW INCREDIBLE JUST ONE FLYING MAN WOULD HAVE SEEMED. HOW MUCH HE WOULD HAVE BEEN TALKED ABOUT-- SPECULATED ON.

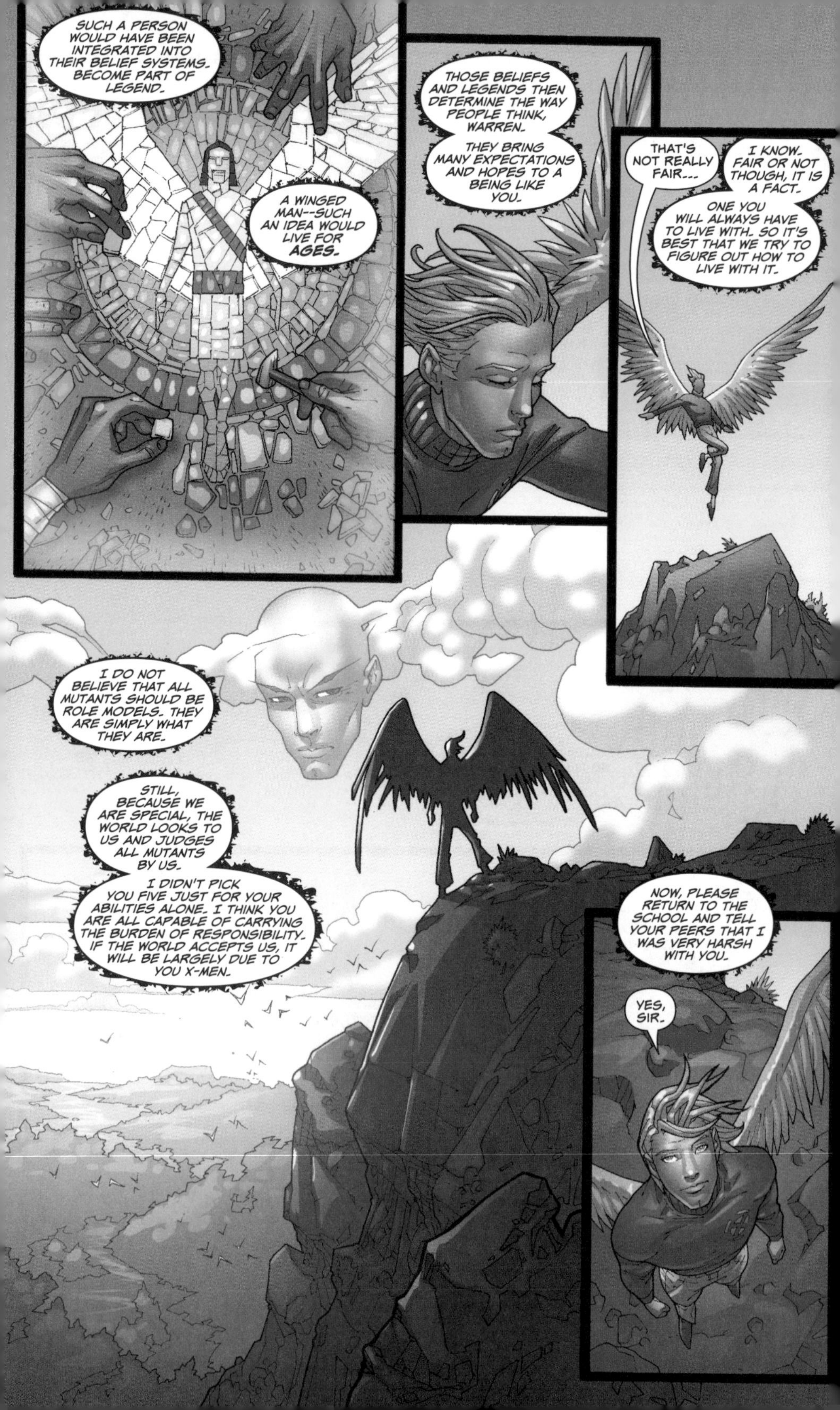

SUCH A PERSON WOULD HAVE BEEN INTEGRATED INTO THEIR BELIEF SYSTEMS. BECOME PART OF LEGEND.
A WINGED MAN--SUCH AN IDEA WOULD LIVE FOR AGES.
THOSE BELIEFS AND LEGENDS THEN DETERMINE THE WAY PEOPLE THINK, WARREN.
THEY BRING MANY EXPECTATIONS AND HOPES TO A BEING LIKE YOU.
THAT'S NOT REALLY FAIR...
I KNOW. FAIR OR NOT THOUGH, IT IS A FACT.
ONE YOU WILL ALWAYS HAVE TO LIVE WITH. SO IT'S BEST THAT WE TRY TO FIGURE OUT HOW TO LIVE WITH IT.
I DO NOT BELIEVE THAT ALL MUTANTS SHOULD BE ROLE MODELS. THEY ARE SIMPLY WHAT THEY ARE.
STILL, BECAUSE WE ARE SPECIAL, THE WORLD LOOKS TO US AND JUDGES ALL MUTANTS BY US.
I DIDN'T PICK YOU FIVE JUST FOR YOUR ABILITIES ALONE. I THINK YOU ARE ALL CAPABLE OF CARRYING THE BURDEN OF RESPONSIBILITY. IF THE WORLD ACCEPTS US, IT WILL BE LARGELY DUE TO YOU X-MEN.
NOW, PLEASE RETURN TO THE SCHOOL AND TELL YOUR PEERS THAT I WAS VERY HARSH WITH YOU.
YES, SIR.

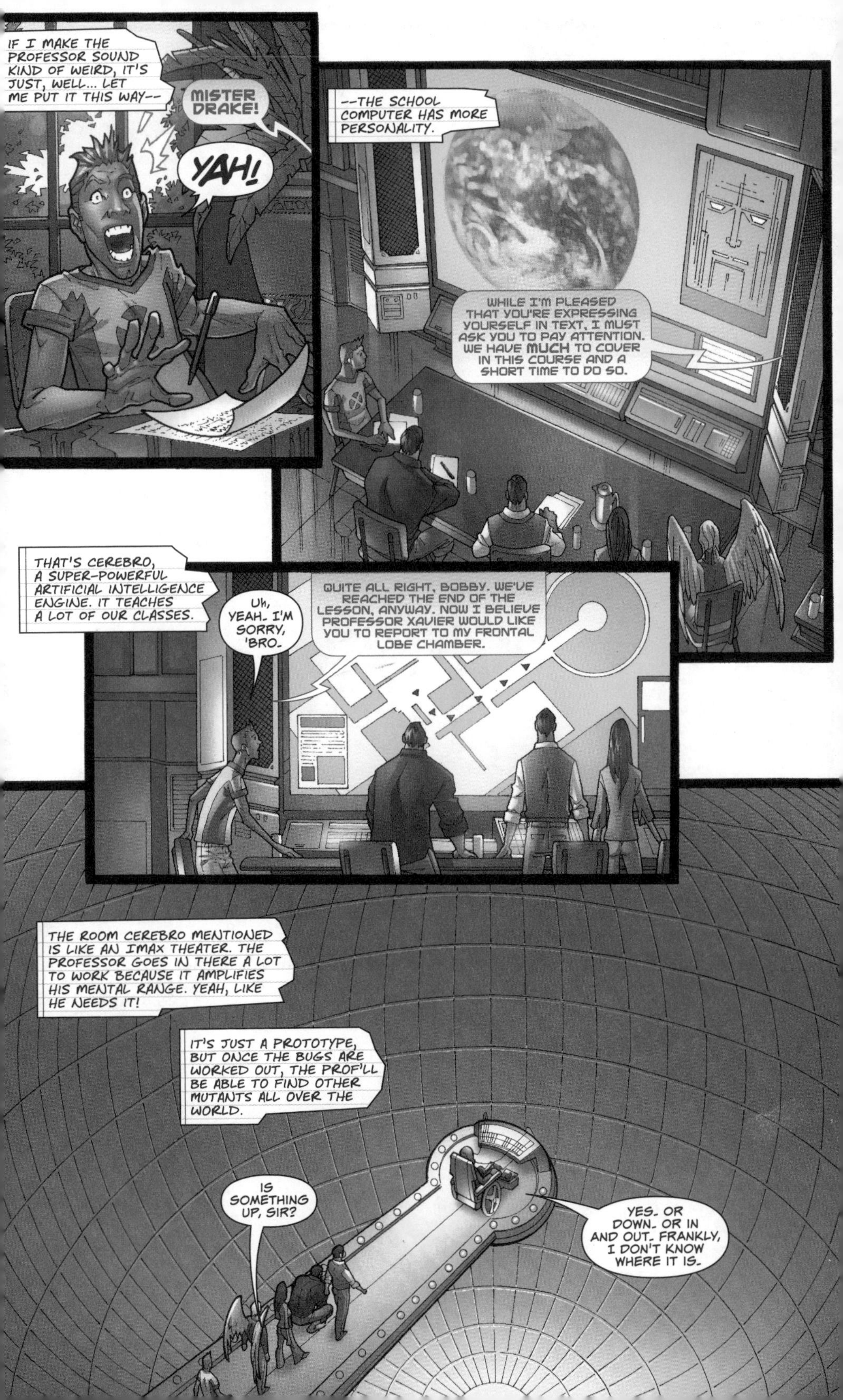
IF I MAKE THE PROFESSOR SOUND KIND OF WEIRD, IT'S JUST, WELL... LET ME PUT IT THIS WAY--
MISTER DRAKE!
YAH!
--THE SCHOOL COMPUTER HAS MORE PERSONALITY.
WHILE I'M PLEASED THAT YOU'RE EXPRESSING YOURSELF IN TEXT, I MUST ASK YOU TO PAY ATTENTION. WE HAVE MUCH TO COVER IN THIS COURSE AND A SHORT TIME TO DO SO.
THAT'S CEREBRO, A SUPER-POWERFUL ARTIFICIAL INTELLIGENCE ENGINE. IT TEACHES A LOT OF OUR CLASSES.
Uh, YEAH. I'M SORRY, 'BRO.
QUITE ALL RIGHT, BOBBY. WE'VE REACHED THE END OF THE LESSON, ANYWAY. NOW I BELIEVE PROFESSOR XAVIER WOULD LIKE YOU TO REPORT TO MY FRONTAL LOBE CHAMBER.
THE ROOM CEREBRO MENTIONED IS LIKE AN IMAX THEATER. THE PROFESSOR GOES IN THERE A LOT TO WORK BECAUSE IT AMPLIFIES HIS MENTAL RANGE. YEAH, LIKE HE NEEDS IT!
IT'S JUST A PROTOTYPE, BUT ONCE THE BUGS ARE WORKED OUT, THE PROF'LL BE ABLE TO FIND OTHER MUTANTS ALL OVER THE WORLD.
IS SOMETHING UP, SIR?
YES. OR DOWN. OR IN AND OUT. FRANKLY, I DON'T KNOW WHERE IT IS.

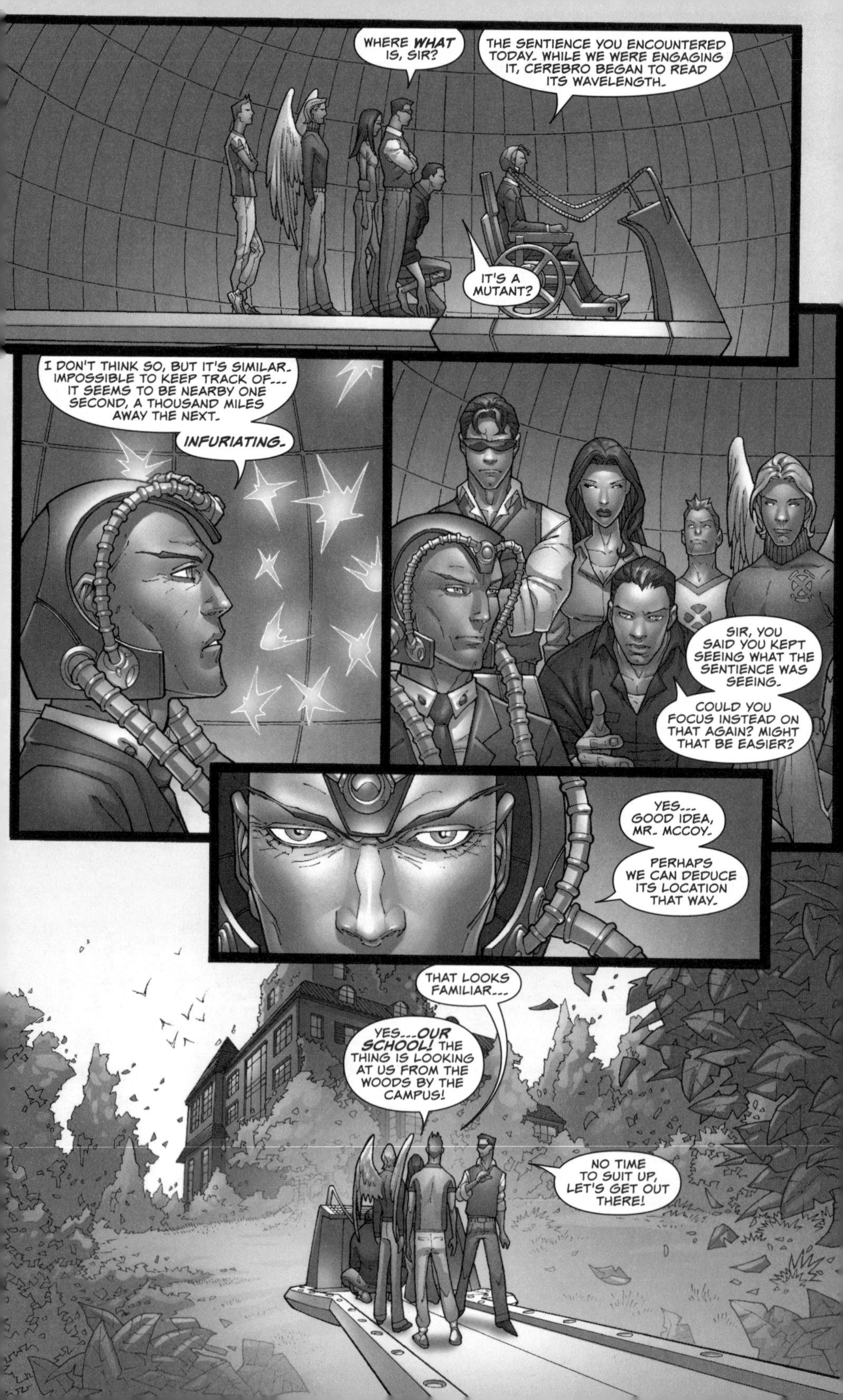
WHERE WHAT IS, SIR?
THE SENTIENCE YOU ENCOUNTERED TODAY. WHILE WE WERE ENGAGING IT, CEREBRO BEGAN TO READ ITS WAVELENGTH.
IT'S A MUTANT?
I DON'T THINK SO, BUT IT'S SIMILAR. IMPOSSIBLE TO KEEP TRACK OF--- IT SEEMS TO BE NEARBY ONE SECOND, A THOUSAND MILES AWAY THE NEXT.
INFURIATING.
SIR, YOU SAID YOU KEPT SEEING WHAT THE SENTIENCE WAS SEEING.
COULD YOU FOCUS INSTEAD ON THAT AGAIN? MIGHT THAT BE EASIER?
YES... GOOD IDEA, MR. MCCOY.
PERHAPS WE CAN DEDUCE ITS LOCATION THAT WAY.
THAT LOOKS FAMILIAR...
YES...OUR SCHOOL! THE THING IS LOOKING AT US FROM THE WOODS BY THE CAMPUS!
NO TIME TO SUIT UP, LET'S GET OUT THERE!

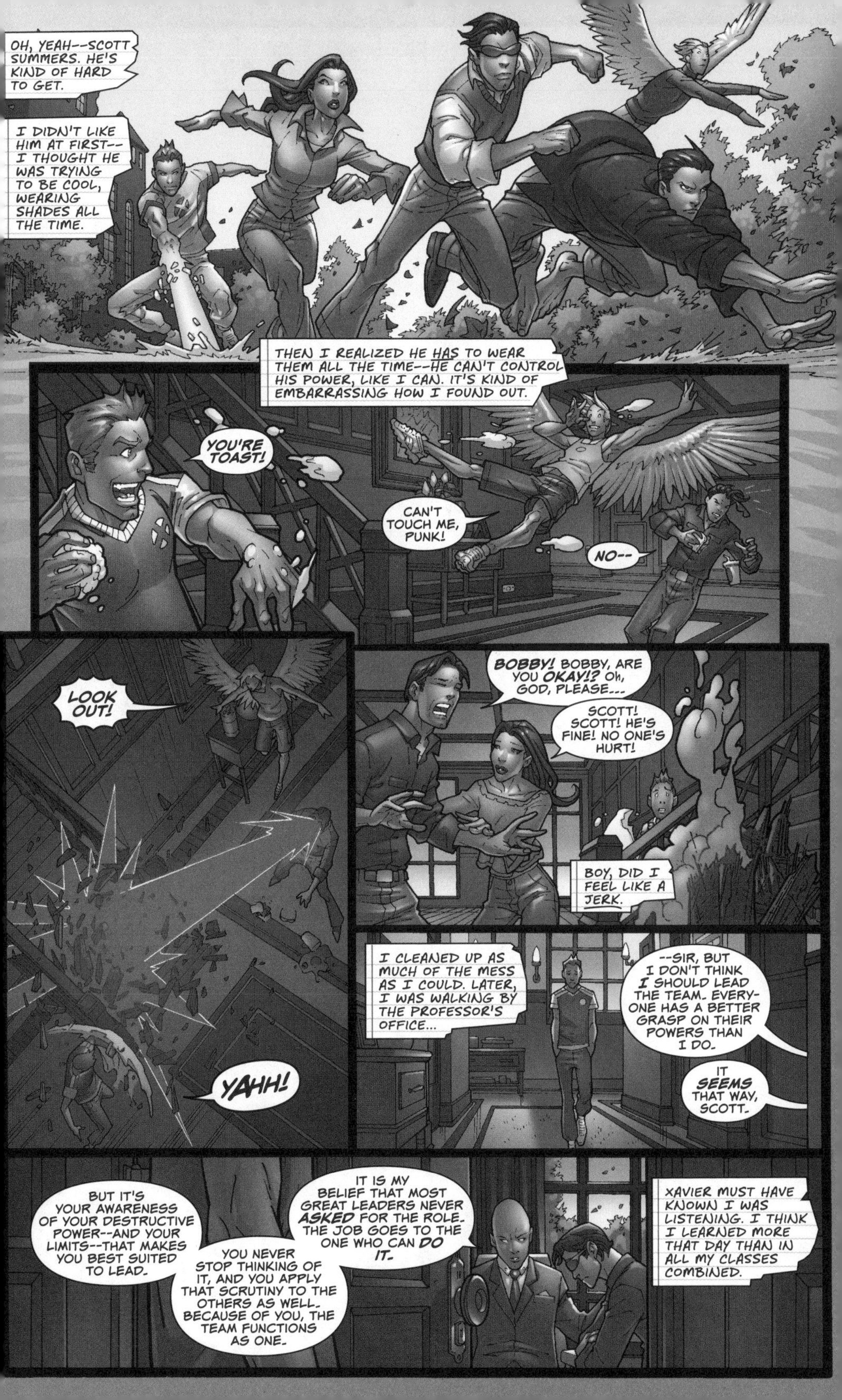

OH, YEAH--SCOTT SUMMERS. HE'S KIND OF HARD TO GET.
I DIDN'T LIKE HIM AT FIRST-- I THOUGHT HE WAS TRYING TO BE COOL, WEARING SHADES ALL THE TIME.
THEN I REALIZED HE HAS TO WEAR THEM ALL THE TIME--HE CAN'T CONTROL HIS POWER, LIKE I CAN. IT'S KIND OF EMBARRASSING HOW I FOUND OUT.
YOU'RE TOAST!
CAN'T TOUCH ME, PUNK!
NO--
LOOK OUT!
YAHH!
BOBBY! BOBBY, ARE YOU OKAY!? Oh, GOD, PLEASE...
SCOTT! SCOTT! HE'S FINE! NO ONE'S HURT!
BOY, DID I FEEL LIKE A JERK.
I CLEANED UP AS MUCH OF THE MESS AS I COULD. LATER, I WAS WALKING BY THE PROFESSOR'S OFFICE...
--SIR, BUT I DON'T THINK I SHOULD LEAD THE TEAM. EVERYONE HAS A BETTER GRASP ON THEIR POWERS THAN I DO.
IT SEEMS THAT WAY, SCOTT.
BUT IT'S YOUR AWARENESS OF YOUR DESTRUCTIVE POWER--AND YOUR LIMITS--THAT MAKES YOU BEST SUITED TO LEAD.
YOU NEVER STOP THINKING OF IT, AND YOU APPLY THAT SCRUTINY TO THE OTHERS AS WELL. BECAUSE OF YOU, THE TEAM FUNCTIONS AS ONE.
IT IS MY BELIEF THAT MOST GREAT LEADERS NEVER ASKED FOR THE ROLE. THE JOB GOES TO THE ONE WHO CAN DO IT.
XAVIER MUST HAVE KNOWN I WAS LISTENING. I THINK I LEARNED MORE THAT DAY THAN IN ALL MY CLASSES COMBINED.

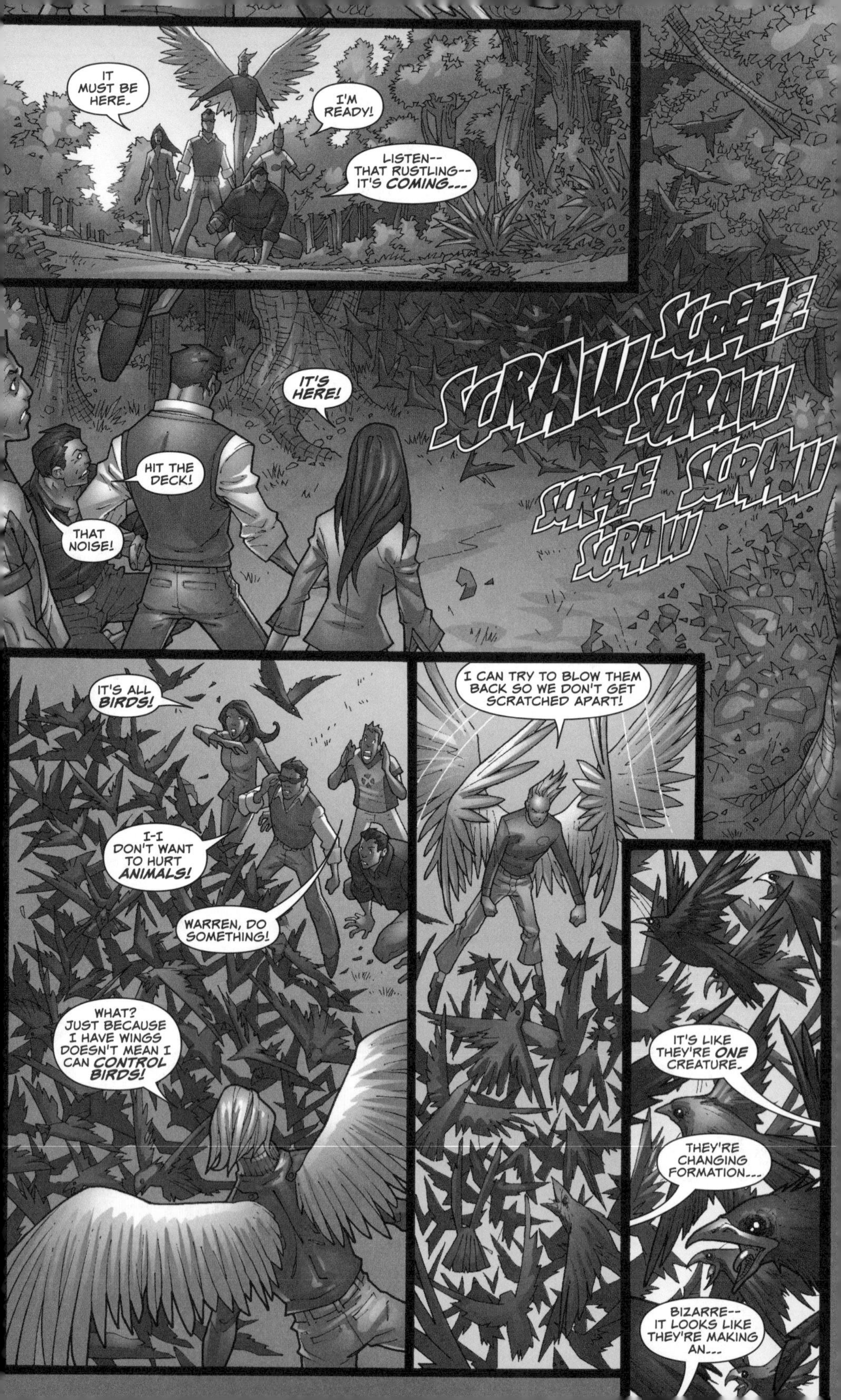

IT MUST BE HERE.
I'M READY!
LISTEN-- THAT RUSTLING-- IT'S COMING...
IT'S HERE!
SCRAW SCREEE SCRAW
SCREEE SCRAW SCRAW
HIT THE DECK!
THAT NOISE!
IT'S ALL BIRDS!
I-I DON'T WANT TO HURT ANIMALS!
WARREN, DO SOMETHING!
WHAT? JUST BECAUSE I HAVE WINGS DOESN'T MEAN I CAN CONTROL BIRDS!
I CAN TRY TO BLOW THEM BACK SO WE DON'T GET SCRATCHED APART!
IT'S LIKE THEY'RE ONE CREATURE.
THEY'RE CHANGING FORMATION...
BIZARRE-- IT LOOKS LIKE THEY'RE MAKING AN...

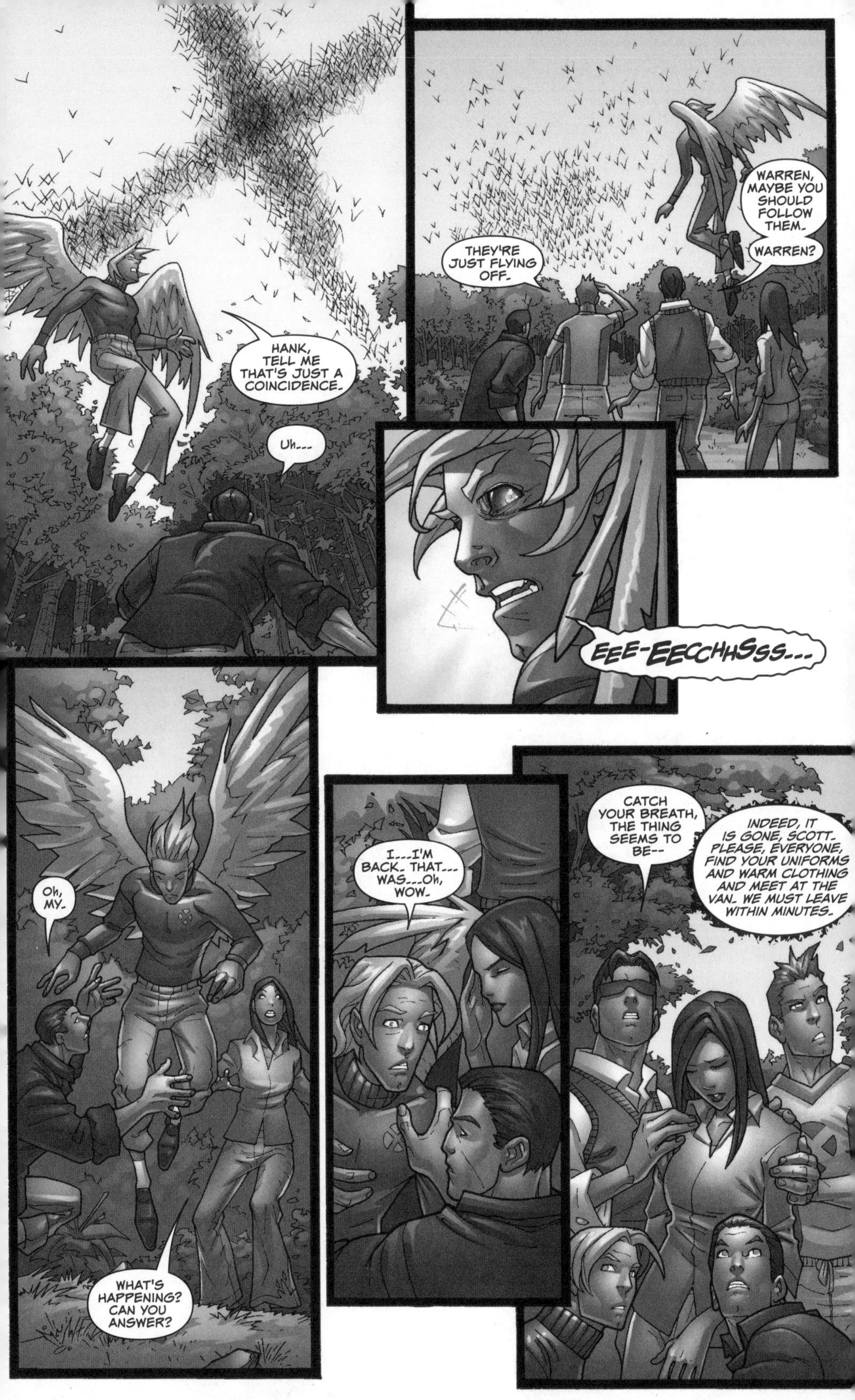
HANK, TELL ME THAT'S JUST A COINCIDENCE.
Uh...
THEY'RE JUST FLYING OFF.
WARREN, MAYBE YOU SHOULD FOLLOW THEM.
WARREN?
EEE-EECCHHSSS...
Oh, MY.
WHAT'S HAPPENING? CAN YOU ANSWER?
I...I'M BACK. THAT... WAS...Oh, WOW.
CATCH YOUR BREATH, THE THING SEEMS TO BE--
INDEED, IT IS GONE, SCOTT. PLEASE, EVERYONE, FIND YOUR UNIFORMS AND WARM CLOTHING AND MEET AT THE VAN. WE MUST LEAVE WITHIN MINUTES.

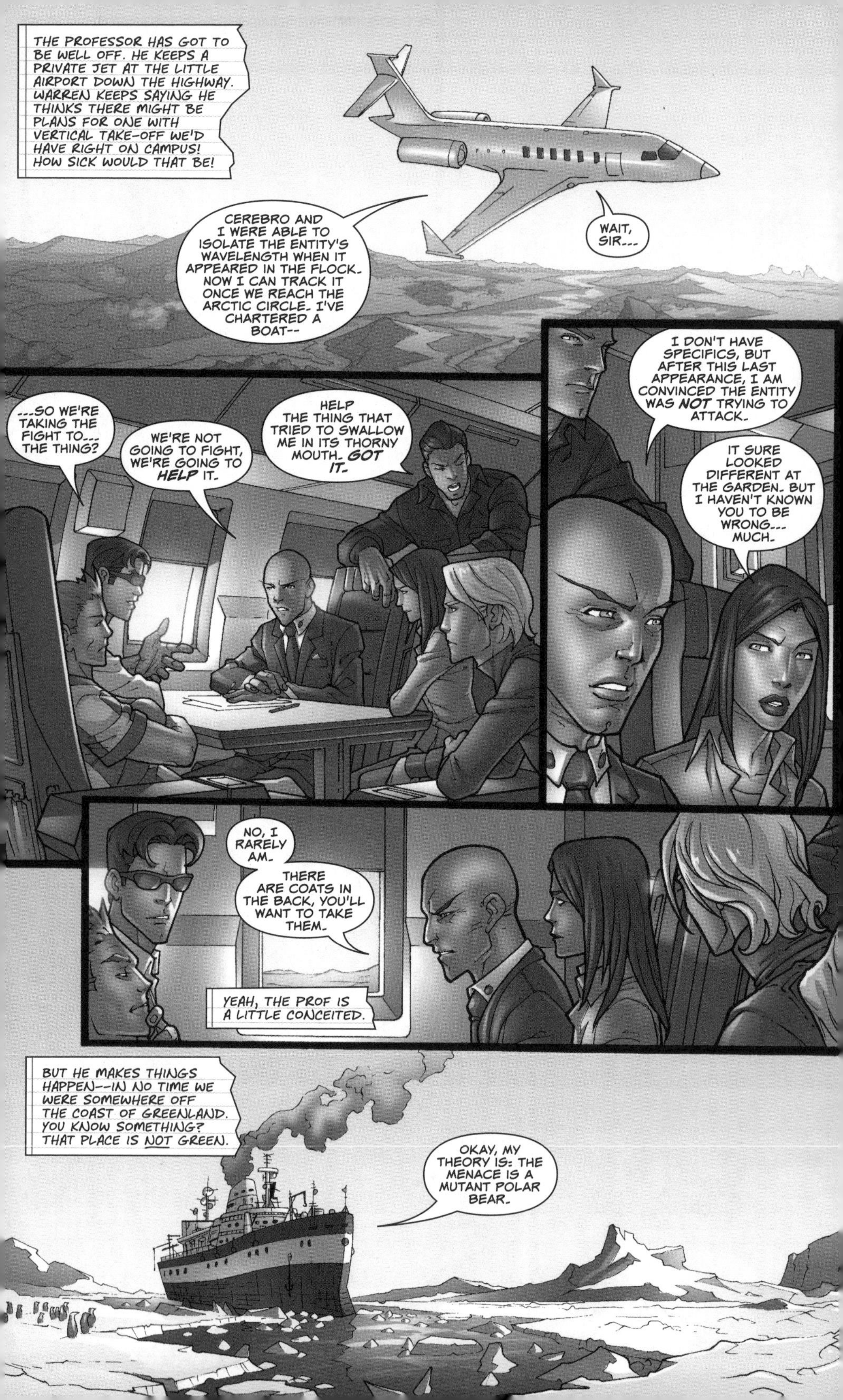
THE PROFESSOR HAS GOT TO BE WELL OFF. HE KEEPS A PRIVATE JET AT THE LITTLE AIRPORT DOWN THE HIGHWAY. WARREN KEEPS SAYING HE THINKS THERE MIGHT BE PLANS FOR ONE WITH VERTICAL TAKE-OFF WE'D HAVE RIGHT ON CAMPUS! HOW SICK WOULD THAT BE!
CEREBRO AND I WERE ABLE TO ISOLATE THE ENTITY'S WAVELENGTH WHEN IT APPEARED IN THE FLOCK. NOW I CAN TRACK IT ONCE WE REACH THE ARCTIC CIRCLE. I'VE CHARTERED A BOAT--
WAIT, SIR...
...SO WE'RE TAKING THE FIGHT TO... THE THING?
WE'RE NOT GOING TO FIGHT, WE'RE GOING TO HELP IT.
HELP THE THING THAT TRIED TO SWALLOW ME IN ITS THORNY MOUTH. GOT IT.
I DON'T HAVE SPECIFICS, BUT AFTER THIS LAST APPEARANCE, I AM CONVINCED THE ENTITY WAS NOT TRYING TO ATTACK.
IT SURE LOOKED DIFFERENT AT THE GARDEN. BUT I HAVEN'T KNOWN YOU TO BE WRONG... MUCH.
NO, I RARELY AM.
THERE ARE COATS IN THE BACK, YOU'LL WANT TO TAKE THEM.
YEAH, THE PROF IS A LITTLE CONCEITED.
BUT HE MAKES THINGS HAPPEN--IN NO TIME WE WERE SOMEWHERE OFF THE COAST OF GREENLAND. YOU KNOW SOMETHING? THAT PLACE IS NOT GREEN.
OKAY, MY THEORY IS: THE MENACE IS A MUTANT POLAR BEAR.

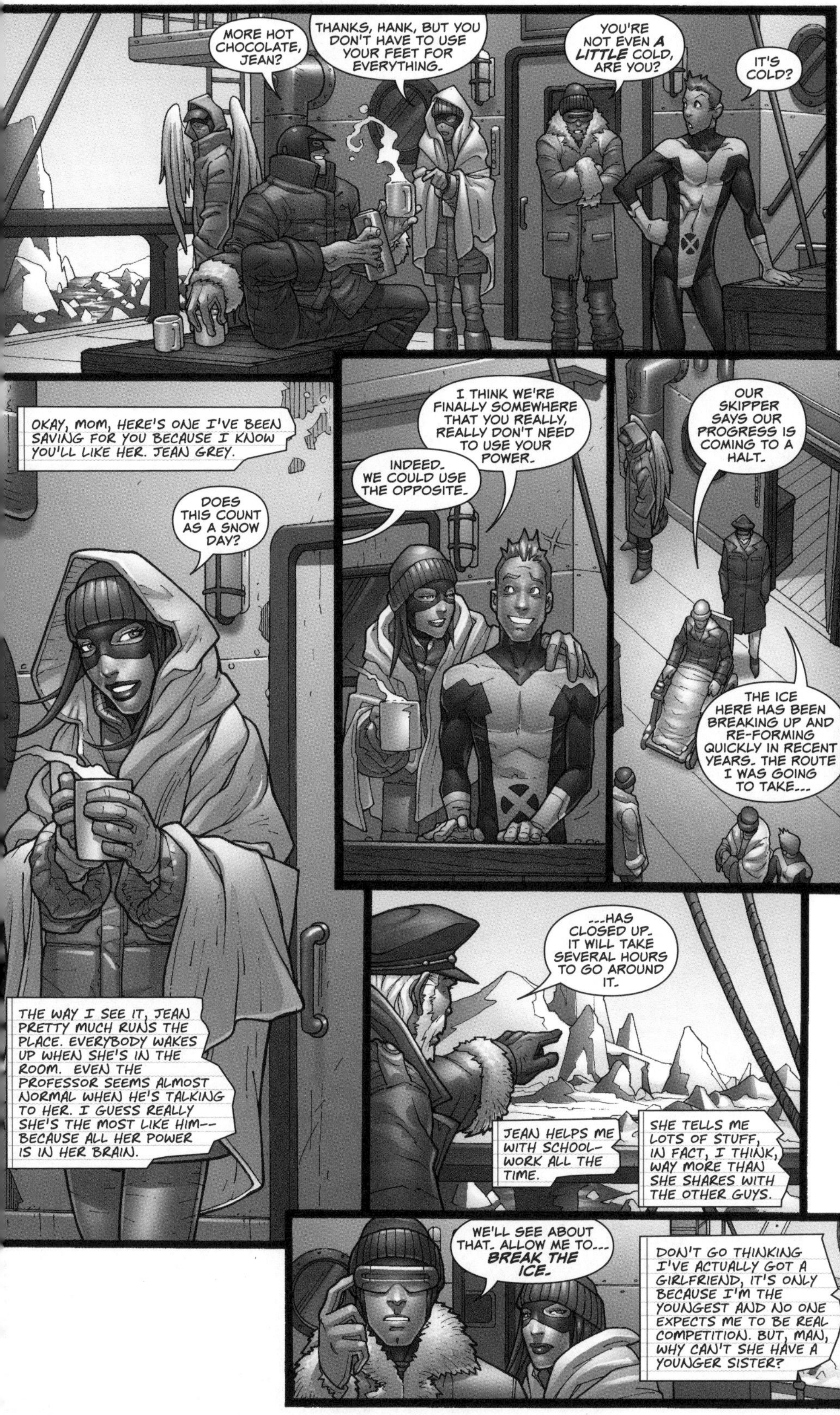
MORE HOT CHOCOLATE, JEAN?
THANKS, HANK, BUT YOU DON'T HAVE TO USE YOUR FEET FOR EVERYTHING.
YOU'RE NOT EVEN A LITTLE COLD, ARE YOU?
IT'S COLD?
OKAY, MOM, HERE'S ONE I'VE BEEN SAVING FOR YOU BECAUSE I KNOW YOU'LL LIKE HER. JEAN GREY.
DOES THIS COUNT AS A SNOW DAY?
THE WAY I SEE IT, JEAN PRETTY MUCH RUNS THE PLACE. EVERYBODY WAKES UP WHEN SHE'S IN THE ROOM. EVEN THE PROFESSOR SEEMS ALMOST NORMAL WHEN HE'S TALKING TO HER. I GUESS REALLY SHE'S THE MOST LIKE HIM--BECAUSE ALL HER POWER IS IN HER BRAIN.
I THINK WE'RE FINALLY SOMEWHERE THAT YOU REALLY, REALLY DON'T NEED TO USE YOUR POWER.
INDEED. WE COULD USE THE OPPOSITE.
OUR SKIPPER SAYS OUR PROGRESS IS COMING TO A HALT.
THE ICE HERE HAS BEEN BREAKING UP AND RE-FORMING QUICKLY IN RECENT YEARS. THE ROUTE I WAS GOING TO TAKE---
---HAS CLOSED UP. IT WILL TAKE SEVERAL HOURS TO GO AROUND IT.
JEAN HELPS ME WITH SCHOOL-WORK ALL THE TIME.
SHE TELLS ME LOTS OF STUFF, IN FACT, I THINK, WAY MORE THAN SHE SHARES WITH THE OTHER GUYS.
WE'LL SEE ABOUT THAT. ALLOW ME TO... BREAK THE ICE.
DON'T GO THINKING I'VE ACTUALLY GOT A GIRLFRIEND, IT'S ONLY BECAUSE I'M THE YOUNGEST AND NO ONE EXPECTS ME TO BE REAL COMPETITION. BUT, MAN, WHY CAN'T SHE HAVE A YOUNGER SISTER?

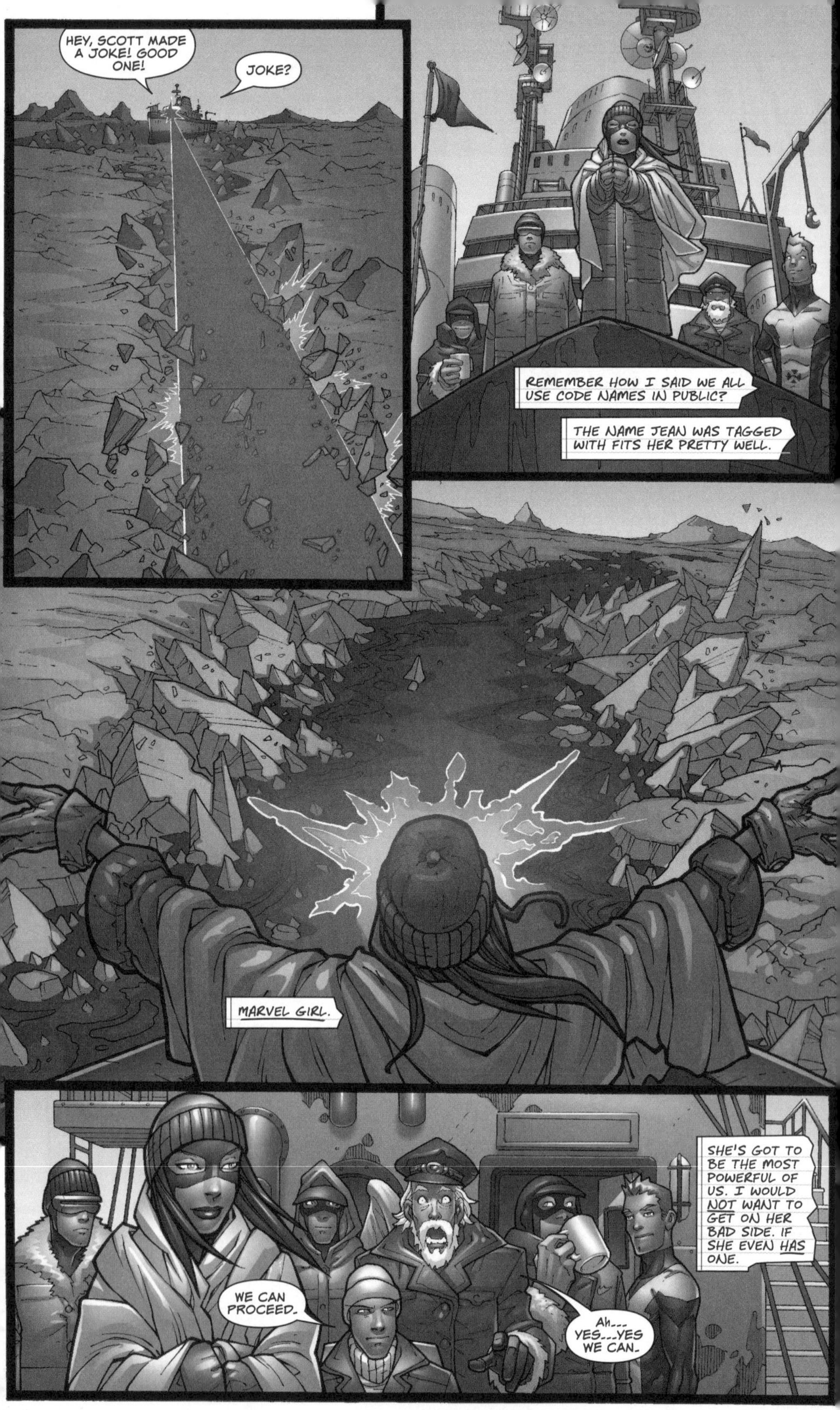
HEY, SCOTT MADE A JOKE! GOOD ONE!
JOKE?
REMEMBER HOW I SAID WE ALL USE CODE NAMES IN PUBLIC?
THE NAME JEAN WAS TAGGED WITH FITS HER PRETTY WELL.
MARVEL GIRL.
SHE'S GOT TO BE THE MOST POWERFUL OF US. I WOULD NOT WANT TO GET ON HER BAD SIDE. IF SHE EVEN HAS ONE.
WE CAN PROCEED.
Ah... YES...YES WE CAN.

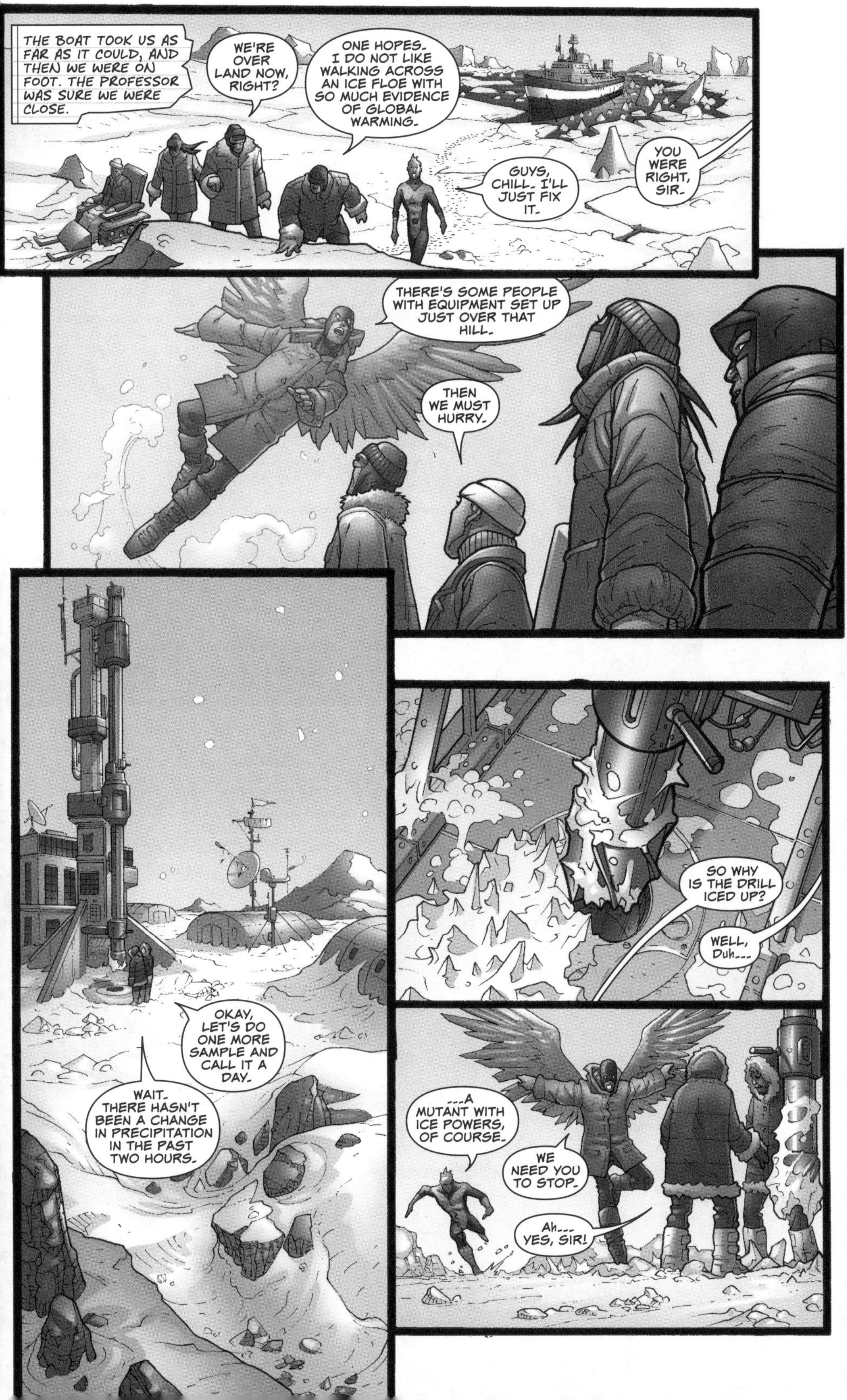
THE BOAT TOOK US AS FAR AS IT COULD, AND THEN WE WERE ON FOOT. THE PROFESSOR WAS SURE WE WERE CLOSE.
WE'RE OVER LAND NOW, RIGHT?
ONE HOPES. I DO NOT LIKE WALKING ACROSS AN ICE FLOE WITH SO MUCH EVIDENCE OF GLOBAL WARMING.
GUYS, CHILL. I'LL JUST FIX IT.
YOU WERE RIGHT, SIR.
THERE'S SOME PEOPLE WITH EQUIPMENT SET UP JUST OVER THAT HILL.
THEN WE MUST HURRY.
OKAY, LET'S DO ONE MORE SAMPLE AND CALL IT A DAY.
WAIT. THERE HASN'T BEEN A CHANGE IN PRECIPITATION IN THE PAST TWO HOURS.
SO WHY IS THE DRILL ICED UP?
WELL, Duh...
...A MUTANT WITH ICE POWERS, OF COURSE.
WE NEED YOU TO STOP.
Ah... YES, SIR!

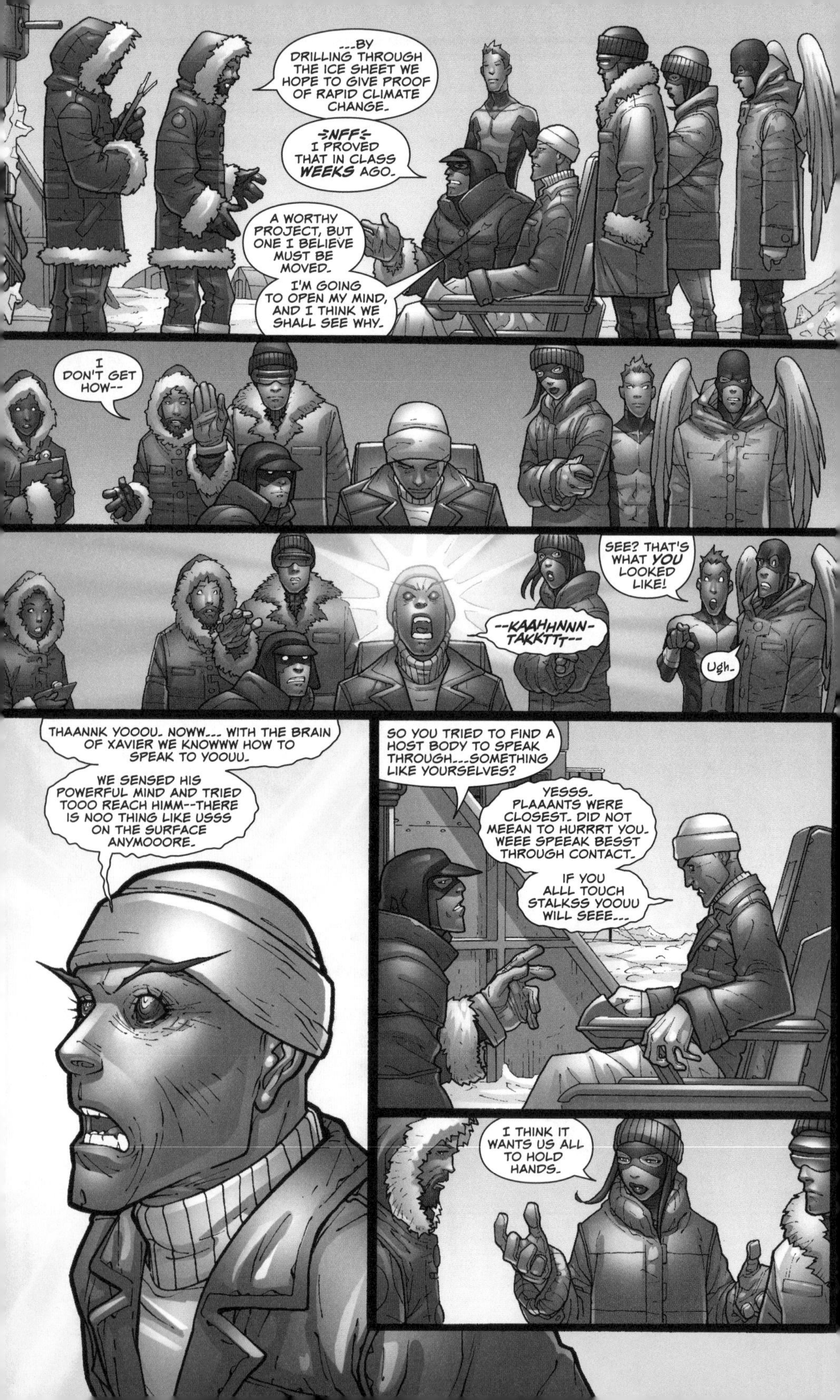

---BY DRILLING THROUGH THE ICE SHEET WE HOPE TO GIVE PROOF OF RAPID CLIMATE CHANGE.
NFF I PROVED THAT IN CLASS **WEEKS** AGO.
A WORTHY PROJECT, BUT ONE I BELIEVE MUST BE MOVED.
I'M GOING TO OPEN MY MIND, AND I THINK WE SHALL SEE WHY.
I DON'T GET HOW--
--KAAHHNNN-TAKKTTT--
SEE? THAT'S WHAT **YOU** LOOKED LIKE!
Ugh.
THAANNK YOOOU. NOWW... WITH THE BRAIN OF XAVIER WE KNOWWW HOW TO SPEAK TO YOOUU.
WE SENSED HIS POWERFUL MIND AND TRIED TOOO REACH HIMM--THERE IS NOO THING LIKE USSS ON THE SURFACE ANYMOOORE.
SO YOU TRIED TO FIND A HOST BODY TO SPEAK THROUGH...SOMETHING LIKE YOURSELVES?
YESSS. PLAAANTS WERE CLOSEST. DID NOT MEEAN TO HURRRT YOU. WEEE SPEEAK BESST THROUGH CONTACT.
IF YOU ALLL TOUCH STALKSS YOOUU WILL SEEE...
I THINK IT WANTS US ALL TO HOLD HANDS.

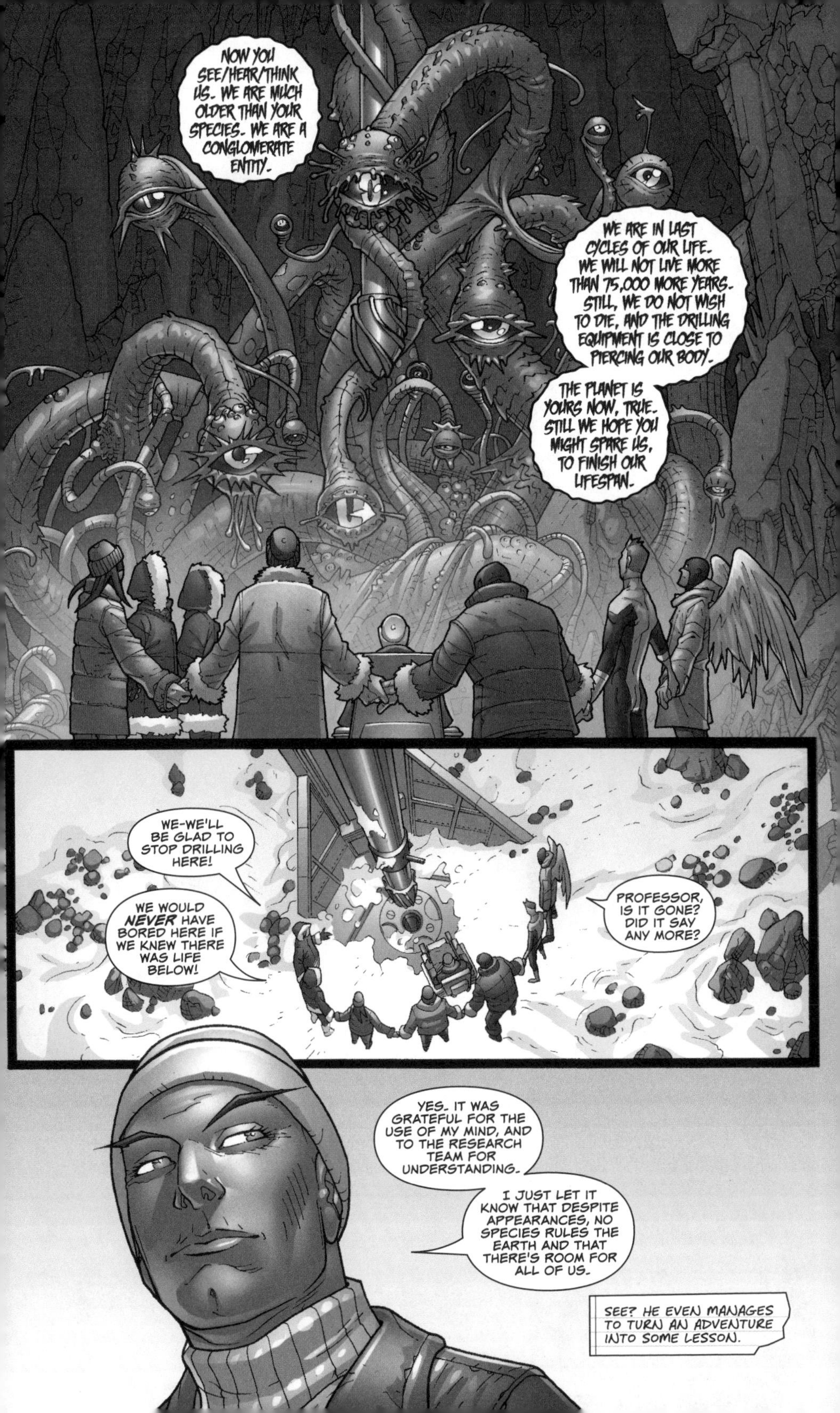
NOW YOU SEE/HEAR/THINK US. WE ARE MUCH OLDER THAN YOUR SPECIES. WE ARE A CONGLOMERATE ENTITY.
WE ARE IN LAST CYCLES OF OUR LIFE. WE WILL NOT LIVE MORE THAN 75,000 MORE YEARS. STILL, WE DO NOT WISH TO DIE, AND THE DRILLING EQUIPMENT IS CLOSE TO PIERCING OUR BODY.
THE PLANET IS YOURS NOW, TRUE. STILL WE HOPE YOU MIGHT SPARE US, TO FINISH OUR LIFESPAN.
WE-WE'LL BE GLAD TO STOP DRILLING HERE!
WE WOULD NEVER HAVE BORED HERE IF WE KNEW THERE WAS LIFE BELOW!
PROFESSOR, IS IT GONE? DID IT SAY ANY MORE?
YES. IT WAS GRATEFUL FOR THE USE OF MY MIND, AND TO THE RESEARCH TEAM FOR UNDERSTANDING.
I JUST LET IT KNOW THAT DESPITE APPEARANCES, NO SPECIES RULES THE EARTH AND THAT THERE'S ROOM FOR ALL OF US.
SEE? HE EVEN MANAGES TO TURN AN ADVENTURE INTO SOME LESSON.

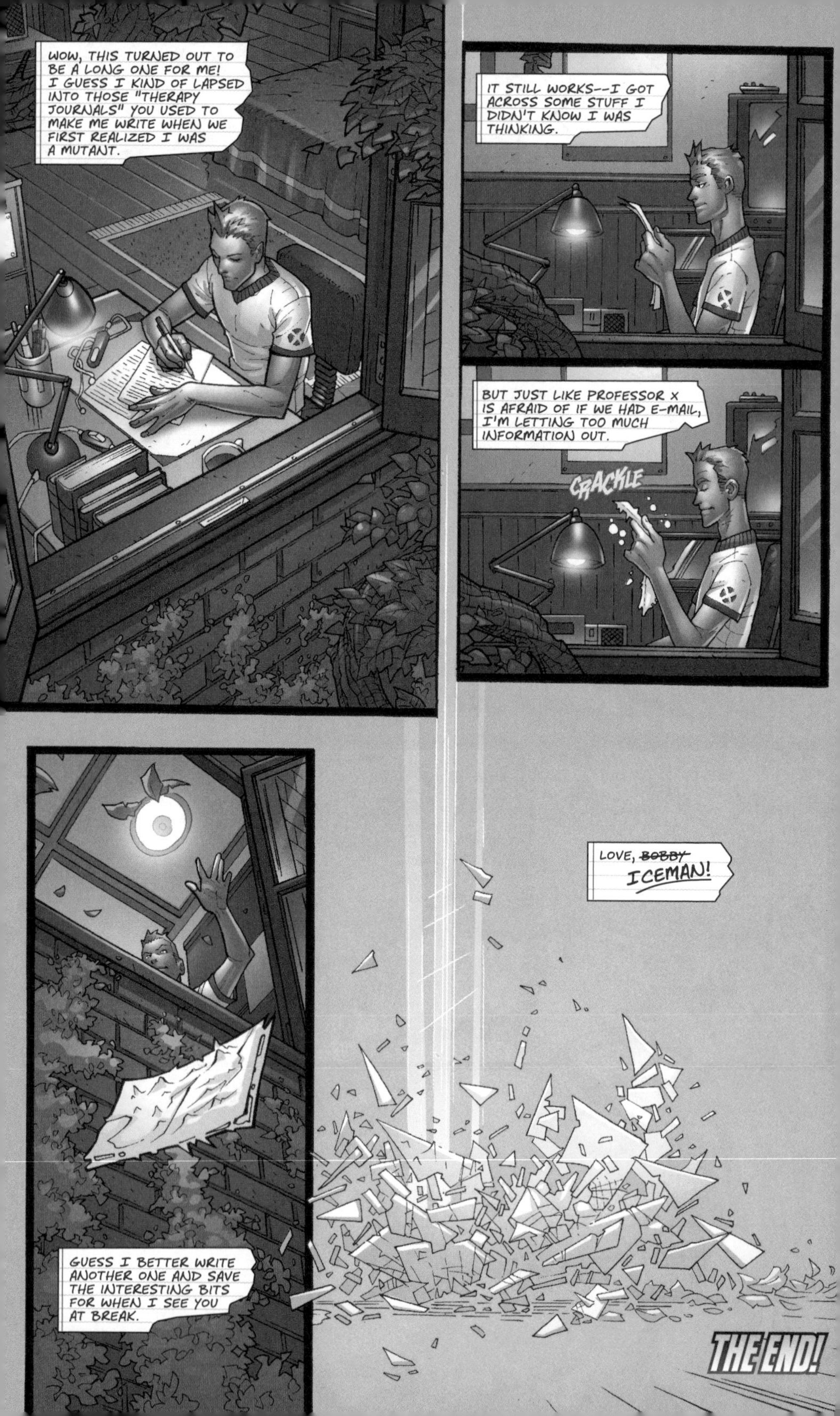

WOW, THIS TURNED OUT TO BE A LONG ONE FOR ME! I GUESS I KIND OF LAPSED INTO THOSE "THERAPY JOURNALS" YOU USED TO MAKE ME WRITE WHEN WE FIRST REALIZED I WAS A MUTANT.
IT STILL WORKS--I GOT ACROSS SOME STUFF I DIDN'T KNOW I WAS THINKING.
BUT JUST LIKE PROFESSOR X IS AFRAID OF IF WE HAD E-MAIL, I'M LETTING TOO MUCH INFORMATION OUT.
CRACKLE
GUESS I BETTER WRITE ANOTHER ONE AND SAVE THE INTERESTING BITS FOR WHEN I SEE YOU AT BREAK.
LOVE, ~~BOBBY~~ ICEMAN!
THE END!

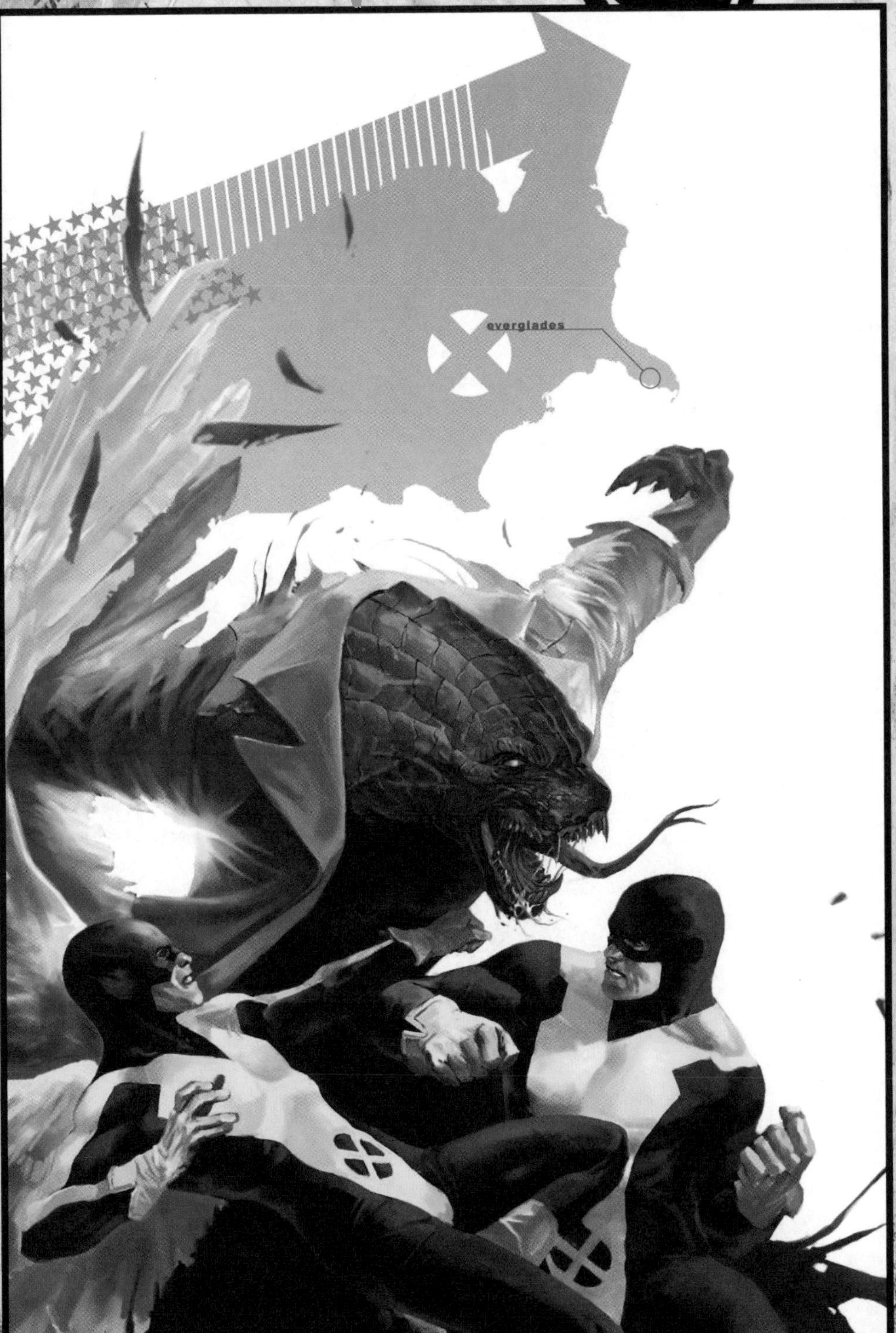
everglades

X-Men: First Class (2006) **#2**

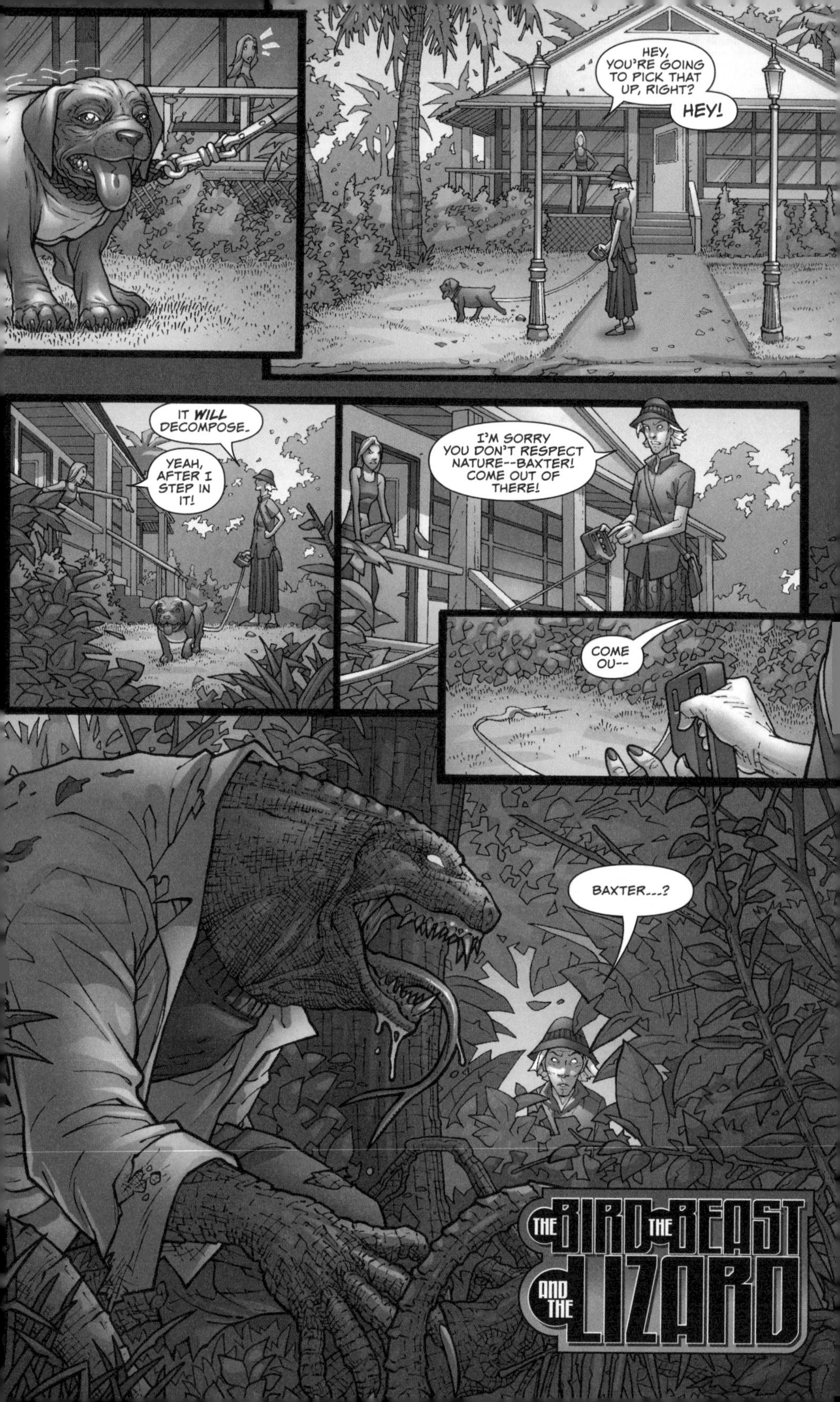
HEY, YOU'RE GOING TO PICK THAT UP, RIGHT?
HEY!
IT WILL DECOMPOSE.
YEAH, AFTER I STEP IN IT!
I'M SORRY YOU DON'T RESPECT NATURE--BAXTER! COME OUT OF THERE!
COME OU--
BAXTER...?
THE BIRD THE BEAST AND THE LIZARD

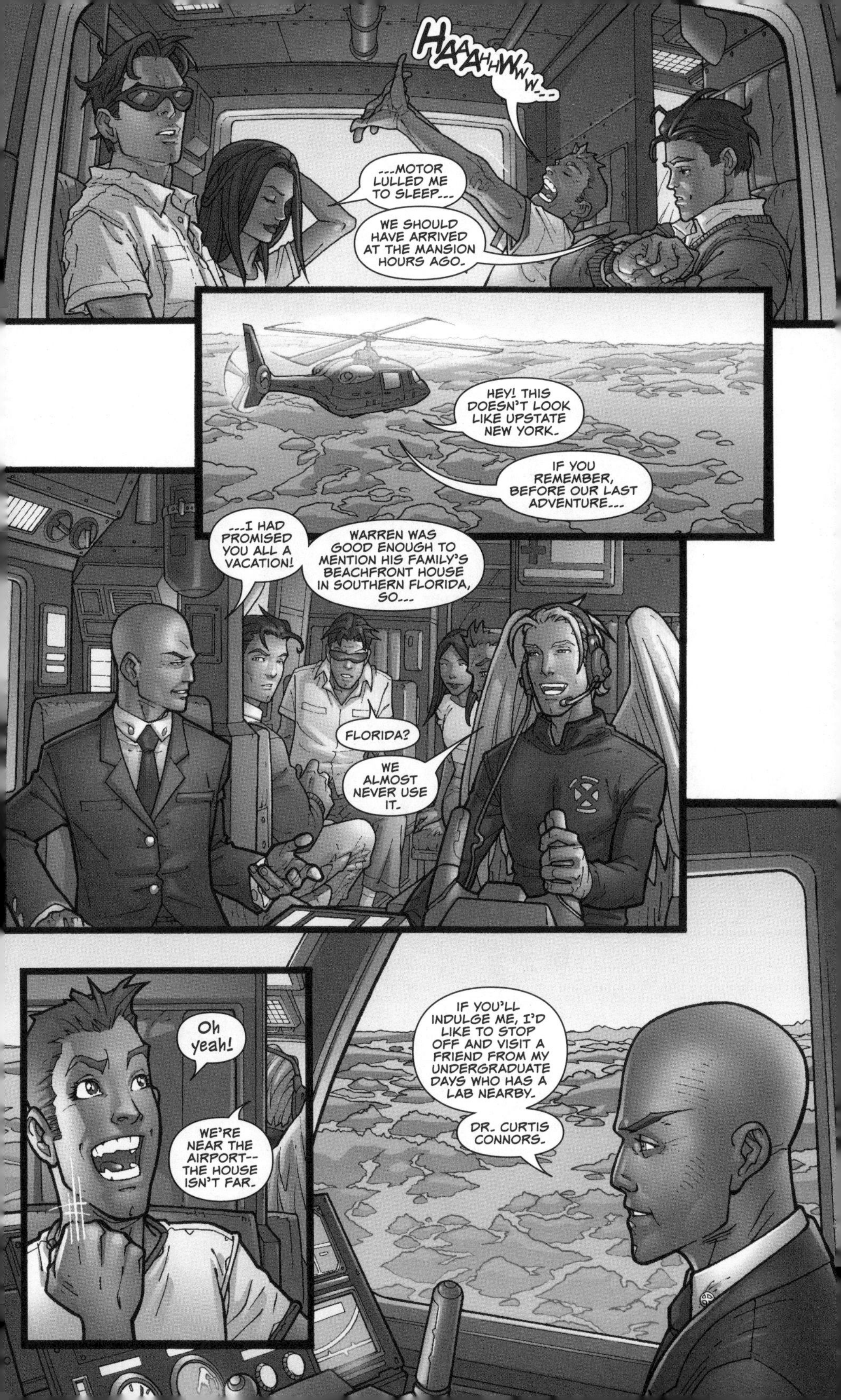
HAAAHHWWW---
---MOTOR LULLED ME TO SLEEP---
WE SHOULD HAVE ARRIVED AT THE MANSION HOURS AGO.
HEY! THIS DOESN'T LOOK LIKE UPSTATE NEW YORK.
IF YOU REMEMBER, BEFORE OUR LAST ADVENTURE---
---I HAD PROMISED YOU ALL A VACATION!
WARREN WAS GOOD ENOUGH TO MENTION HIS FAMILY'S BEACHFRONT HOUSE IN SOUTHERN FLORIDA, SO---
FLORIDA?
WE ALMOST NEVER USE IT.
Oh yeah!
WE'RE NEAR THE AIRPORT-- THE HOUSE ISN'T FAR.
IF YOU'LL INDULGE ME, I'D LIKE TO STOP OFF AND VISIT A FRIEND FROM MY UNDERGRADUATE DAYS WHO HAS A LAB NEARBY.
DR. CURTIS CONNORS.

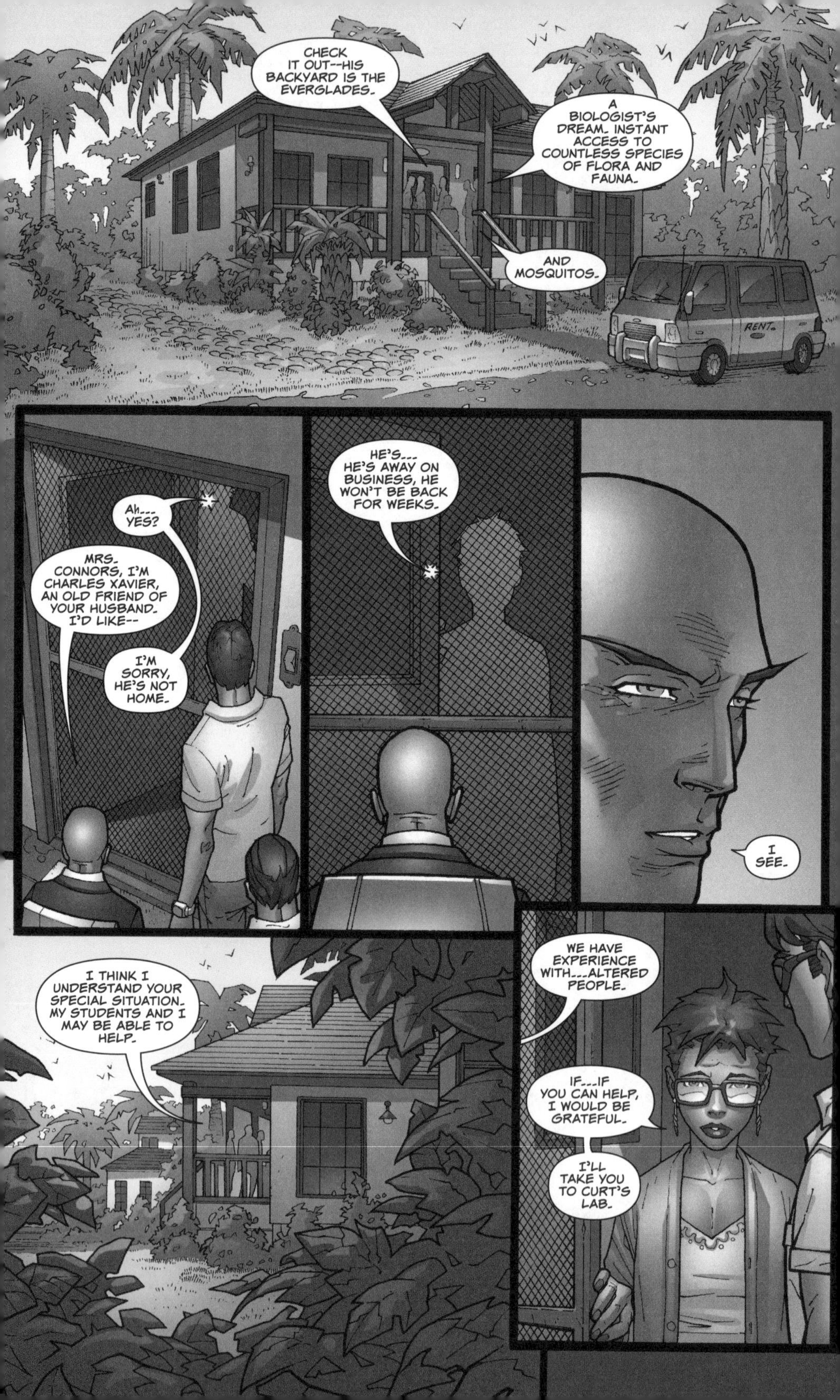
CHECK IT OUT--HIS BACKYARD IS THE EVERGLADES.
A BIOLOGIST'S DREAM. INSTANT ACCESS TO COUNTLESS SPECIES OF FLORA AND FAUNA.
AND MOSQUITOS.
RENT.
Ah... YES?
MRS. CONNORS, I'M CHARLES XAVIER, AN OLD FRIEND OF YOUR HUSBAND. I'D LIKE--
I'M SORRY, HE'S NOT HOME.
HE'S... HE'S AWAY ON BUSINESS, HE WON'T BE BACK FOR WEEKS.
I SEE.
I THINK I UNDERSTAND YOUR SPECIAL SITUATION. MY STUDENTS AND I MAY BE ABLE TO HELP.
WE HAVE EXPERIENCE WITH...ALTERED PEOPLE.
IF...IF YOU CAN HELP, I WOULD BE GRATEFUL.
I'LL TAKE YOU TO CURT'S LAB.

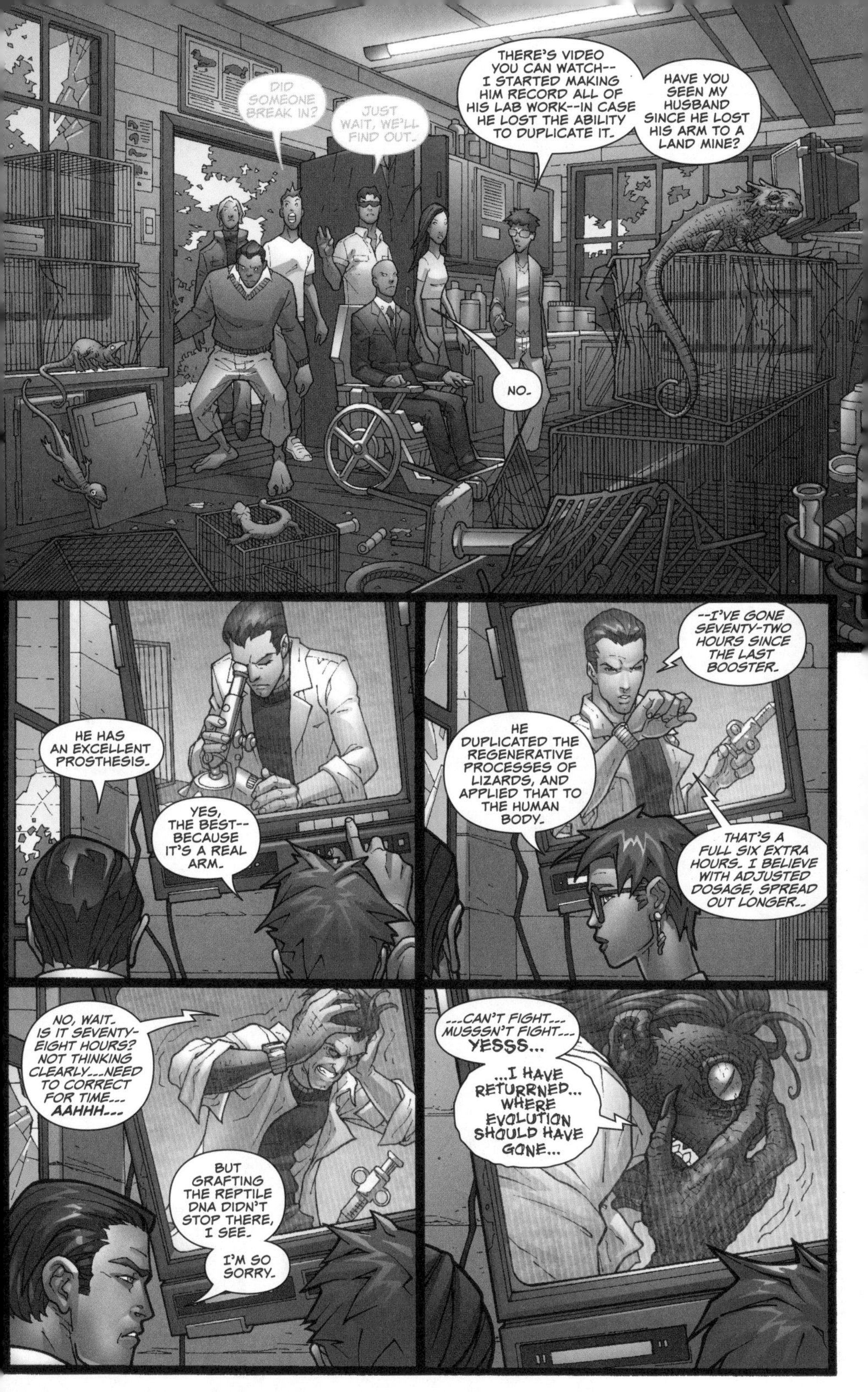
DID SOMEONE BREAK IN?
JUST WAIT, WE'LL FIND OUT.
THERE'S VIDEO YOU CAN WATCH-- I STARTED MAKING HIM RECORD ALL OF HIS LAB WORK--IN CASE HE LOST THE ABILITY TO DUPLICATE IT.
HAVE YOU SEEN MY HUSBAND SINCE HE LOST HIS ARM TO A LAND MINE?
NO.
HE HAS AN EXCELLENT PROSTHESIS.
YES, THE BEST-- BECAUSE IT'S A REAL ARM.
--I'VE GONE SEVENTY-TWO HOURS SINCE THE LAST BOOSTER.
HE DUPLICATED THE REGENERATIVE PROCESSES OF LIZARDS, AND APPLIED THAT TO THE HUMAN BODY.
THAT'S A FULL SIX EXTRA HOURS. I BELIEVE WITH ADJUSTED DOSAGE, SPREAD OUT LONGER..
NO, WAIT. IS IT SEVENTY-EIGHT HOURS? NOT THINKING CLEARLY...NEED TO CORRECT FOR TIME... AAHHH...
BUT GRAFTING THE REPTILE DNA DIDN'T STOP THERE, I SEE.
I'M SO SORRY.
...CAN'T FIGHT... MUSSSN'T FIGHT... YESSS...
...I HAVE RETURRNED... WHERE EVOLUTION SHOULD HAVE GONE...

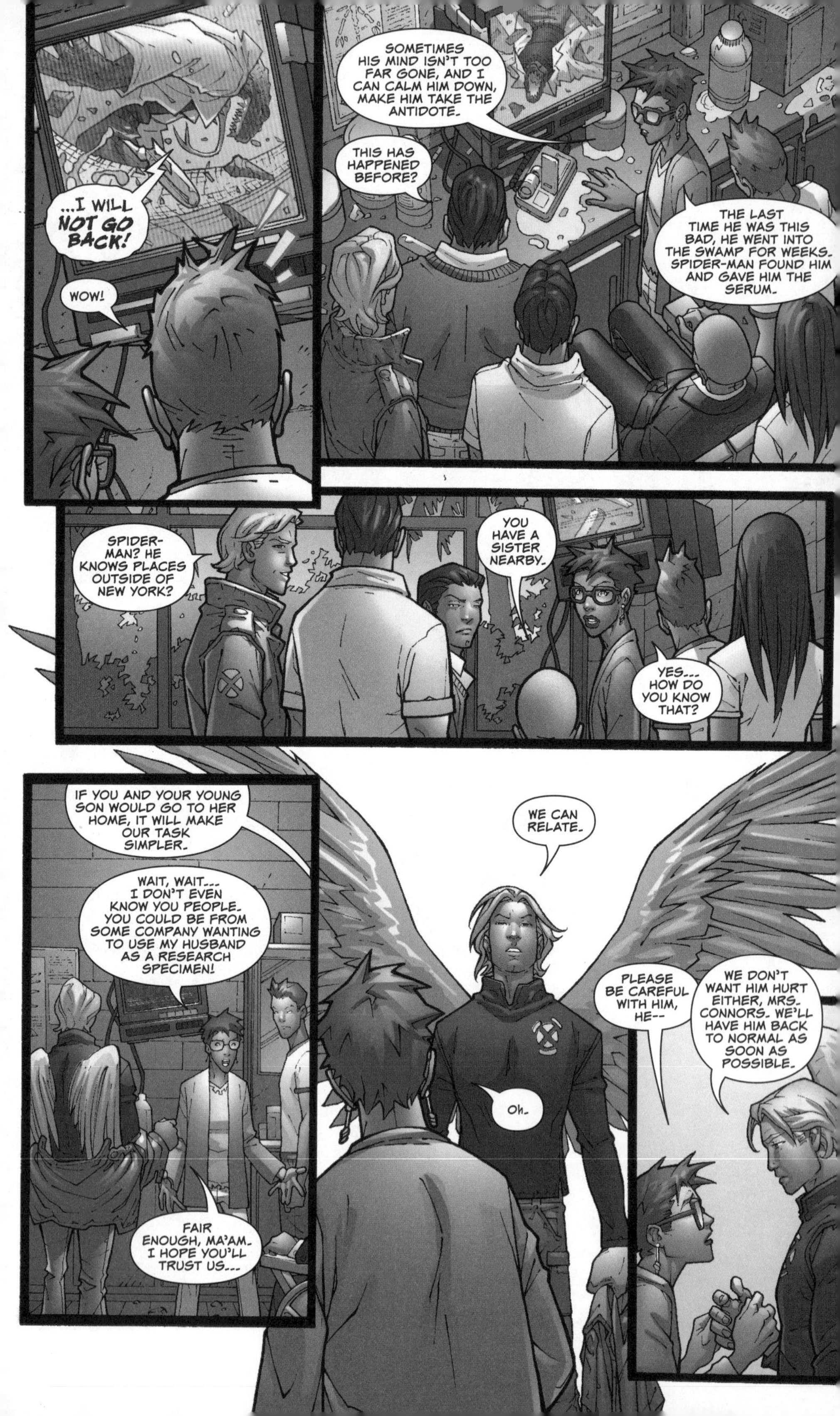
...I WILL NOT GO BACK!
WOW!
SOMETIMES HIS MIND ISN'T TOO FAR GONE, AND I CAN CALM HIM DOWN, MAKE HIM TAKE THE ANTIDOTE.
THIS HAS HAPPENED BEFORE?
THE LAST TIME HE WAS THIS BAD, HE WENT INTO THE SWAMP FOR WEEKS. SPIDER-MAN FOUND HIM AND GAVE HIM THE SERUM.
SPIDER-MAN? HE KNOWS PLACES OUTSIDE OF NEW YORK?
YOU HAVE A SISTER NEARBY.
YES... HOW DO YOU KNOW THAT?
IF YOU AND YOUR YOUNG SON WOULD GO TO HER HOME, IT WILL MAKE OUR TASK SIMPLER.
WAIT, WAIT... I DON'T EVEN KNOW YOU PEOPLE. YOU COULD BE FROM SOME COMPANY WANTING TO USE MY HUSBAND AS A RESEARCH SPECIMEN!
FAIR ENOUGH, MA'AM. I HOPE YOU'LL TRUST US...
WE CAN RELATE.
Oh.
PLEASE BE CAREFUL WITH HIM, HE--
WE DON'T WANT HIM HURT EITHER, MRS. CONNORS. WE'LL HAVE HIM BACK TO NORMAL AS SOON AS POSSIBLE.

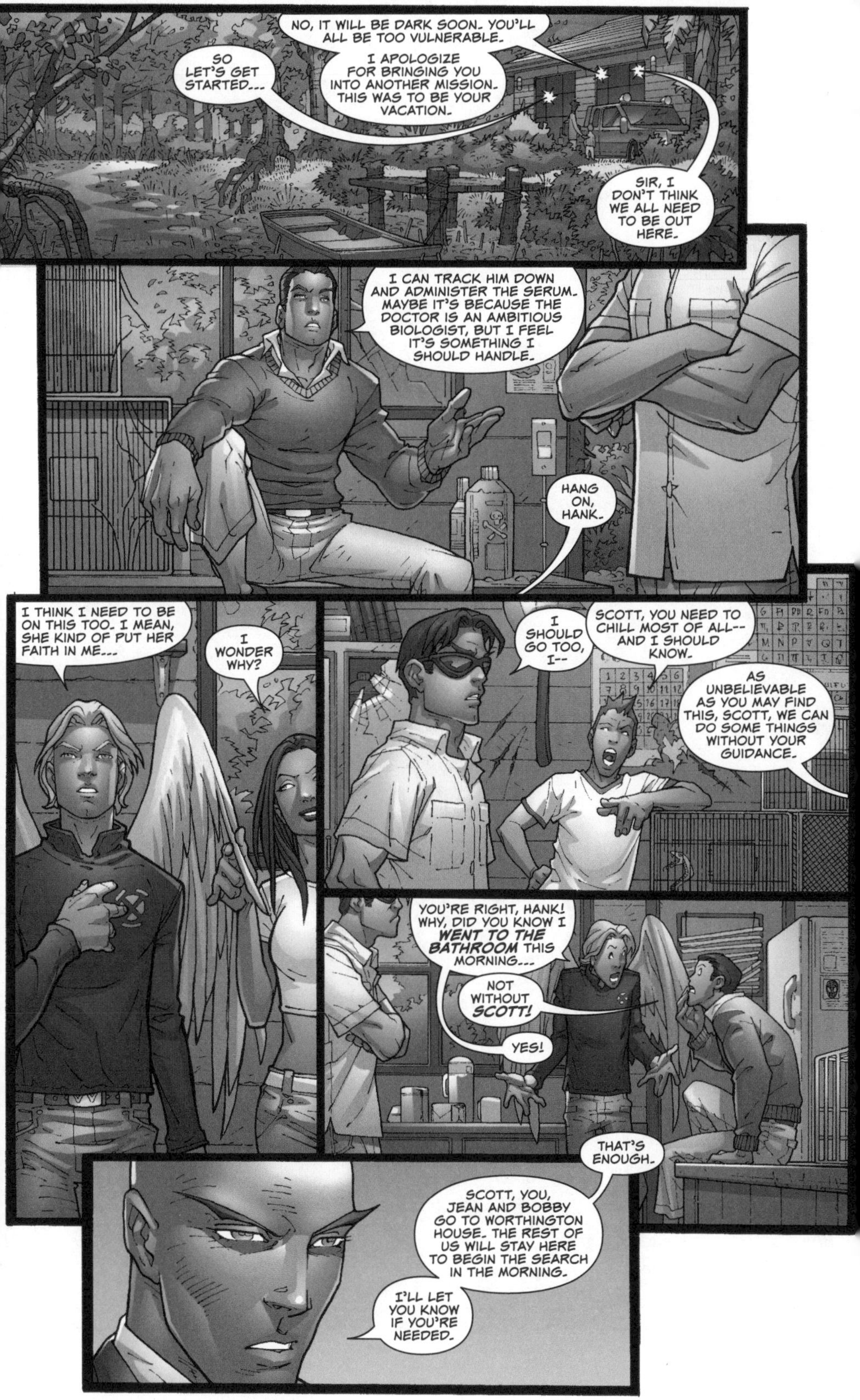

NO, IT WILL BE DARK SOON. YOU'LL ALL BE TOO VULNERABLE.
SO LET'S GET STARTED...
I APOLOGIZE FOR BRINGING YOU INTO ANOTHER MISSION. THIS WAS TO BE YOUR VACATION.
SIR, I DON'T THINK WE ALL NEED TO BE OUT HERE.
I CAN TRACK HIM DOWN AND ADMINISTER THE SERUM. MAYBE IT'S BECAUSE THE DOCTOR IS AN AMBITIOUS BIOLOGIST, BUT I FEEL IT'S SOMETHING I SHOULD HANDLE.
HANG ON, HANK.
I THINK I NEED TO BE ON THIS TOO. I MEAN, SHE KIND OF PUT HER FAITH IN ME...
I WONDER WHY?
I SHOULD GO TOO, I--
SCOTT, YOU NEED TO CHILL MOST OF ALL--AND I SHOULD KNOW.
AS UNBELIEVABLE AS YOU MAY FIND THIS, SCOTT, WE CAN DO SOME THINGS WITHOUT YOUR GUIDANCE.
YOU'RE RIGHT, HANK! WHY, DID YOU KNOW I *WENT TO THE BATHROOM* THIS MORNING...
NOT WITHOUT *SCOTT!*
YES!
THAT'S ENOUGH.
SCOTT, YOU, JEAN AND BOBBY GO TO WORTHINGTON HOUSE. THE REST OF US WILL STAY HERE TO BEGIN THE SEARCH IN THE MORNING.
I'LL LET YOU KNOW IF YOU'RE NEEDED.

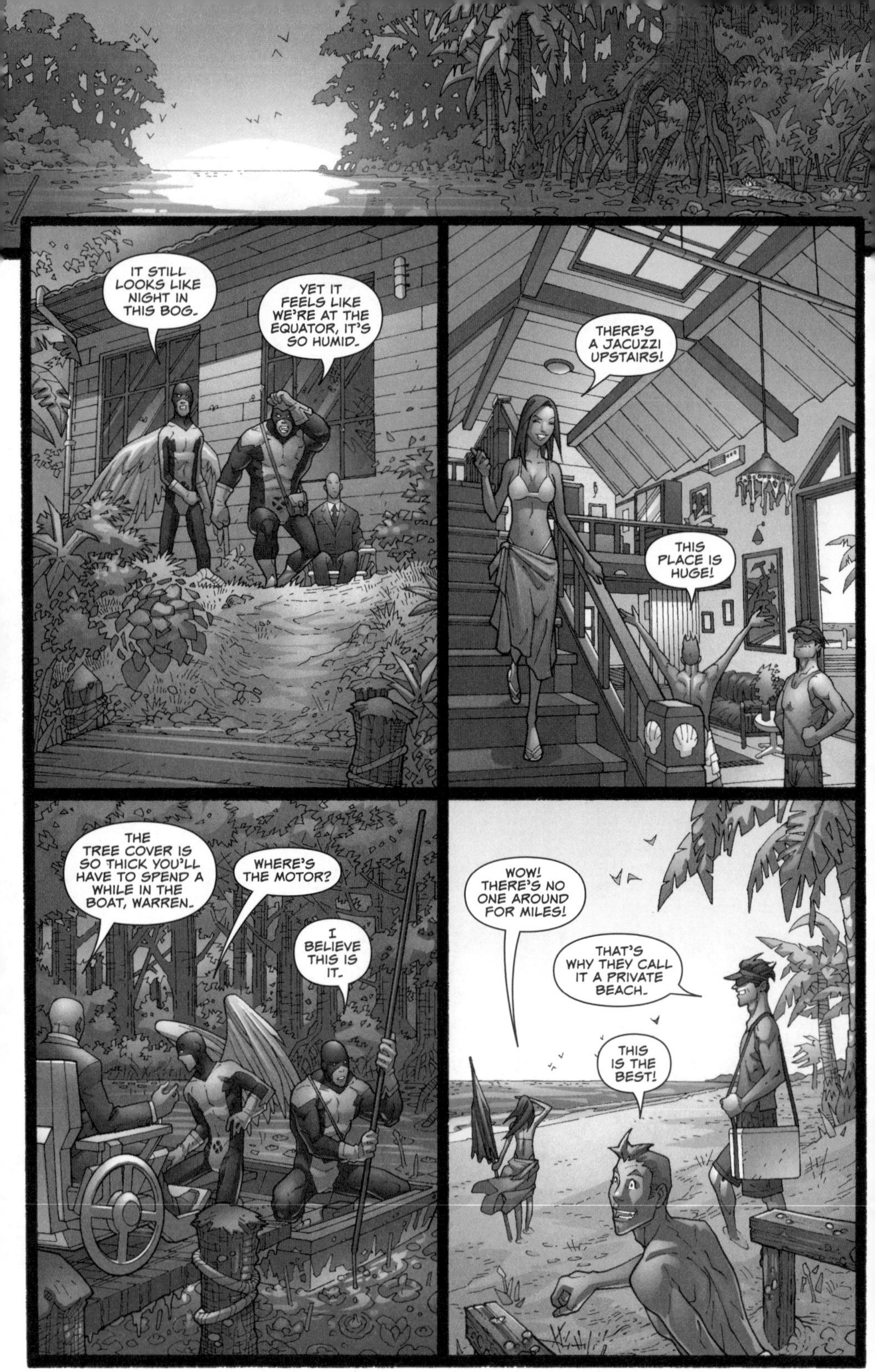
IT STILL LOOKS LIKE NIGHT IN THIS BOG.
YET IT FEELS LIKE WE'RE AT THE EQUATOR, IT'S SO HUMID.
THERE'S A JACUZZI UPSTAIRS!
THIS PLACE IS HUGE!
THE TREE COVER IS SO THICK YOU'LL HAVE TO SPEND A WHILE IN THE BOAT, WARREN.
WHERE'S THE MOTOR?
I BELIEVE THIS IS IT.
WOW! THERE'S NO ONE AROUND FOR MILES!
THAT'S WHY THEY CALL IT A PRIVATE BEACH.
THIS IS THE BEST!

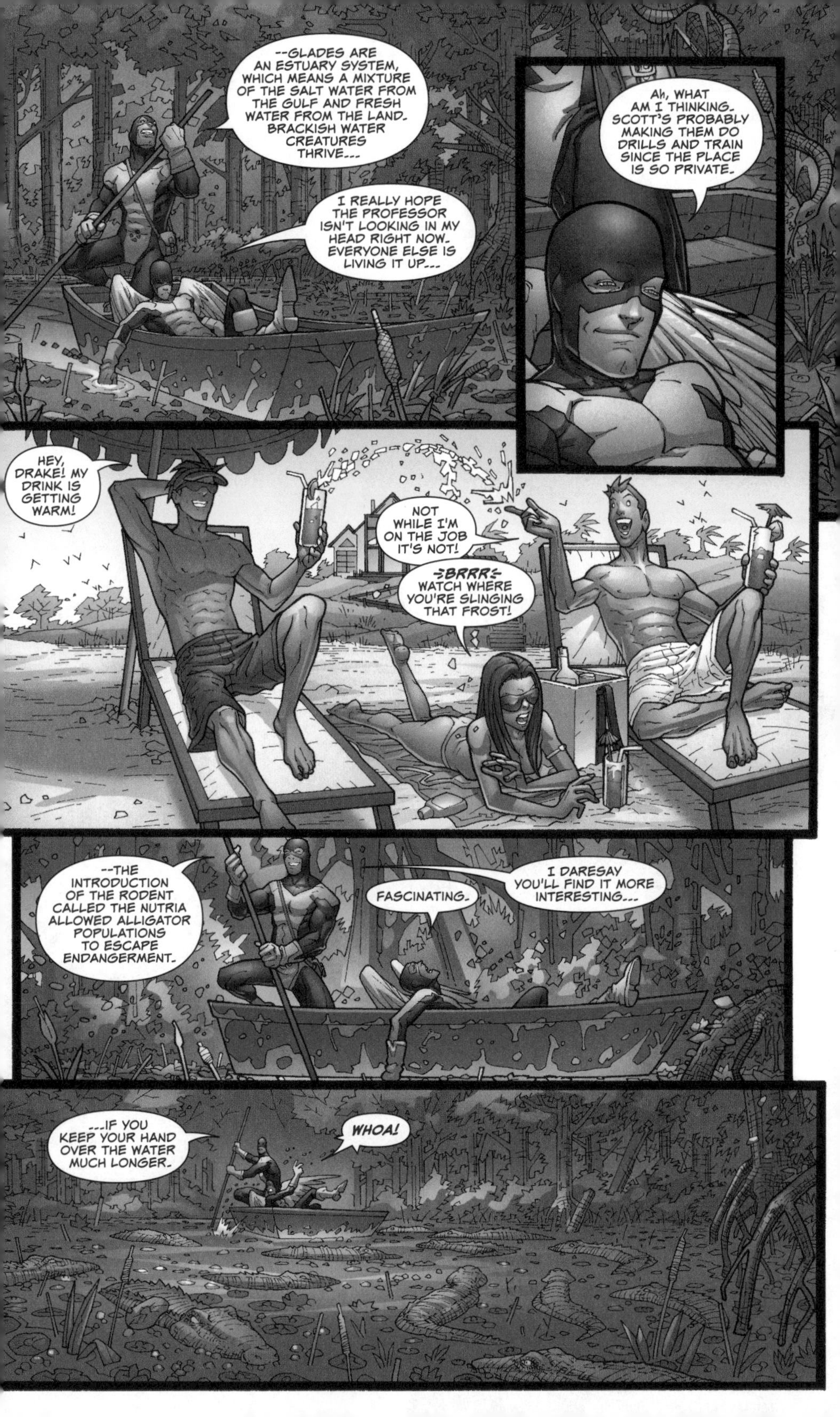
--GLADES ARE AN ESTUARY SYSTEM, WHICH MEANS A MIXTURE OF THE SALT WATER FROM THE GULF AND FRESH WATER FROM THE LAND. BRACKISH WATER CREATURES THRIVE...
I REALLY HOPE THE PROFESSOR ISN'T LOOKING IN MY HEAD RIGHT NOW. EVERYONE ELSE IS LIVING IT UP...
Ah, WHAT AM I THINKING. SCOTT'S PROBABLY MAKING THEM DO DRILLS AND TRAIN SINCE THE PLACE IS SO PRIVATE.
HEY, DRAKE! MY DRINK IS GETTING WARM!
NOT WHILE I'M ON THE JOB IT'S NOT!
BRRR
WATCH WHERE YOU'RE SLINGING THAT FROST!
--THE INTRODUCTION OF THE RODENT CALLED THE NUTRIA ALLOWED ALLIGATOR POPULATIONS TO ESCAPE ENDANGERMENT.
FASCINATING.
I DARESAY YOU'LL FIND IT MORE INTERESTING...
...IF YOU KEEP YOUR HAND OVER THE WATER MUCH LONGER.
WHOA!

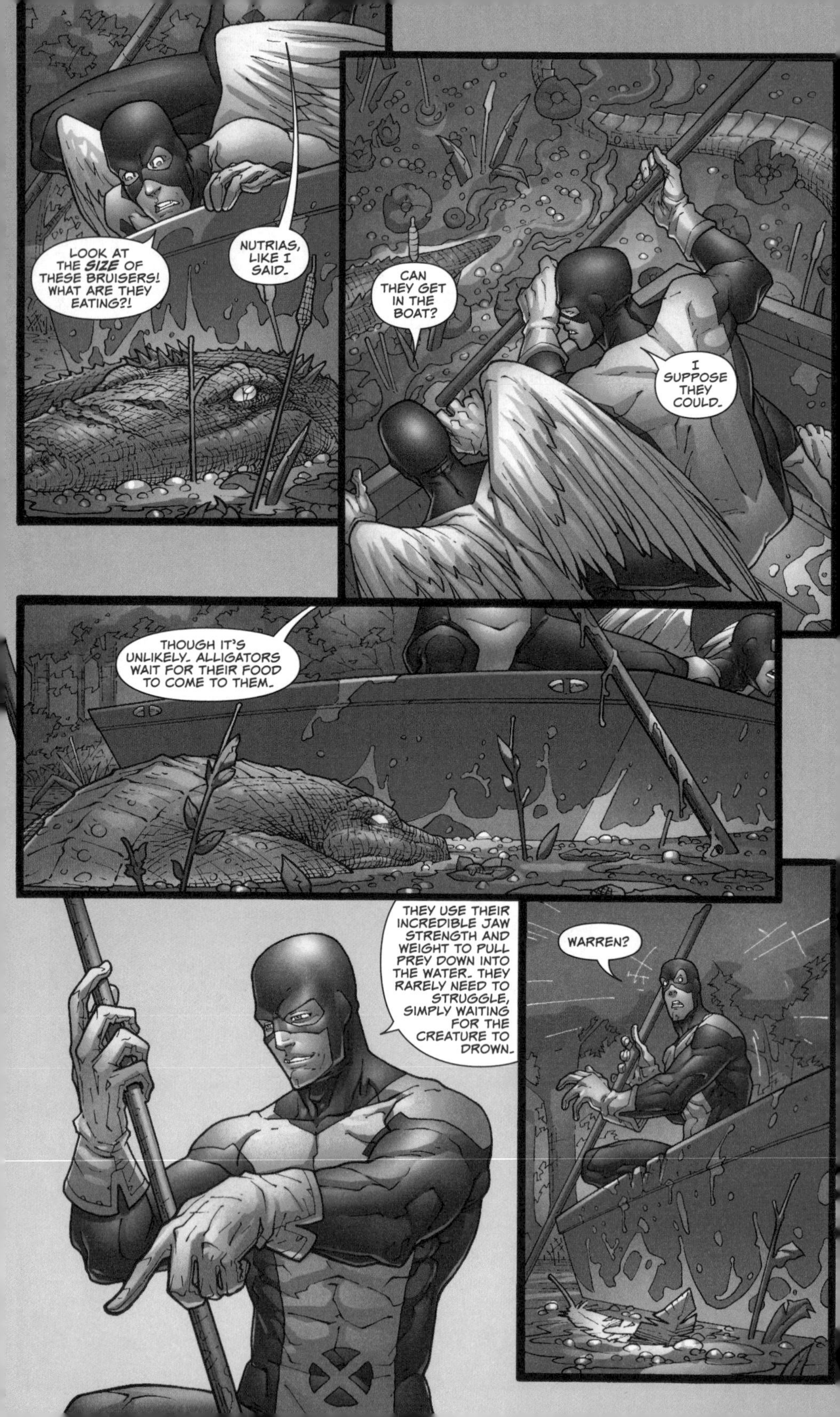
LOOK AT THE SIZE OF THESE BRUISERS! WHAT ARE THEY EATING?!
NUTRIAS, LIKE I SAID.
CAN THEY GET IN THE BOAT?
I SUPPOSE THEY COULD.
THOUGH IT'S UNLIKELY. ALLIGATORS WAIT FOR THEIR FOOD TO COME TO THEM.
THEY USE THEIR INCREDIBLE JAW STRENGTH AND WEIGHT TO PULL PREY DOWN INTO THE WATER. THEY RARELY NEED TO STRUGGLE, SIMPLY WAITING FOR THE CREATURE TO DROWN.
WARREN?

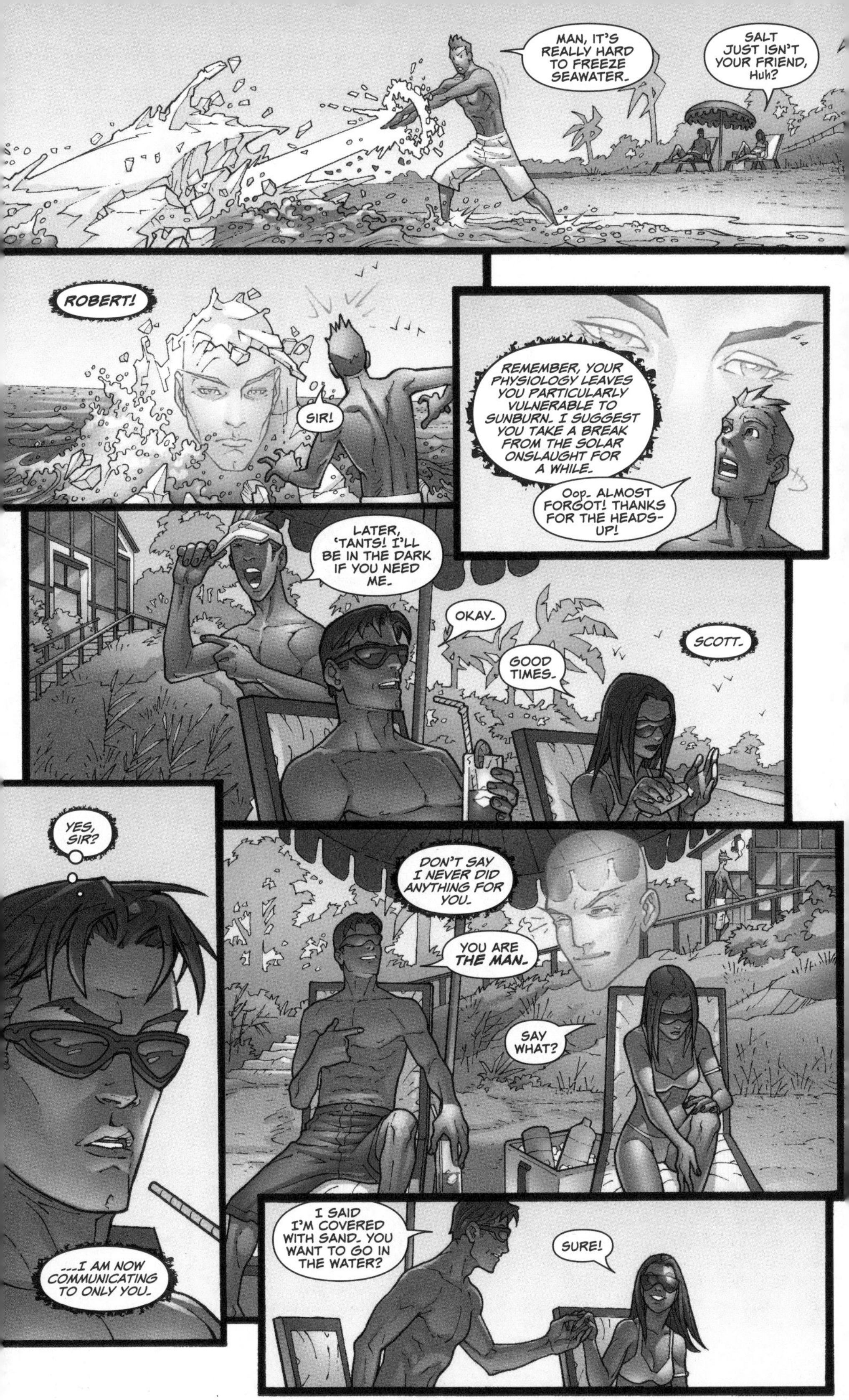
MAN, IT'S REALLY HARD TO FREEZE SEAWATER.
SALT JUST ISN'T YOUR FRIEND, Huh?
ROBERT!
SIR!
REMEMBER, YOUR PHYSIOLOGY LEAVES YOU PARTICULARLY VULNERABLE TO SUNBURN. I SUGGEST YOU TAKE A BREAK FROM THE SOLAR ONSLAUGHT FOR A WHILE.
Oop. ALMOST FORGOT! THANKS FOR THE HEADS-UP!
LATER, 'TANTS! I'LL BE IN THE DARK IF YOU NEED ME.
OKAY.
GOOD TIMES.
SCOTT.
YES, SIR?
...I AM NOW COMMUNICATING TO ONLY YOU.
DON'T SAY I NEVER DID ANYTHING FOR YOU.
YOU ARE THE MAN.
SAY WHAT?
I SAID I'M COVERED WITH SAND. YOU WANT TO GO IN THE WATER?
SURE!

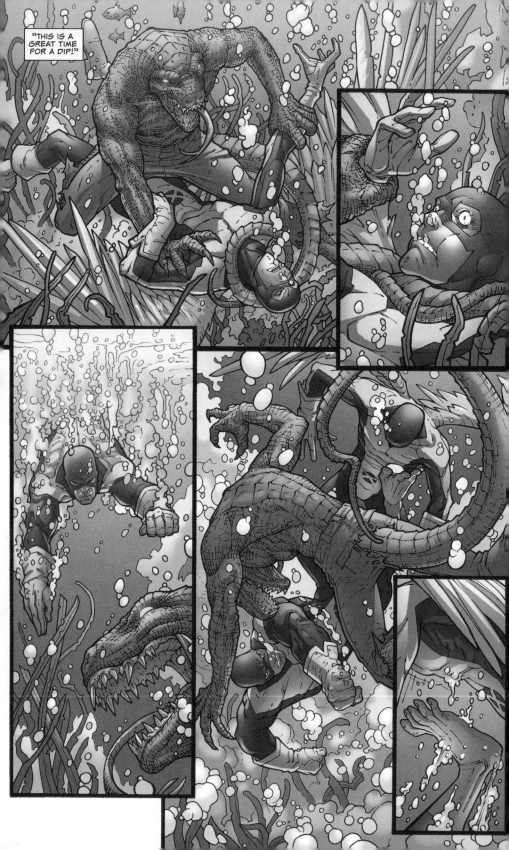

"THIS IS A GREAT TIME FOR A DIP!"

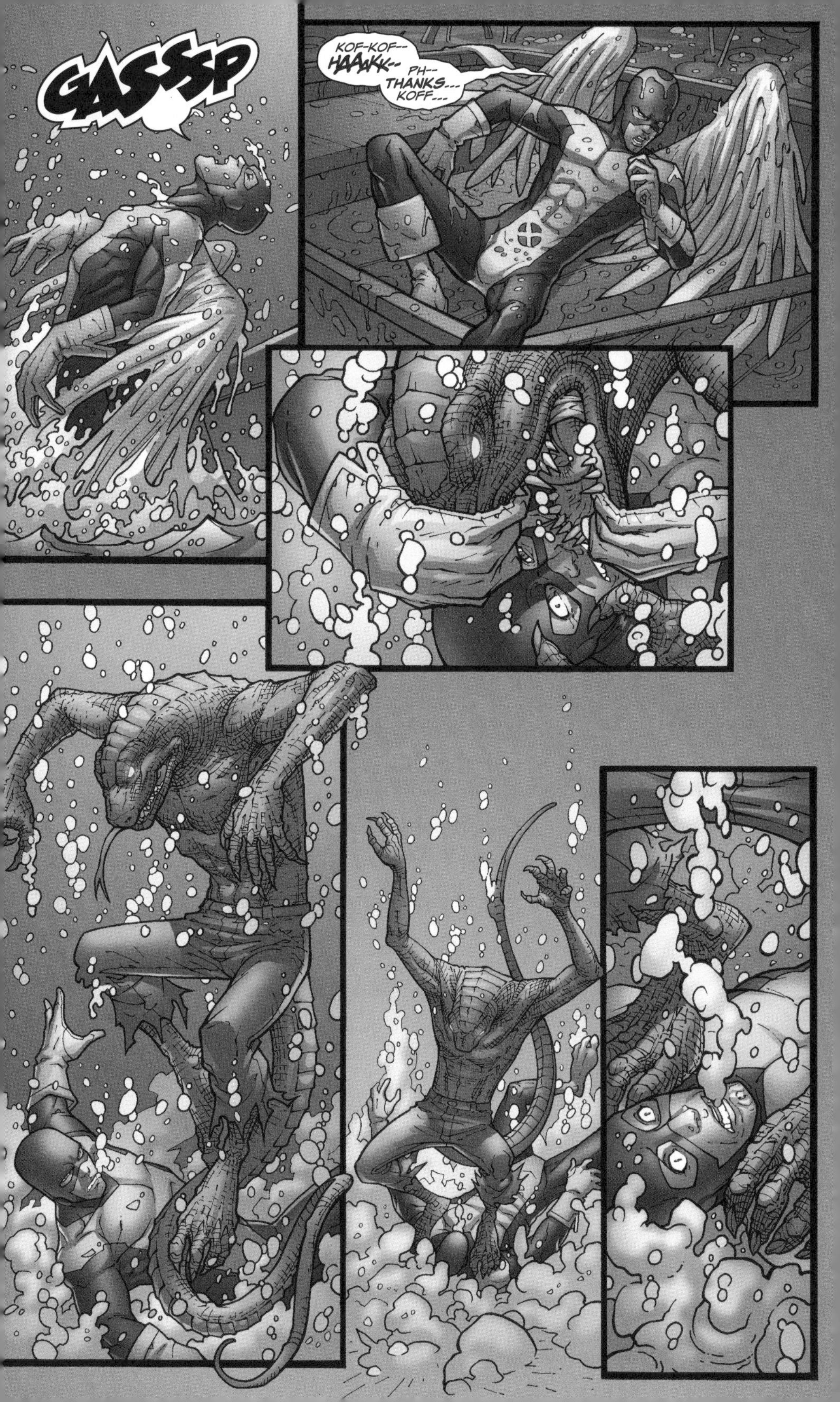
GASSSP
KOF-KOF--
HAAAKK--
PH--
THANKS---
KOFF---

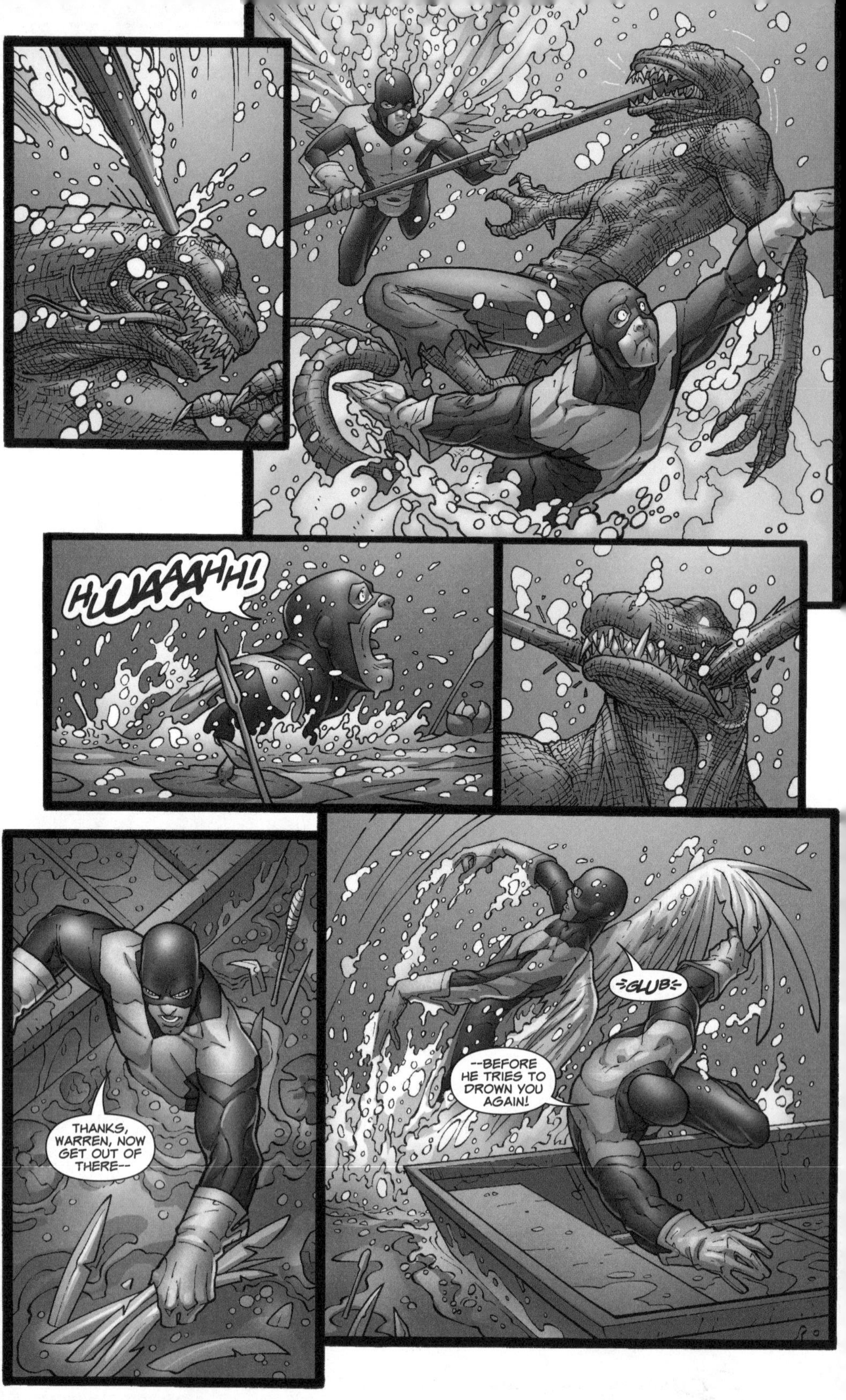
HUUAAAHH!
THANKS, WARREN, NOW GET OUT OF THERE--
GLUB
--BEFORE HE TRIES TO DROWN YOU AGAIN!

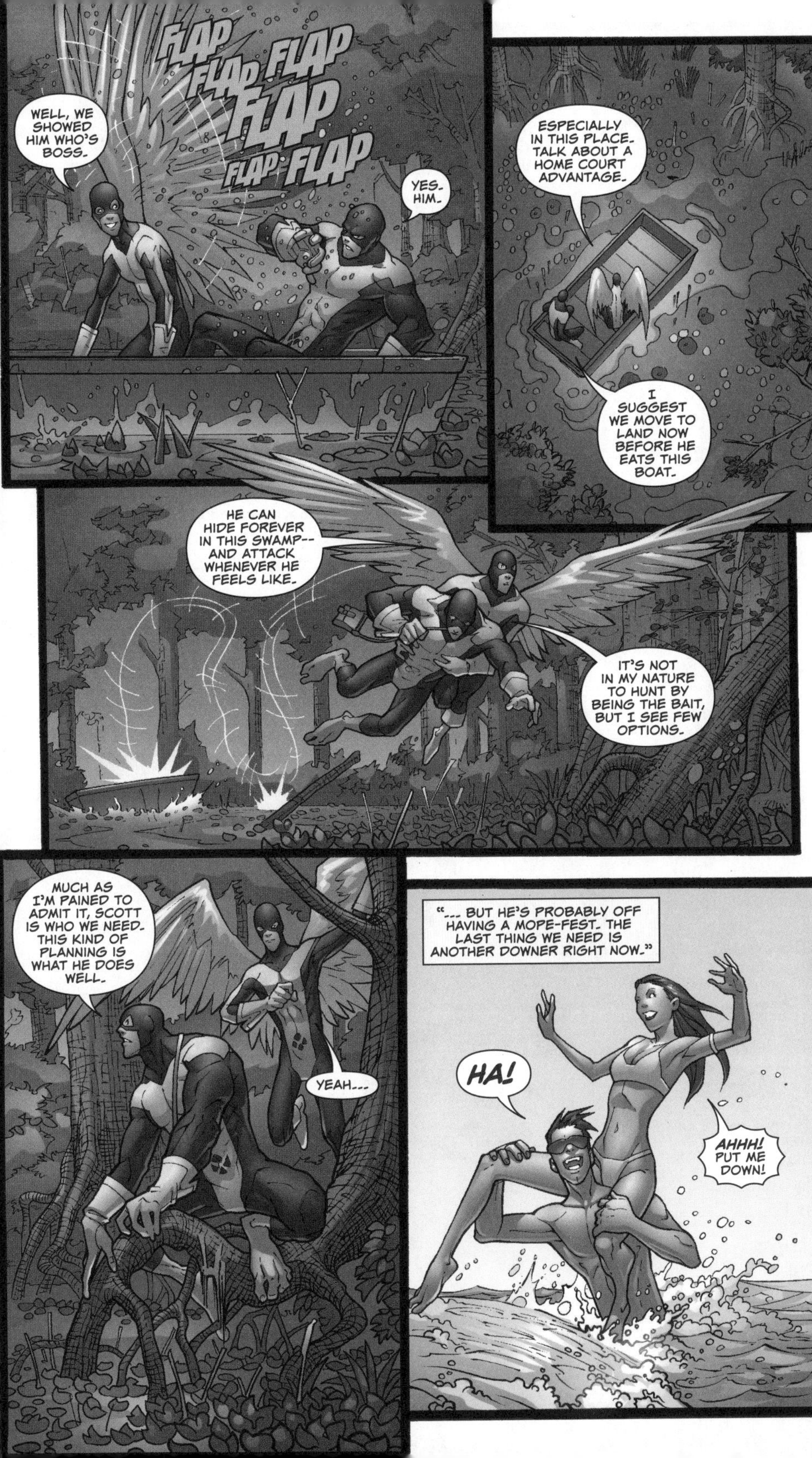
FLAP FLAP FLAP FLAP FLAP FLAP
WELL, WE SHOWED HIM WHO'S BOSS.
YES. HIM.
ESPECIALLY IN THIS PLACE. TALK ABOUT A HOME COURT ADVANTAGE.
I SUGGEST WE MOVE TO LAND NOW BEFORE HE EATS THIS BOAT.
HE CAN HIDE FOREVER IN THIS SWAMP-- AND ATTACK WHENEVER HE FEELS LIKE.
IT'S NOT IN MY NATURE TO HUNT BY BEING THE BAIT, BUT I SEE FEW OPTIONS.
MUCH AS I'M PAINED TO ADMIT IT, SCOTT IS WHO WE NEED. THIS KIND OF PLANNING IS WHAT HE DOES WELL.
YEAH...
"... BUT HE'S PROBABLY OFF HAVING A MOPE-FEST. THE LAST THING WE NEED IS ANOTHER DOWNER RIGHT NOW."
HA!
AHHH! PUT ME DOWN!

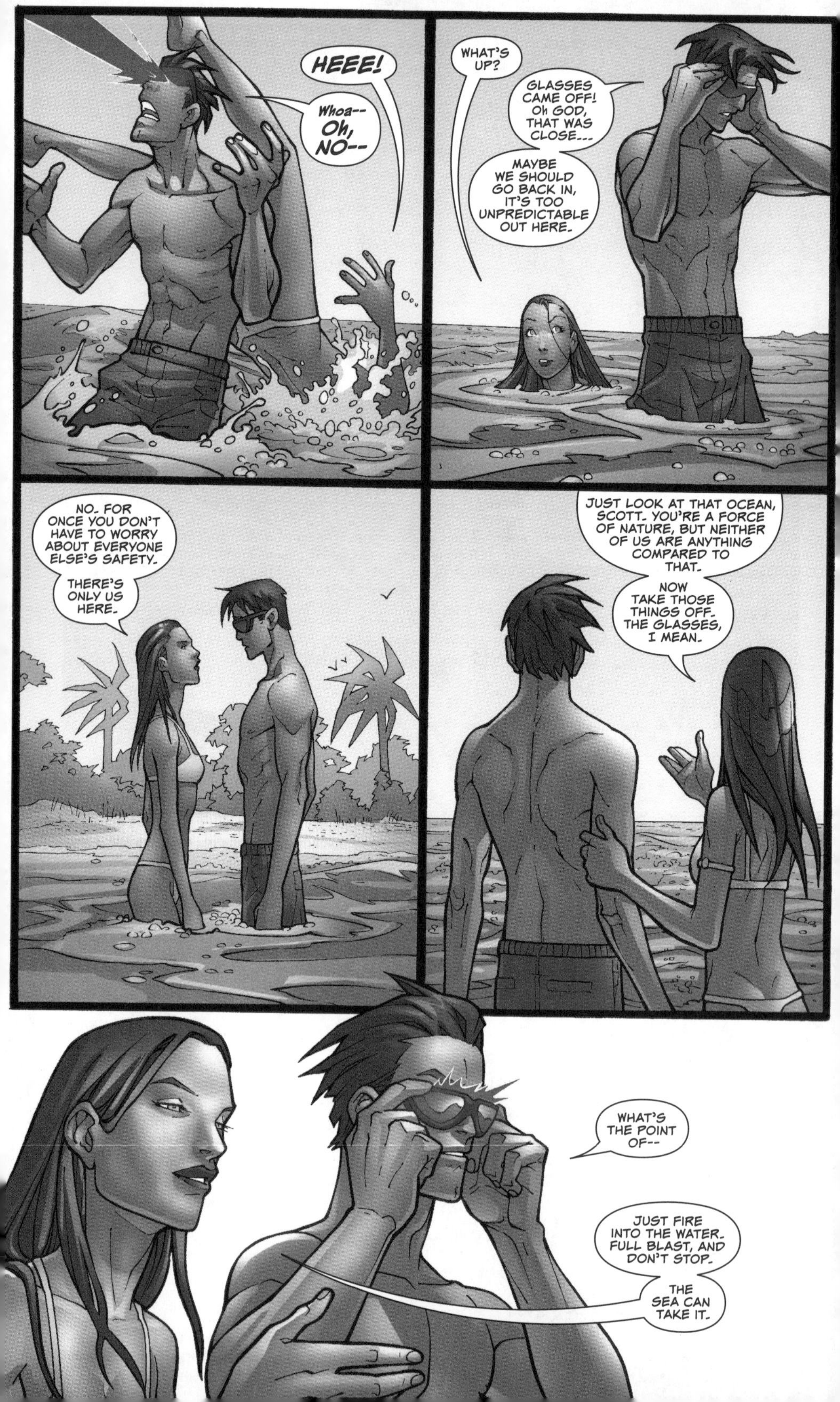
HEEEE!
Whoa-- Oh, NO--
WHAT'S UP?
GLASSES CAME OFF! Oh GOD, THAT WAS CLOSE...
MAYBE WE SHOULD GO BACK IN, IT'S TOO UNPREDICTABLE OUT HERE.
NO. FOR ONCE YOU DON'T HAVE TO WORRY ABOUT EVERYONE ELSE'S SAFETY.
THERE'S ONLY US HERE.
JUST LOOK AT THAT OCEAN, SCOTT. YOU'RE A FORCE OF NATURE, BUT NEITHER OF US ARE ANYTHING COMPARED TO THAT.
NOW TAKE THOSE THINGS OFF. THE GLASSES, I MEAN.
WHAT'S THE POINT OF--
JUST FIRE INTO THE WATER. FULL BLAST, AND DON'T STOP.
THE SEA CAN TAKE IT.

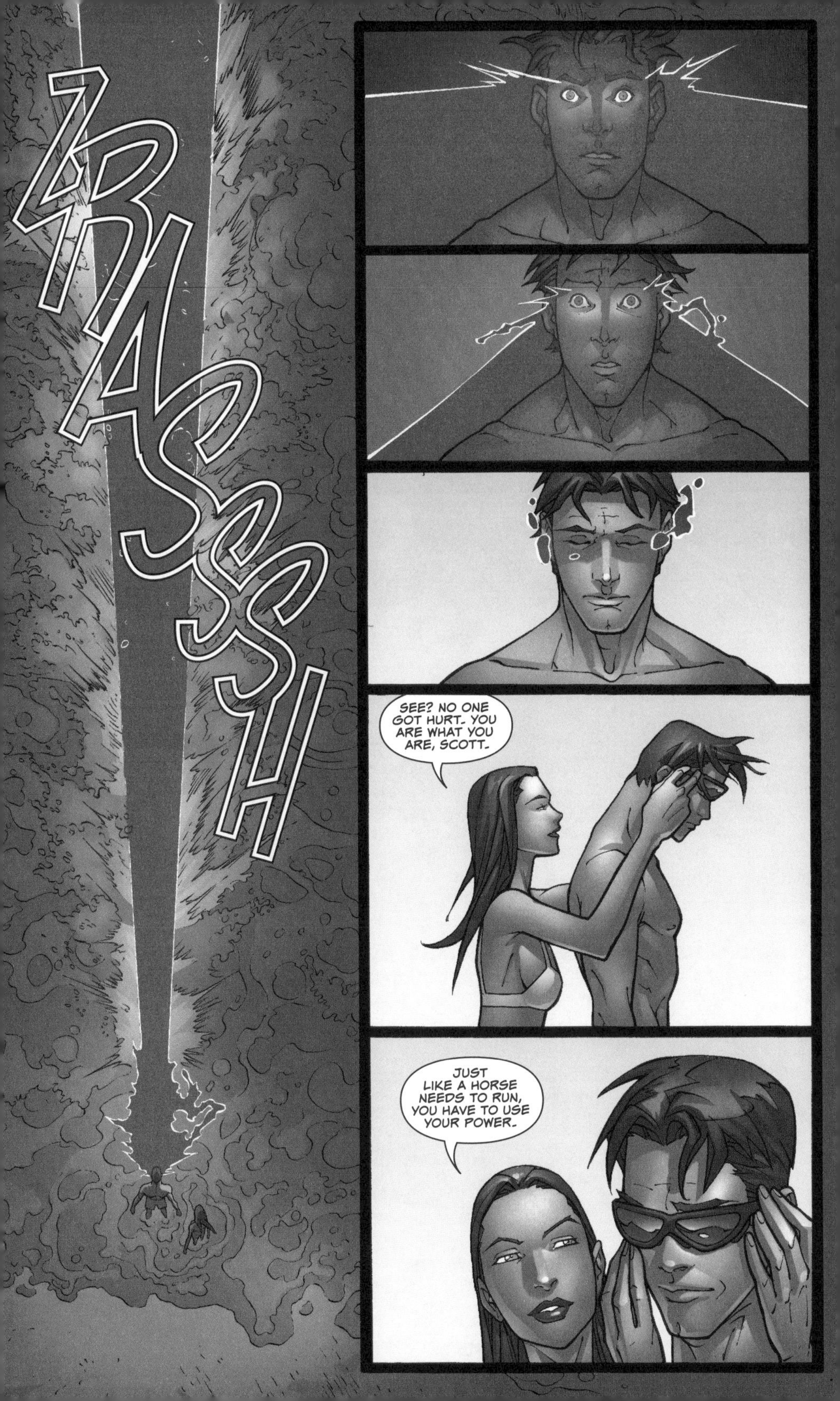
ZRAASSSH
SEE? NO ONE GOT HURT. YOU ARE WHAT YOU ARE, SCOTT.
JUST LIKE A HORSE NEEDS TO RUN, YOU HAVE TO USE YOUR POWER.

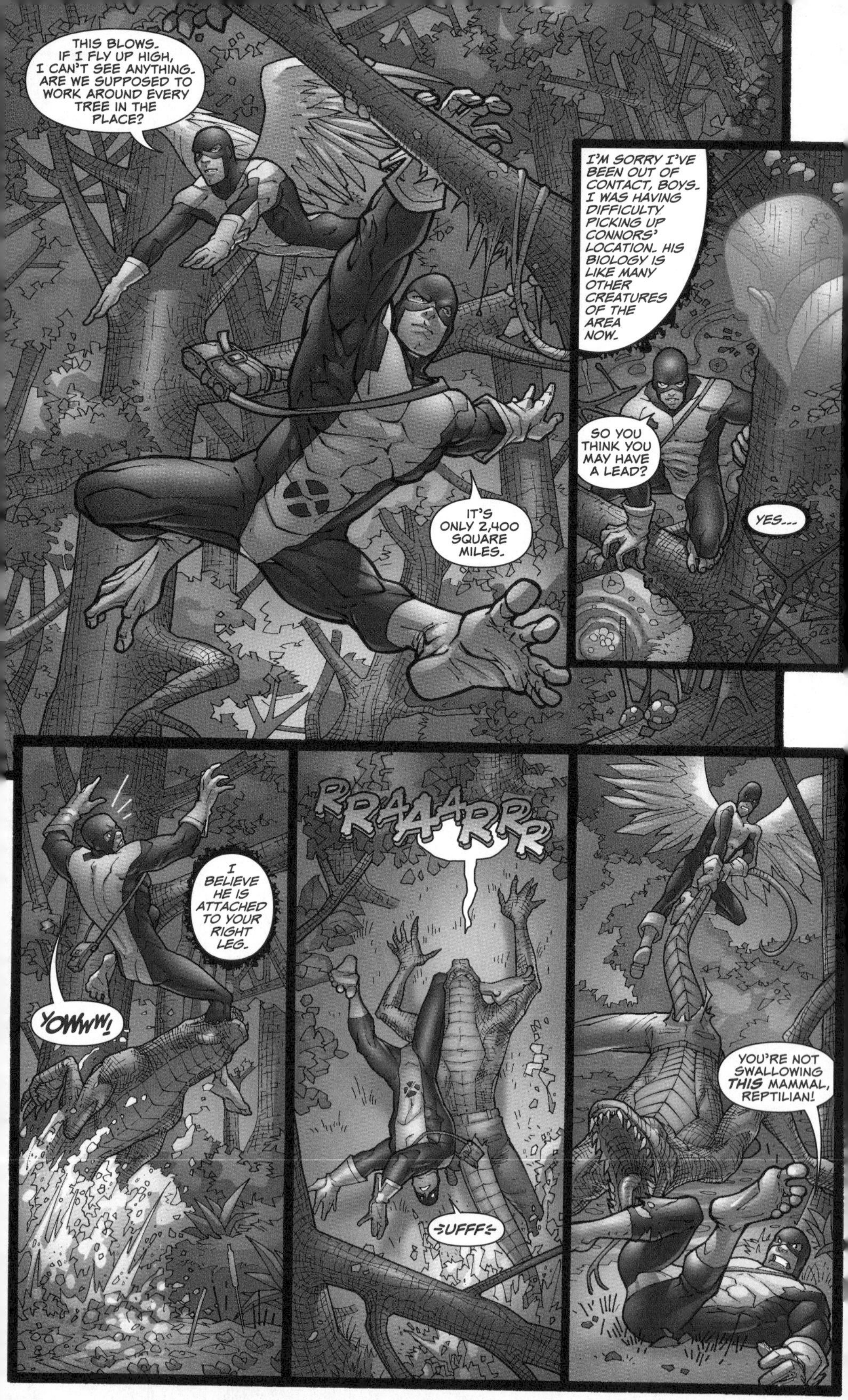
THIS BLOWS. IF I FLY UP HIGH, I CAN'T SEE ANYTHING. ARE WE SUPPOSED TO WORK AROUND EVERY TREE IN THE PLACE?
IT'S ONLY 2,400 SQUARE MILES.
I'M SORRY I'VE BEEN OUT OF CONTACT, BOYS. I WAS HAVING DIFFICULTY PICKING UP CONNORS' LOCATION. HIS BIOLOGY IS LIKE MANY OTHER CREATURES OF THE AREA NOW.
SO YOU THINK YOU MAY HAVE A LEAD?
YES...
I BELIEVE HE IS ATTACHED TO YOUR RIGHT LEG.
YOWWW!
RRAAARRR
UFFF
YOU'RE NOT SWALLOWING THIS MAMMAL, REPTILIAN!

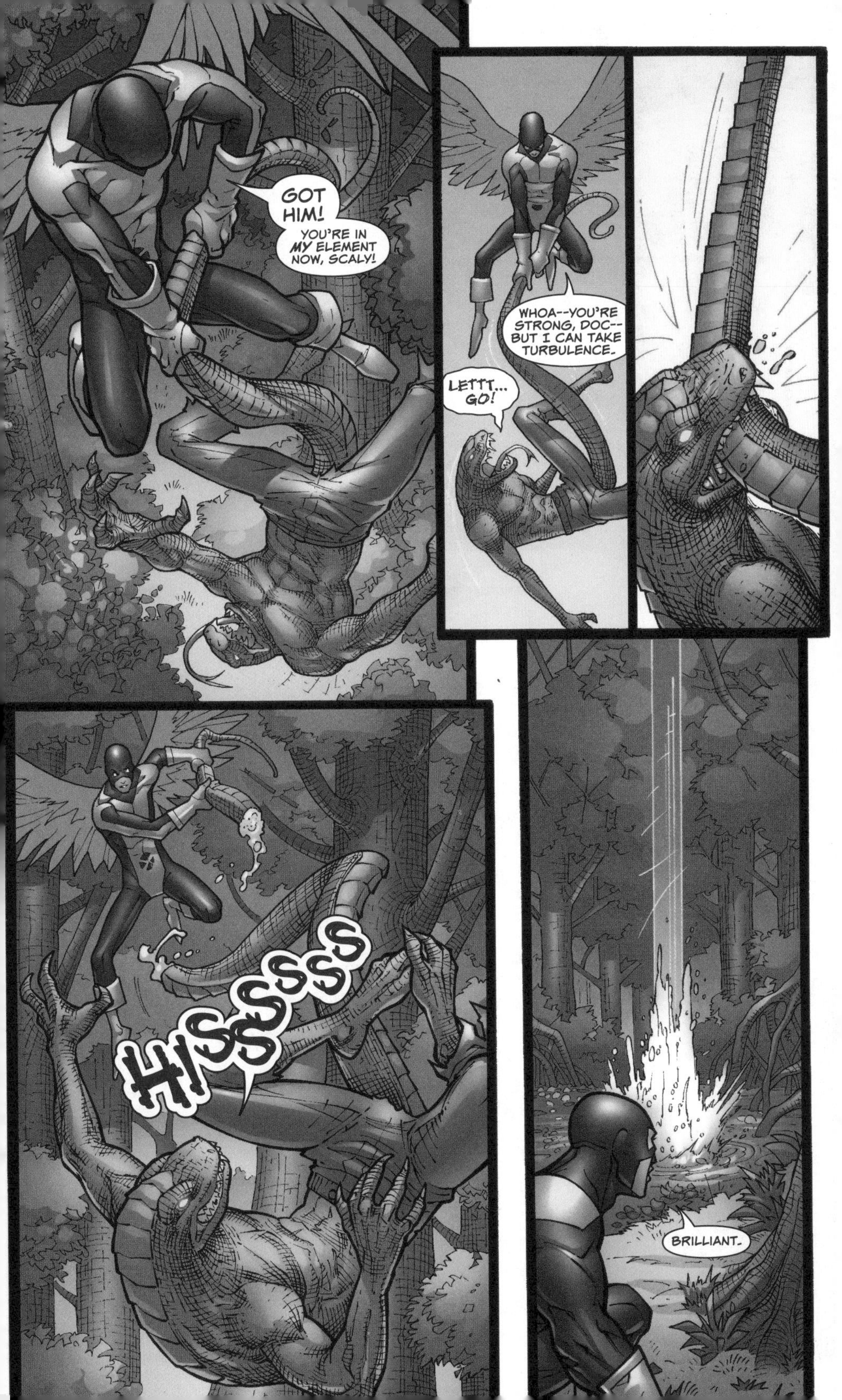

GOT HIM!
YOU'RE IN MY ELEMENT NOW, SCALY!
WHOA--YOU'RE STRONG, DOC--BUT I CAN TAKE TURBULENCE.
LETTT... GO!
HISSSSSS
BRILLIANT.

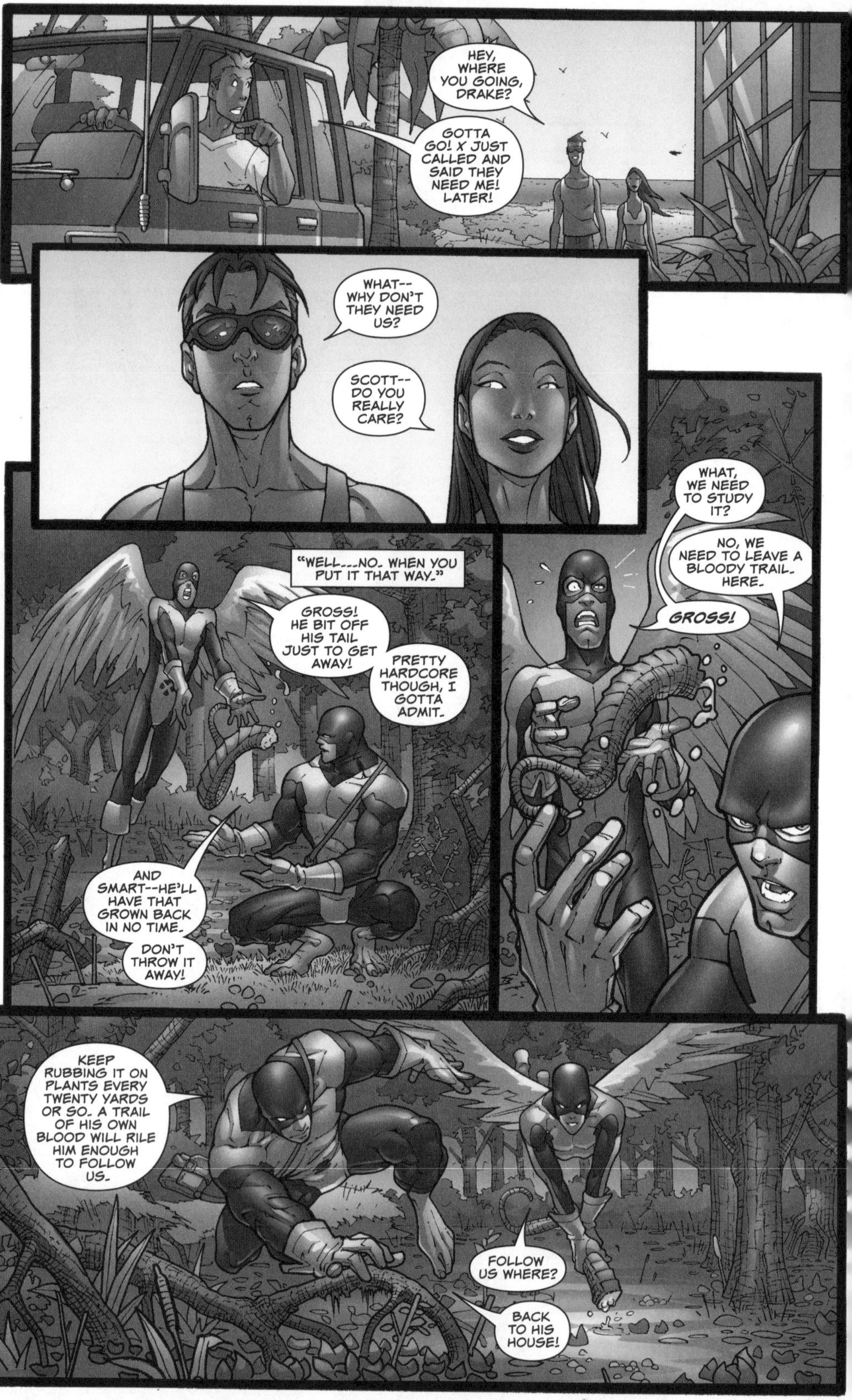
HEY, WHERE YOU GOING, DRAKE?
GOTTA GO! X JUST CALLED AND SAID THEY NEED ME! LATER!
WHAT-- WHY DON'T THEY NEED US?
SCOTT-- DO YOU REALLY CARE?
"WELL...NO. WHEN YOU PUT IT THAT WAY."
GROSS! HE BIT OFF HIS TAIL JUST TO GET AWAY!
PRETTY HARDCORE THOUGH, I GOTTA ADMIT.
AND SMART--HE'LL HAVE THAT GROWN BACK IN NO TIME.
DON'T THROW IT AWAY!
WHAT, WE NEED TO STUDY IT?
NO, WE NEED TO LEAVE A BLOODY TRAIL HERE.
GROSS!
KEEP RUBBING IT ON PLANTS EVERY TWENTY YARDS OR SO. A TRAIL OF HIS OWN BLOOD WILL RILE HIM ENOUGH TO FOLLOW US.
FOLLOW US WHERE?
BACK TO HIS HOUSE!

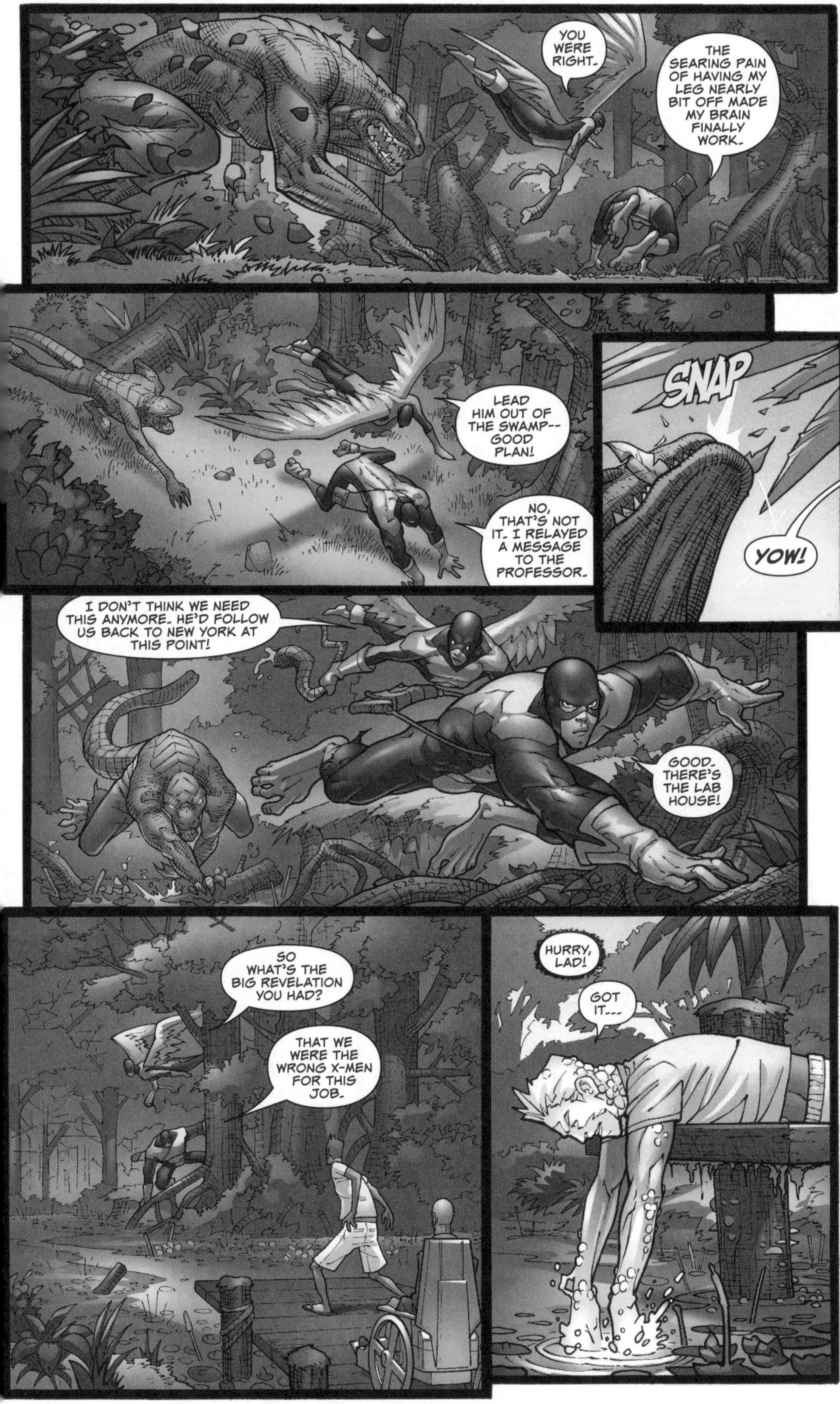

YOU WERE RIGHT.
THE SEARING PAIN OF HAVING MY LEG NEARLY BIT OFF MADE MY BRAIN FINALLY WORK.
LEAD HIM OUT OF THE SWAMP-- GOOD PLAN!
NO, THAT'S NOT IT. I RELAYED A MESSAGE TO THE PROFESSOR.
SNAP
YOW!
I DON'T THINK WE NEED THIS ANYMORE. HE'D FOLLOW US BACK TO NEW YORK AT THIS POINT!
GOOD. THERE'S THE LAB HOUSE!
SO WHAT'S THE BIG REVELATION YOU HAD?
THAT WE WERE THE WRONG X-MEN FOR THIS JOB.
HURRY, LAD!
GOT IT...

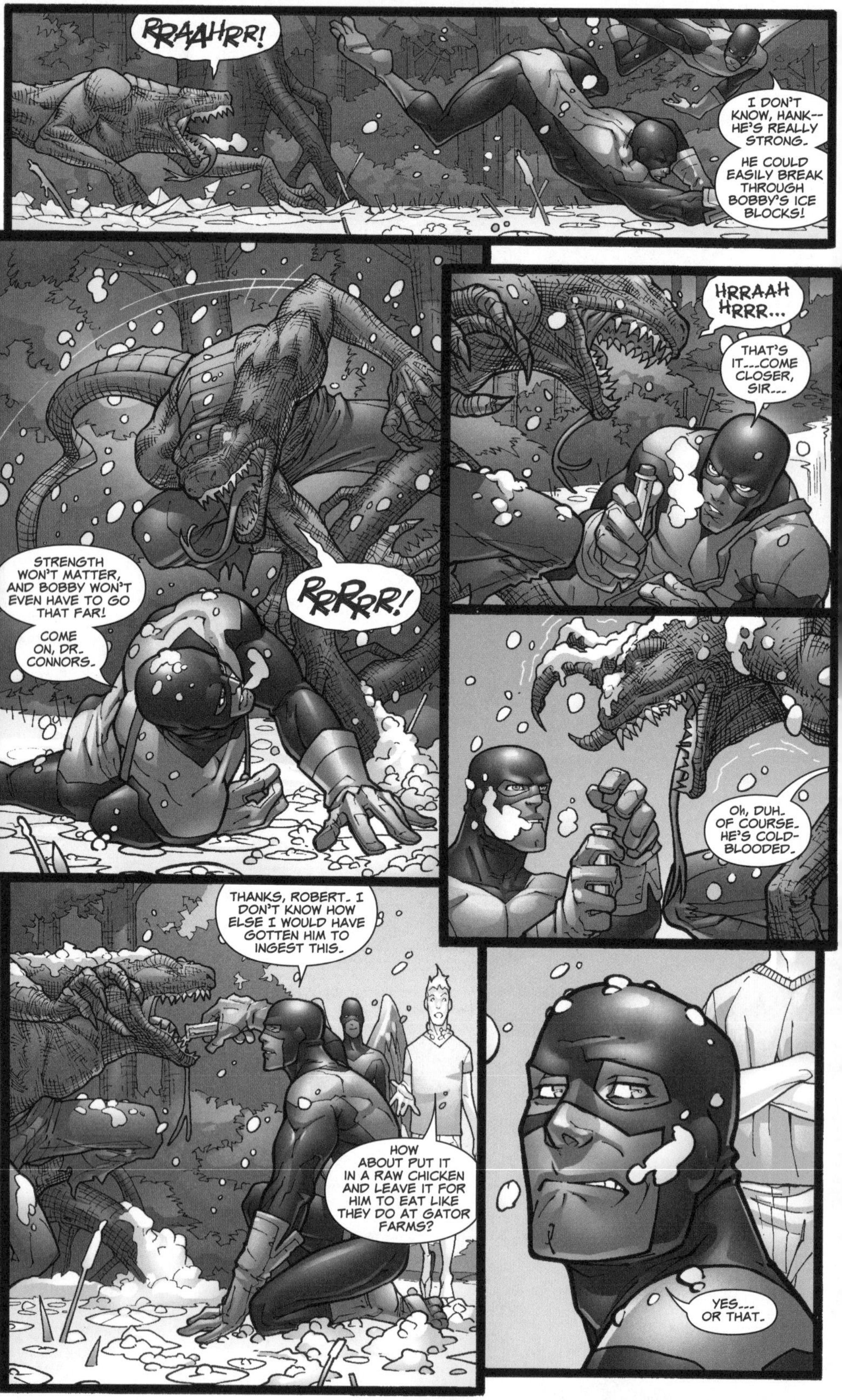
RRAAHRR!
I DON'T KNOW, HANK--HE'S REALLY STRONG.
HE COULD EASILY BREAK THROUGH BOBBY'S ICE BLOCKS!
STRENGTH WON'T MATTER, AND BOBBY WON'T EVEN HAVE TO GO THAT FAR!
COME ON, DR. CONNORS.
RRRRR!
HRRAAH HRRR...
THAT'S IT...COME CLOSER, SIR...
Oh, DUH. OF COURSE. HE'S COLD-BLOODED.
THANKS, ROBERT. I DON'T KNOW HOW ELSE I WOULD HAVE GOTTEN HIM TO INGEST THIS.
HOW ABOUT PUT IT IN A RAW CHICKEN AND LEAVE IT FOR HIM TO EAT LIKE THEY DO AT GATOR FARMS?
YES... OR THAT.

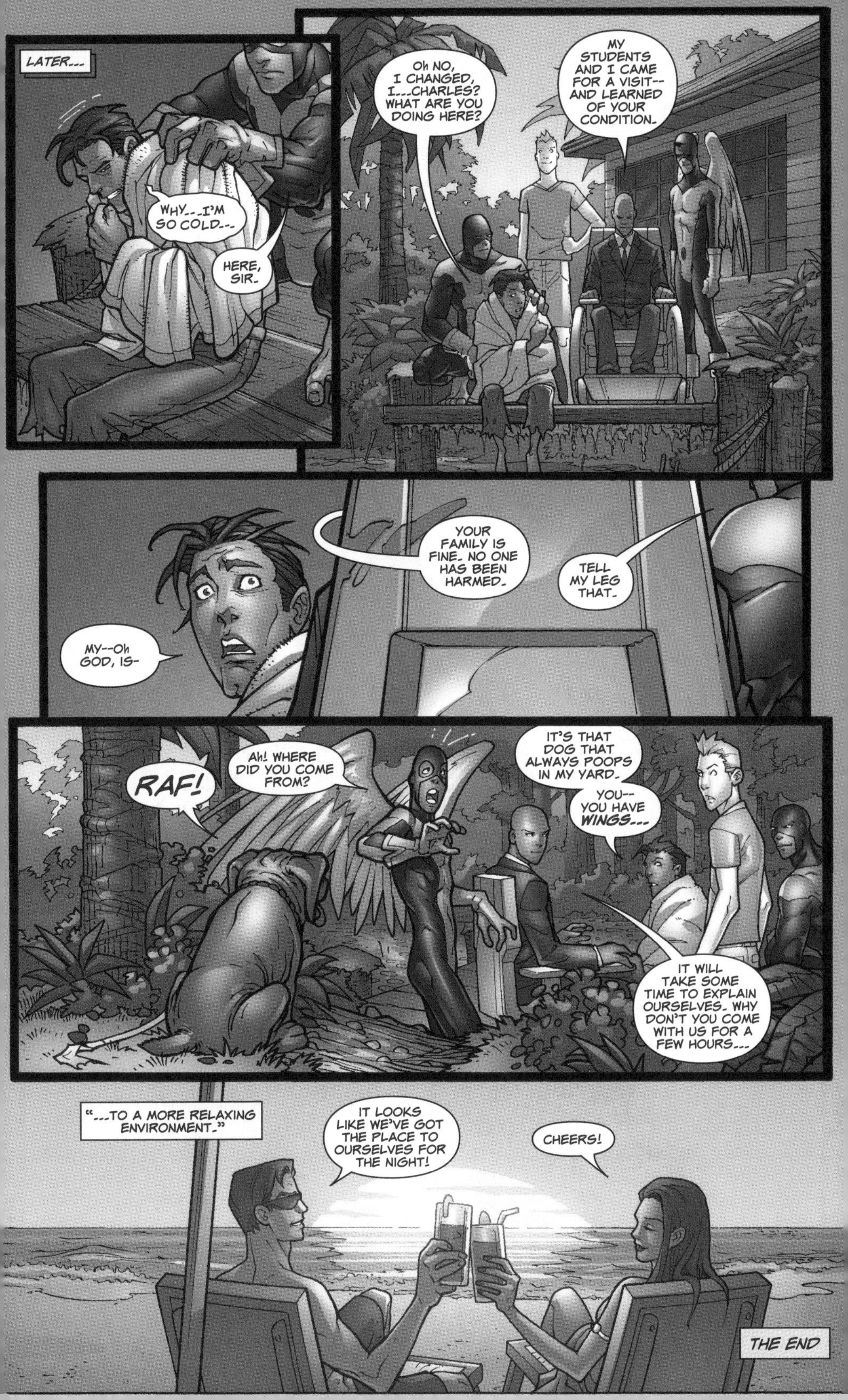
LATER...
WHY...I'M SO COLD...
HERE, SIR.
Oh NO, I CHANGED, I...CHARLES? WHAT ARE YOU DOING HERE?
MY STUDENTS AND I CAME FOR A VISIT-- AND LEARNED OF YOUR CONDITION.
YOUR FAMILY IS FINE. NO ONE HAS BEEN HARMED.
TELL MY LEG THAT.
MY--Oh GOD, IS-
RAF!
Ah! WHERE DID YOU COME FROM?
IT'S THAT DOG THAT ALWAYS POOPS IN MY YARD.
YOU-- YOU HAVE WINGS...
IT WILL TAKE SOME TIME TO EXPLAIN OURSELVES. WHY DON'T YOU COME WITH US FOR A FEW HOURS...
"...TO A MORE RELAXING ENVIRONMENT."
IT LOOKS LIKE WE'VE GOT THE PLACE TO OURSELVES FOR THE NIGHT!
CHEERS!
THE END

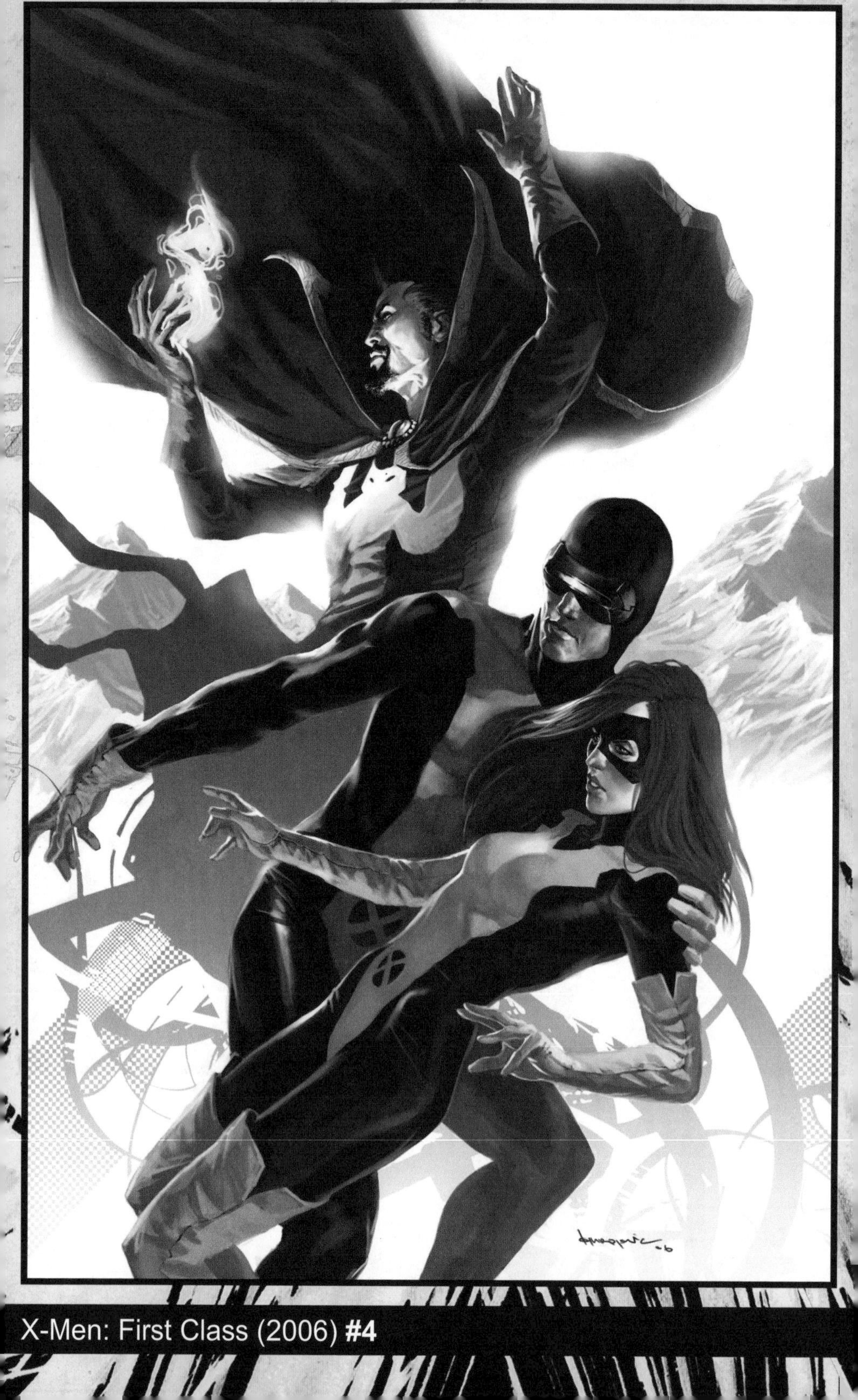

X-Men: First Class (2006) **#4**

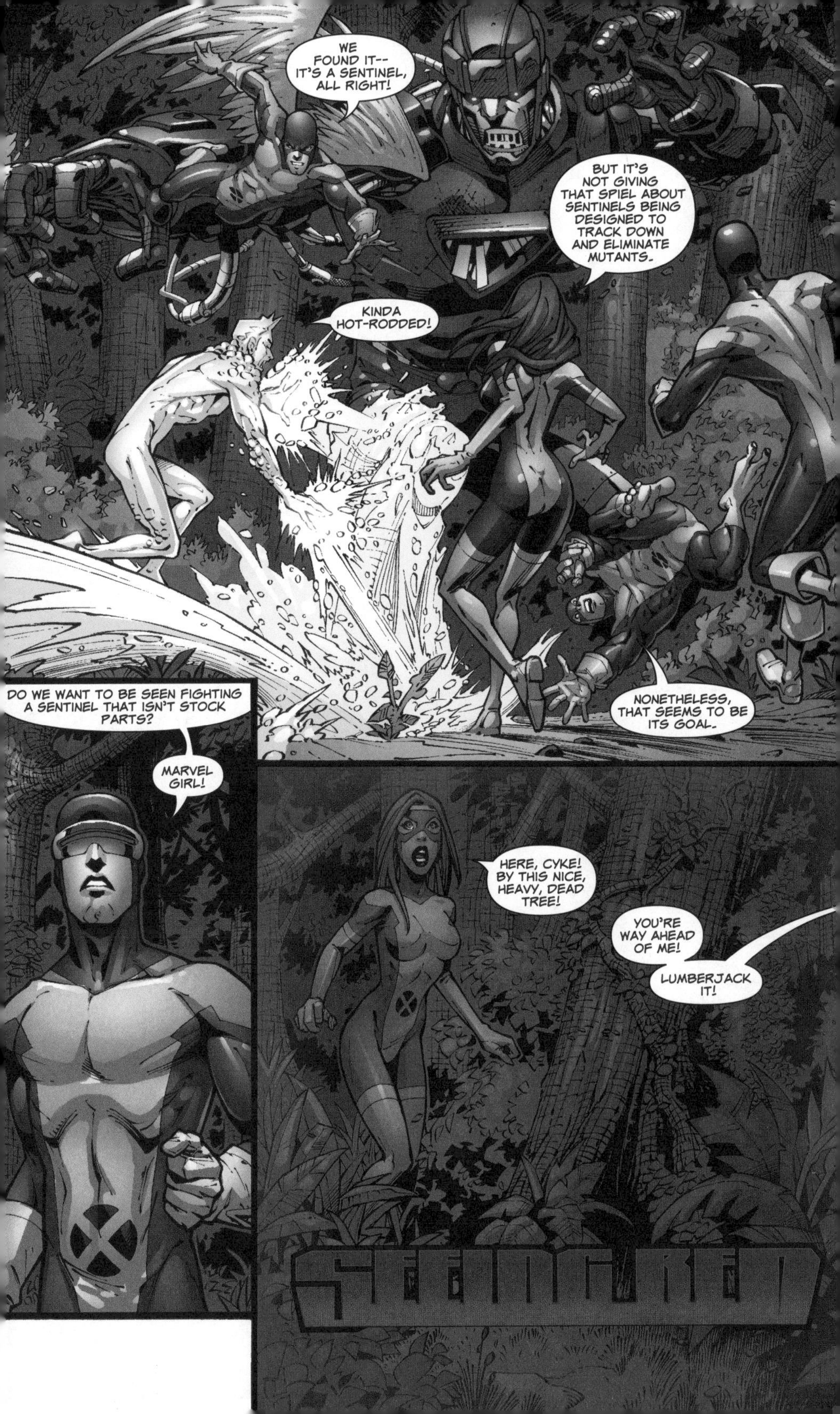
WE FOUND IT-- IT'S A SENTINEL, ALL RIGHT!
BUT IT'S NOT GIVING THAT SPIEL ABOUT SENTINELS BEING DESIGNED TO TRACK DOWN AND ELIMINATE MUTANTS.
KINDA HOT-RODDED!
NONETHELESS, THAT SEEMS TO BE ITS GOAL.
DO WE WANT TO BE SEEN FIGHTING A SENTINEL THAT ISN'T STOCK PARTS?
MARVEL GIRL!
HERE, CYKE! BY THIS NICE, HEAVY, DEAD TREE!
YOU'RE WAY AHEAD OF ME!
LUMBERJACK IT!

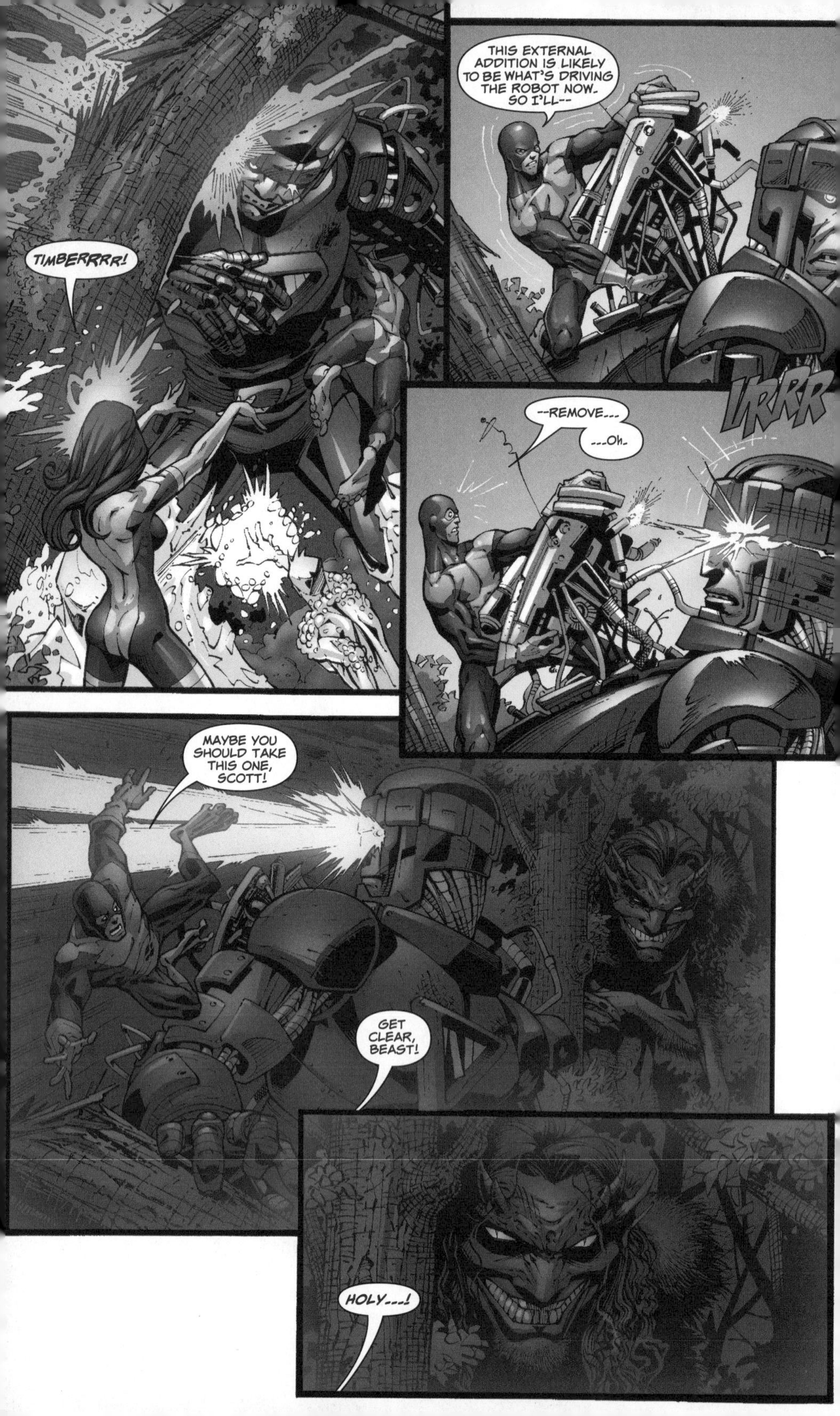
TIMBERRRR!
THIS EXTERNAL ADDITION IS LIKELY TO BE WHAT'S DRIVING THE ROBOT NOW. SO I'LL--
--REMOVE...
...Oh.
URRR
MAYBE YOU SHOULD TAKE THIS ONE, SCOTT!
GET CLEAR, BEAST!
HOLY...!

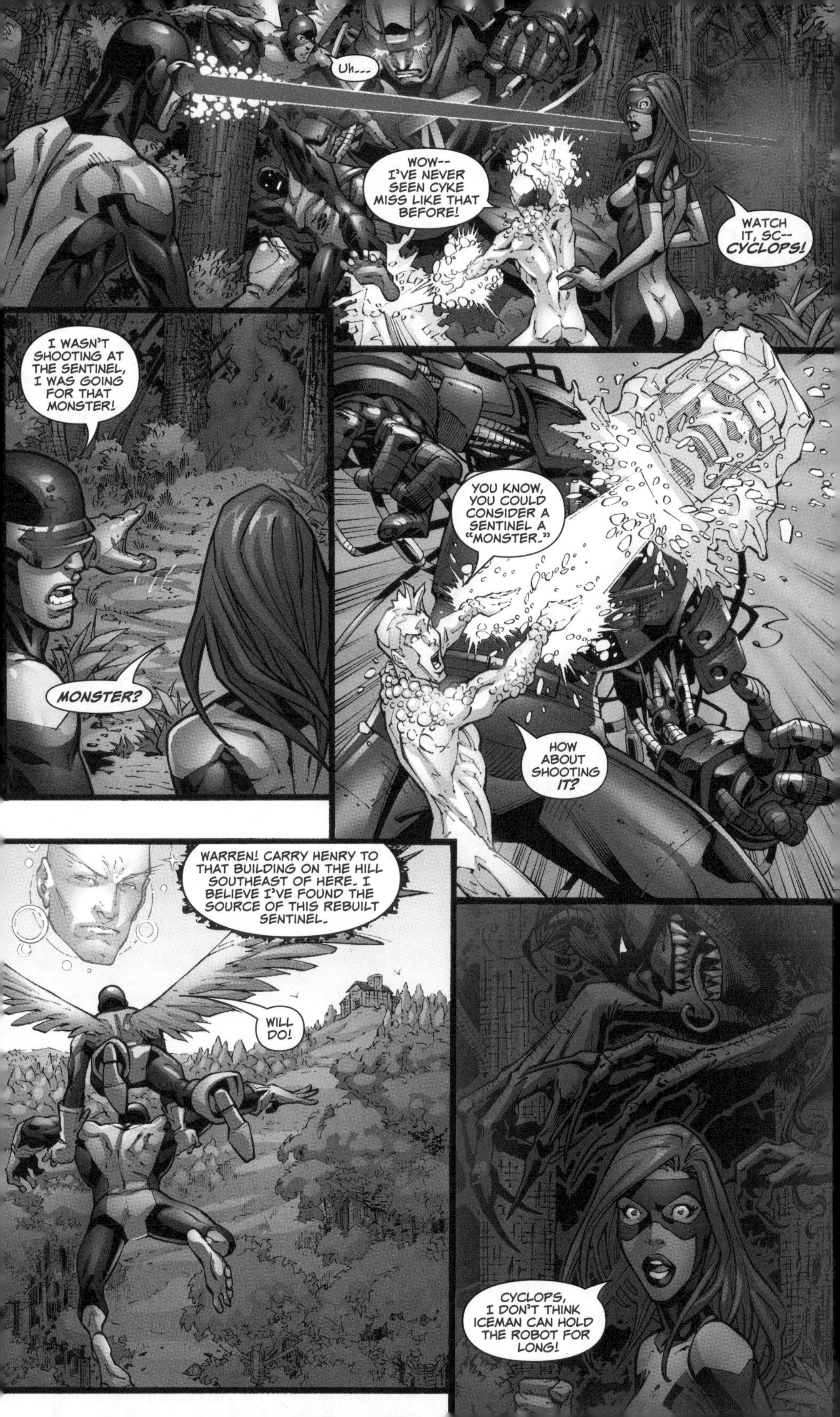
Uh--
WOW-- I'VE NEVER SEEN CYKE MISS LIKE THAT BEFORE!
WATCH IT, SC-- CYCLOPS!
I WASN'T SHOOTING AT THE SENTINEL, I WAS GOING FOR THAT MONSTER!
MONSTER?
YOU KNOW, YOU COULD CONSIDER A SENTINEL A "MONSTER."
HOW ABOUT SHOOTING IT?
WARREN! CARRY HENRY TO THAT BUILDING ON THE HILL SOUTHEAST OF HERE. I BELIEVE I'VE FOUND THE SOURCE OF THIS REBUILT SENTINEL.
WILL DO!
CYCLOPS, I DON'T THINK ICEMAN CAN HOLD THE ROBOT FOR LONG!

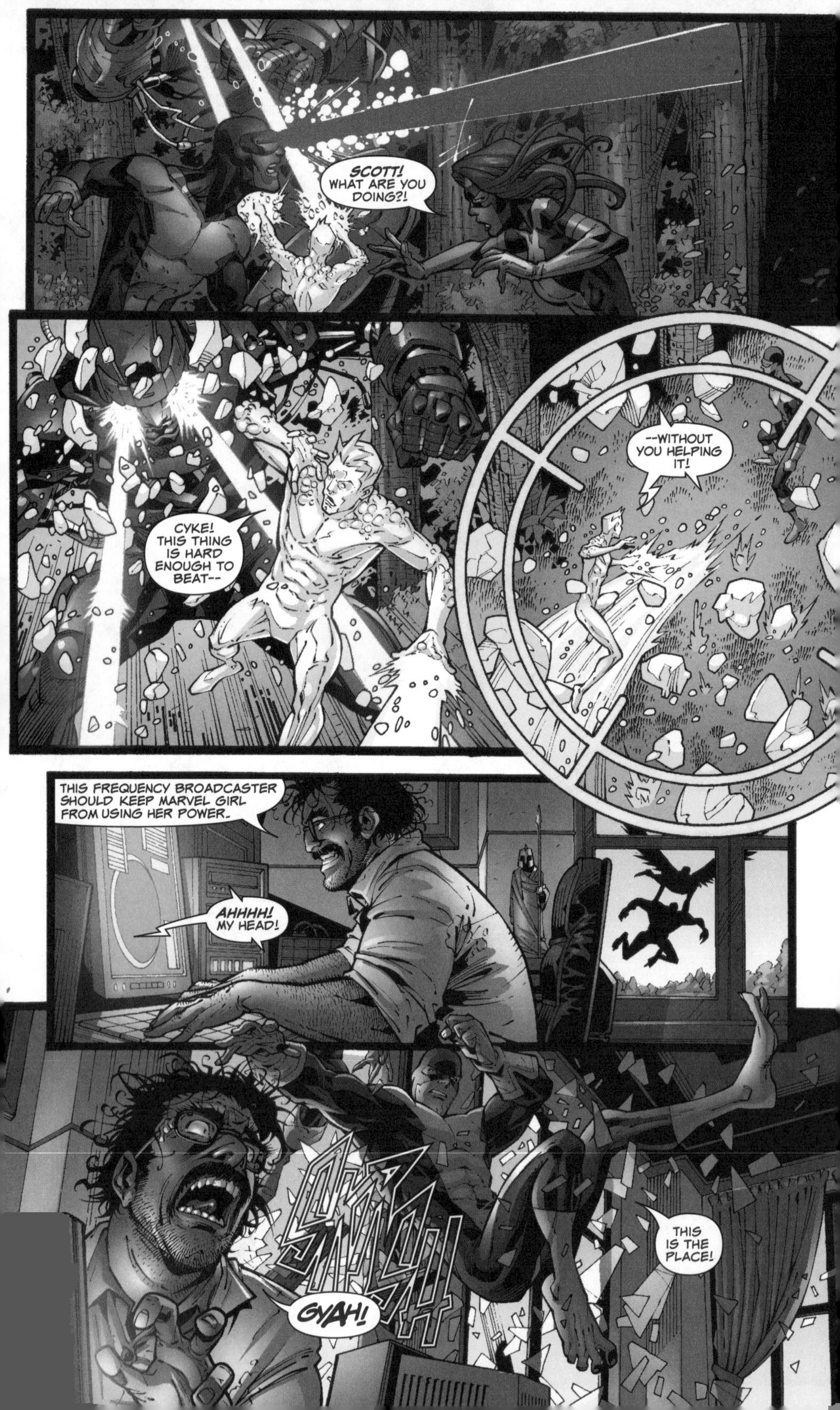
SCOTT! WHAT ARE YOU DOING?!
CYKE! THIS THING IS HARD ENOUGH TO BEAT--
--WITHOUT YOU HELPING IT!
THIS FREQUENCY BROADCASTER SHOULD KEEP MARVEL GIRL FROM USING HER POWER.
AHHHH! MY HEAD!
SMASH
THIS IS THE PLACE!
GYAH!

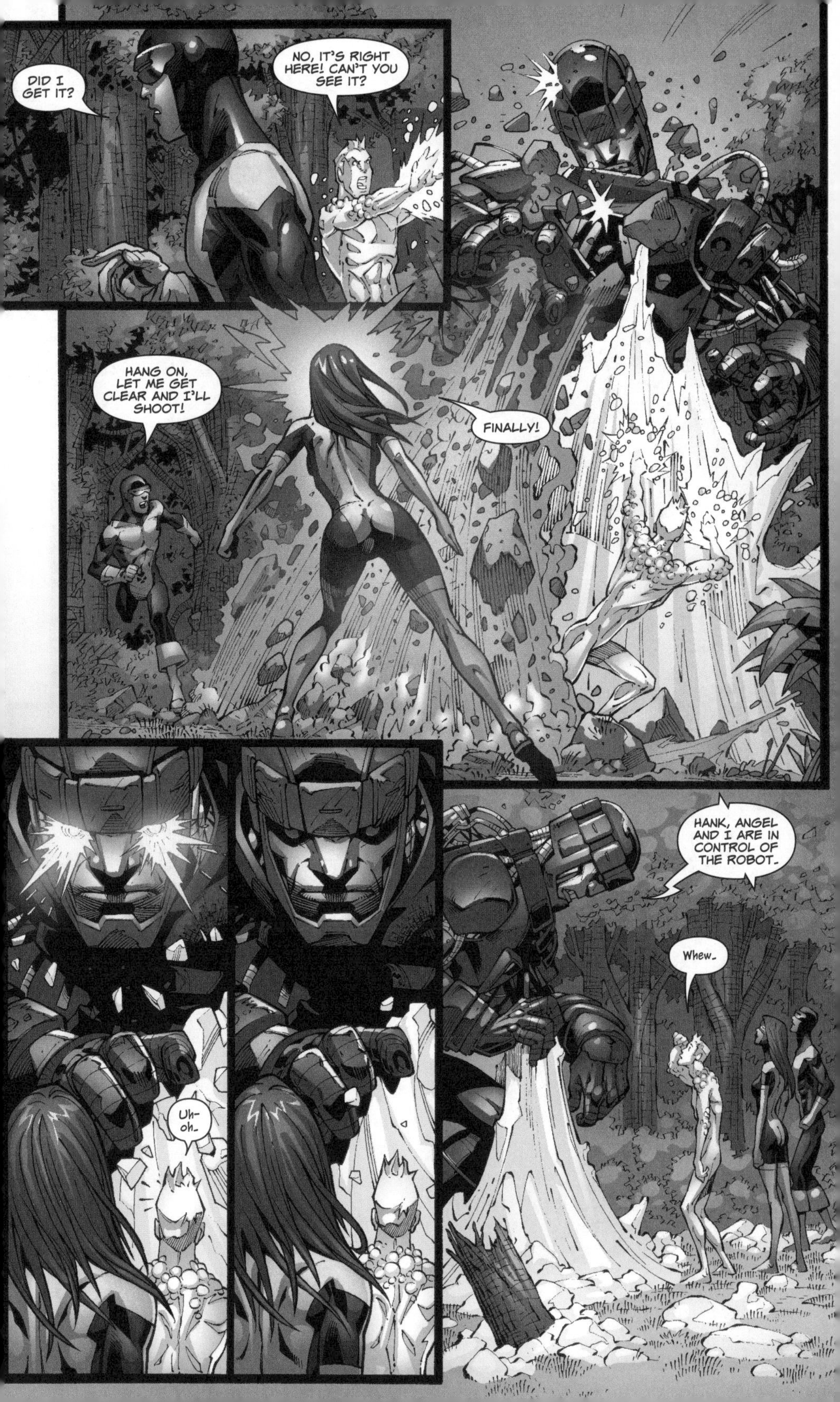
DID I GET IT?
NO, IT'S RIGHT HERE! CAN'T YOU SEE IT?
HANG ON, LET ME GET CLEAR AND I'LL SHOOT!
FINALLY!
Uh-oh.
HANK, ANGEL AND I ARE IN CONTROL OF THE ROBOT.
Whew.

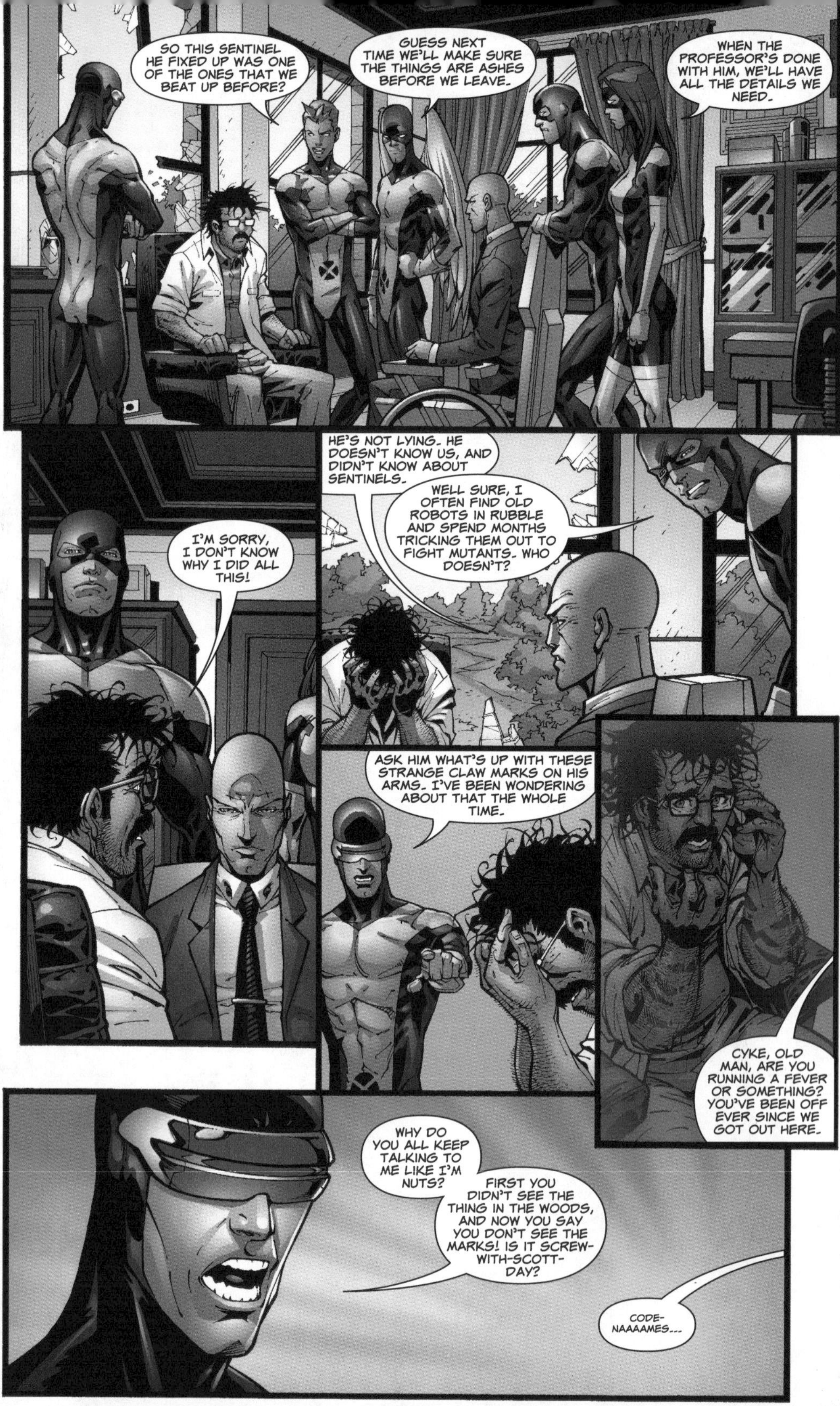

SO THIS SENTINEL HE FIXED UP WAS ONE OF THE ONES THAT WE BEAT UP BEFORE?
GUESS NEXT TIME WE'LL MAKE SURE THE THINGS ARE ASHES BEFORE WE LEAVE.
WHEN THE PROFESSOR'S DONE WITH HIM, WE'LL HAVE ALL THE DETAILS WE NEED.
I'M SORRY, I DON'T KNOW WHY I DID ALL THIS!
HE'S NOT LYING. HE DOESN'T KNOW US, AND DIDN'T KNOW ABOUT SENTINELS.
WELL SURE, I OFTEN FIND OLD ROBOTS IN RUBBLE AND SPEND MONTHS TRICKING THEM OUT TO FIGHT MUTANTS. WHO DOESN'T?
ASK HIM WHAT'S UP WITH THESE STRANGE CLAW MARKS ON HIS ARMS. I'VE BEEN WONDERING ABOUT THAT THE WHOLE TIME.
CYKE, OLD MAN, ARE YOU RUNNING A FEVER OR SOMETHING? YOU'VE BEEN OFF EVER SINCE WE GOT OUT HERE.
WHY DO YOU ALL KEEP TALKING TO ME LIKE I'M NUTS?
FIRST YOU DIDN'T SEE THE THING IN THE WOODS, AND NOW YOU SAY YOU DON'T SEE THE MARKS! IS IT SCREW-WITH-SCOTT-DAY?
CODE-NAAAAMES...

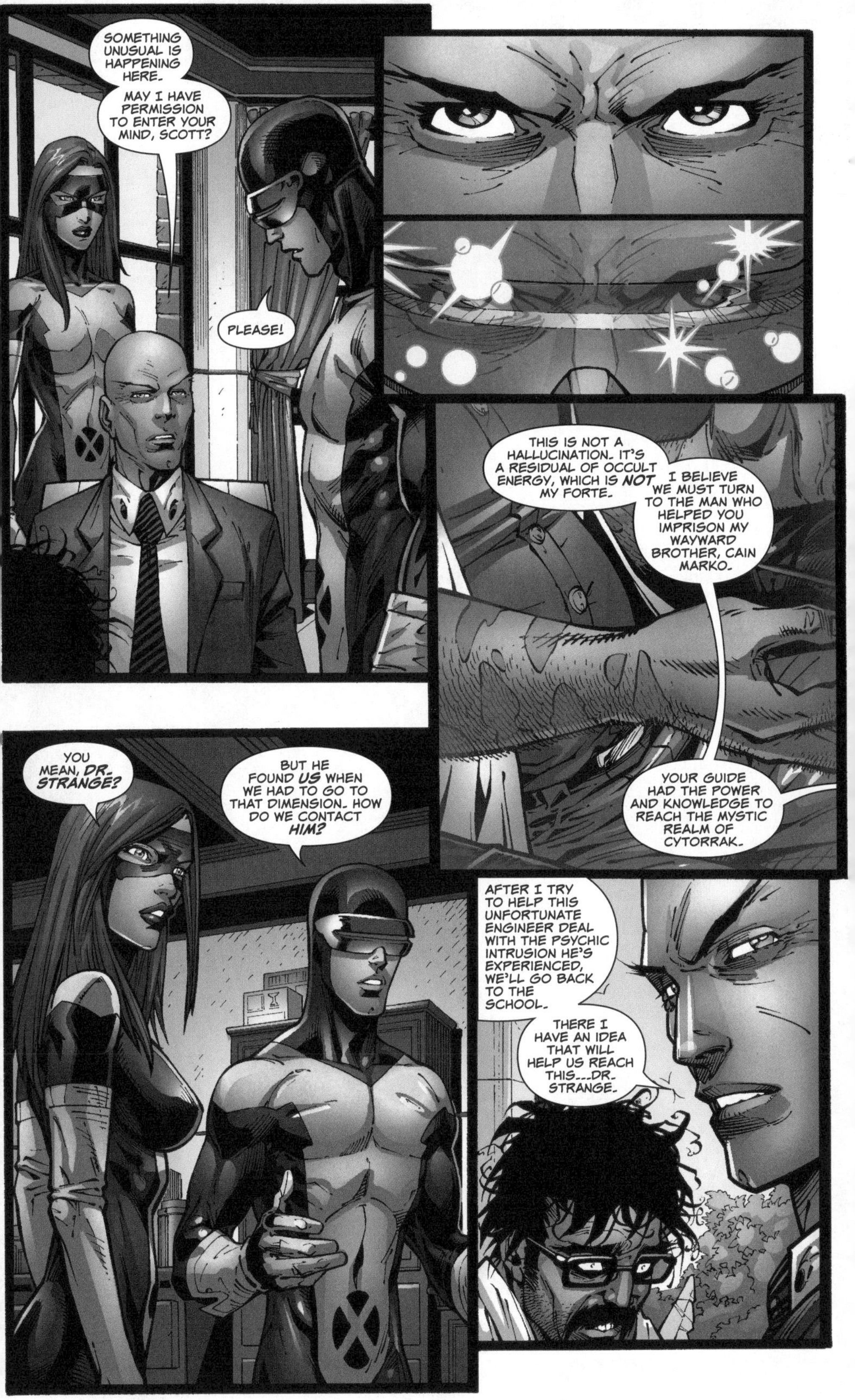

SOMETHING UNUSUAL IS HAPPENING HERE.
MAY I HAVE PERMISSION TO ENTER YOUR MIND, SCOTT?
PLEASE!
THIS IS NOT A HALLUCINATION. IT'S A RESIDUAL OF OCCULT ENERGY, WHICH IS NOT MY FORTE.
I BELIEVE WE MUST TURN TO THE MAN WHO HELPED YOU IMPRISON MY WAYWARD BROTHER, CAIN MARKO.
YOUR GUIDE HAD THE POWER AND KNOWLEDGE TO REACH THE MYSTIC REALM OF CYTORRAK.
YOU MEAN, DR. STRANGE?
BUT HE FOUND US WHEN WE HAD TO GO TO THAT DIMENSION. HOW DO WE CONTACT HIM?
AFTER I TRY TO HELP THIS UNFORTUNATE ENGINEER DEAL WITH THE PSYCHIC INTRUSION HE'S EXPERIENCED, WE'LL GO BACK TO THE SCHOOL.
THERE I HAVE AN IDEA THAT WILL HELP US REACH THIS...DR. STRANGE.

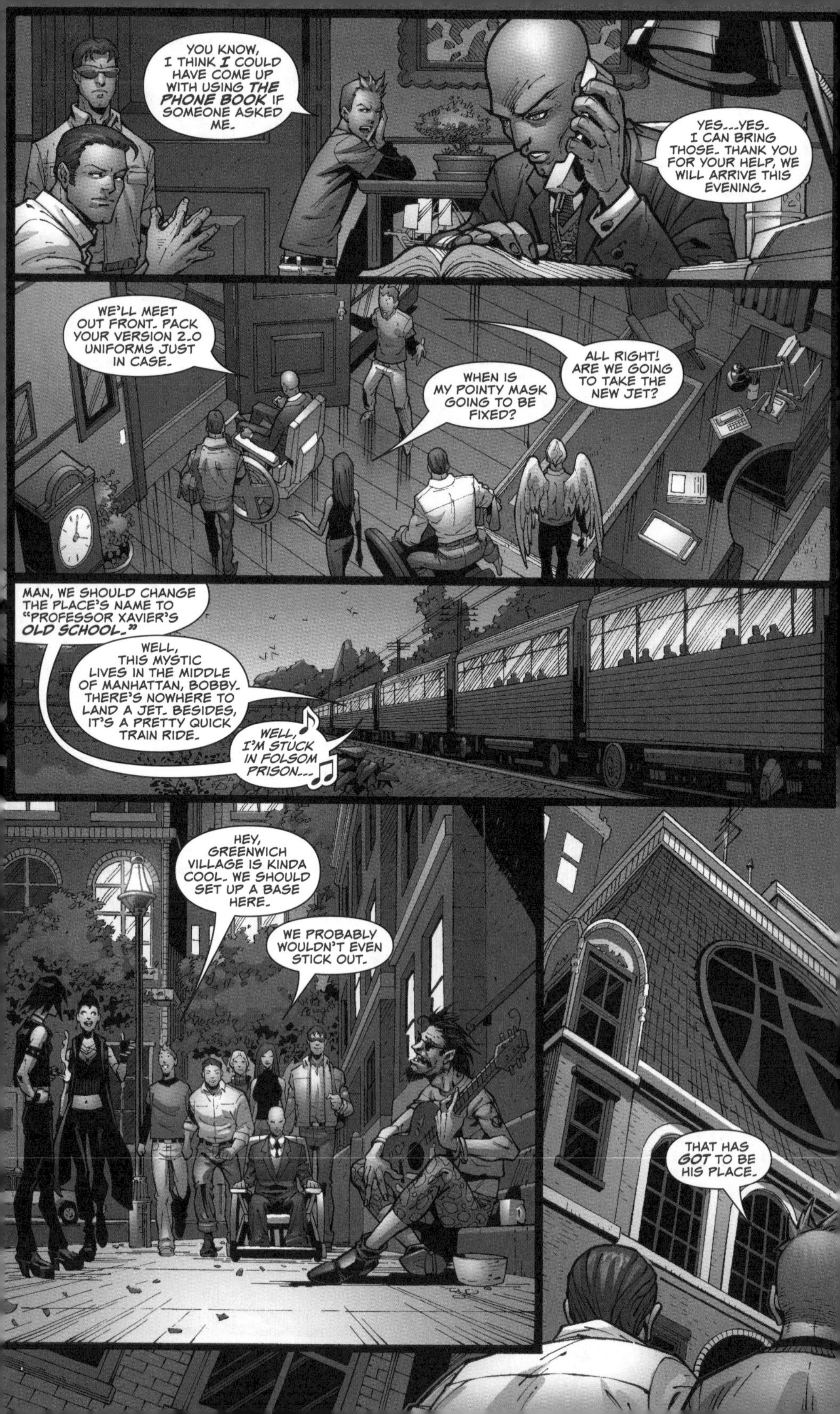
YOU KNOW, I THINK I COULD HAVE COME UP WITH USING THE PHONE BOOK IF SOMEONE ASKED ME.
YES...YES. I CAN BRING THOSE. THANK YOU FOR YOUR HELP, WE WILL ARRIVE THIS EVENING.
WE'LL MEET OUT FRONT. PACK YOUR VERSION 2.0 UNIFORMS JUST IN CASE.
ALL RIGHT! ARE WE GOING TO TAKE THE NEW JET?
WHEN IS MY POINTY MASK GOING TO BE FIXED?
MAN, WE SHOULD CHANGE THE PLACE'S NAME TO "PROFESSOR XAVIER'S OLD SCHOOL."
WELL, THIS MYSTIC LIVES IN THE MIDDLE OF MANHATTAN, BOBBY. THERE'S NOWHERE TO LAND A JET. BESIDES, IT'S A PRETTY QUICK TRAIN RIDE.
WELL, I'M STUCK IN FOLSOM PRISON...
HEY, GREENWICH VILLAGE IS KINDA COOL. WE SHOULD SET UP A BASE HERE.
WE PROBABLY WOULDN'T EVEN STICK OUT.
THAT HAS GOT TO BE HIS PLACE.

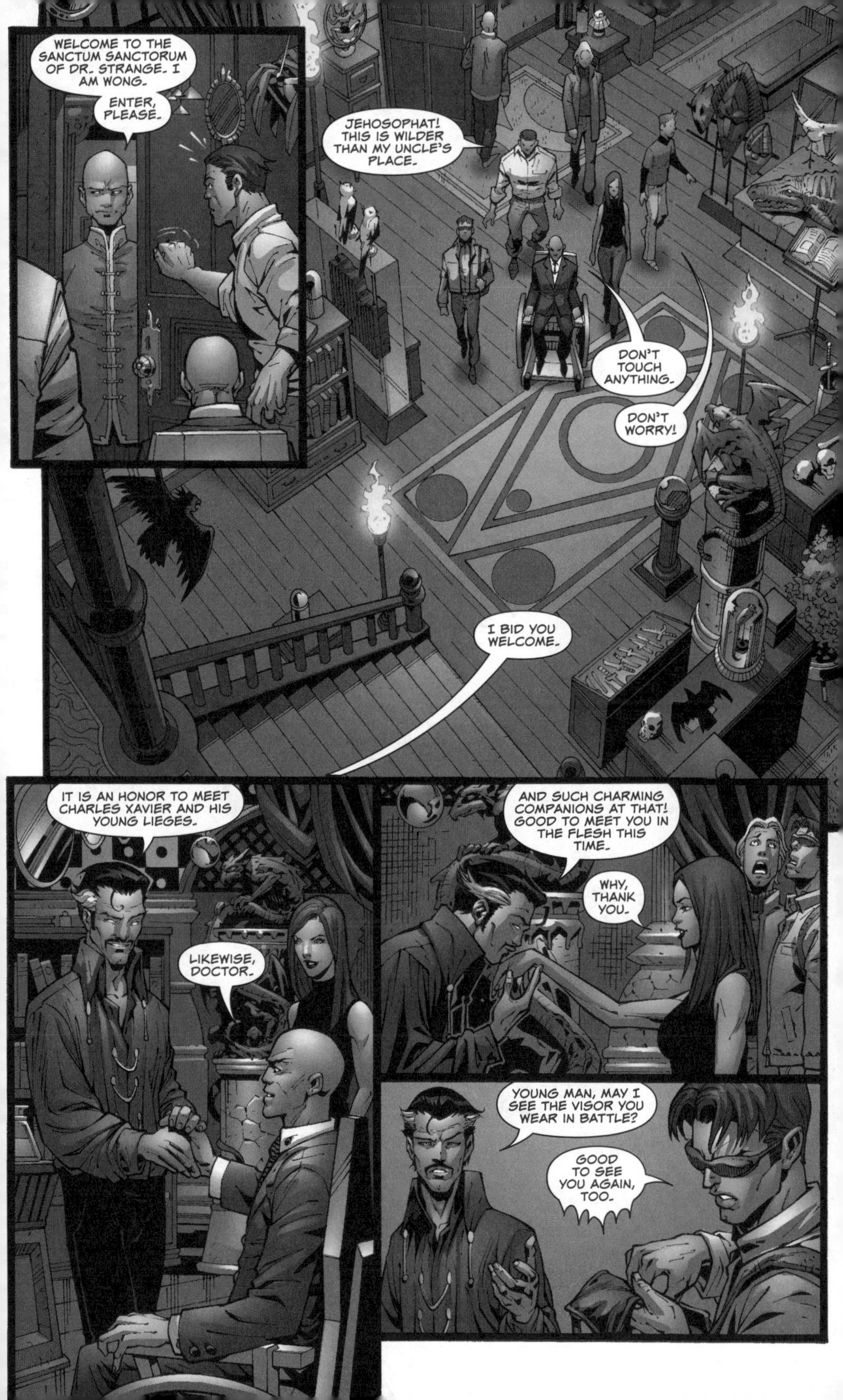
WELCOME TO THE SANCTUM SANCTORUM OF DR. STRANGE. I AM WONG.
ENTER, PLEASE.
JEHOSOPHAT! THIS IS WILDER THAN MY UNCLE'S PLACE.
DON'T TOUCH ANYTHING.
DON'T WORRY!
I BID YOU WELCOME.
IT IS AN HONOR TO MEET CHARLES XAVIER AND HIS YOUNG LIEGES.
LIKEWISE, DOCTOR.
AND SUCH CHARMING COMPANIONS AT THAT! GOOD TO MEET YOU IN THE FLESH THIS TIME.
WHY, THANK YOU.
YOUNG MAN, MAY I SEE THE VISOR YOU WEAR IN BATTLE?
GOOD TO SEE YOU AGAIN, TOO.

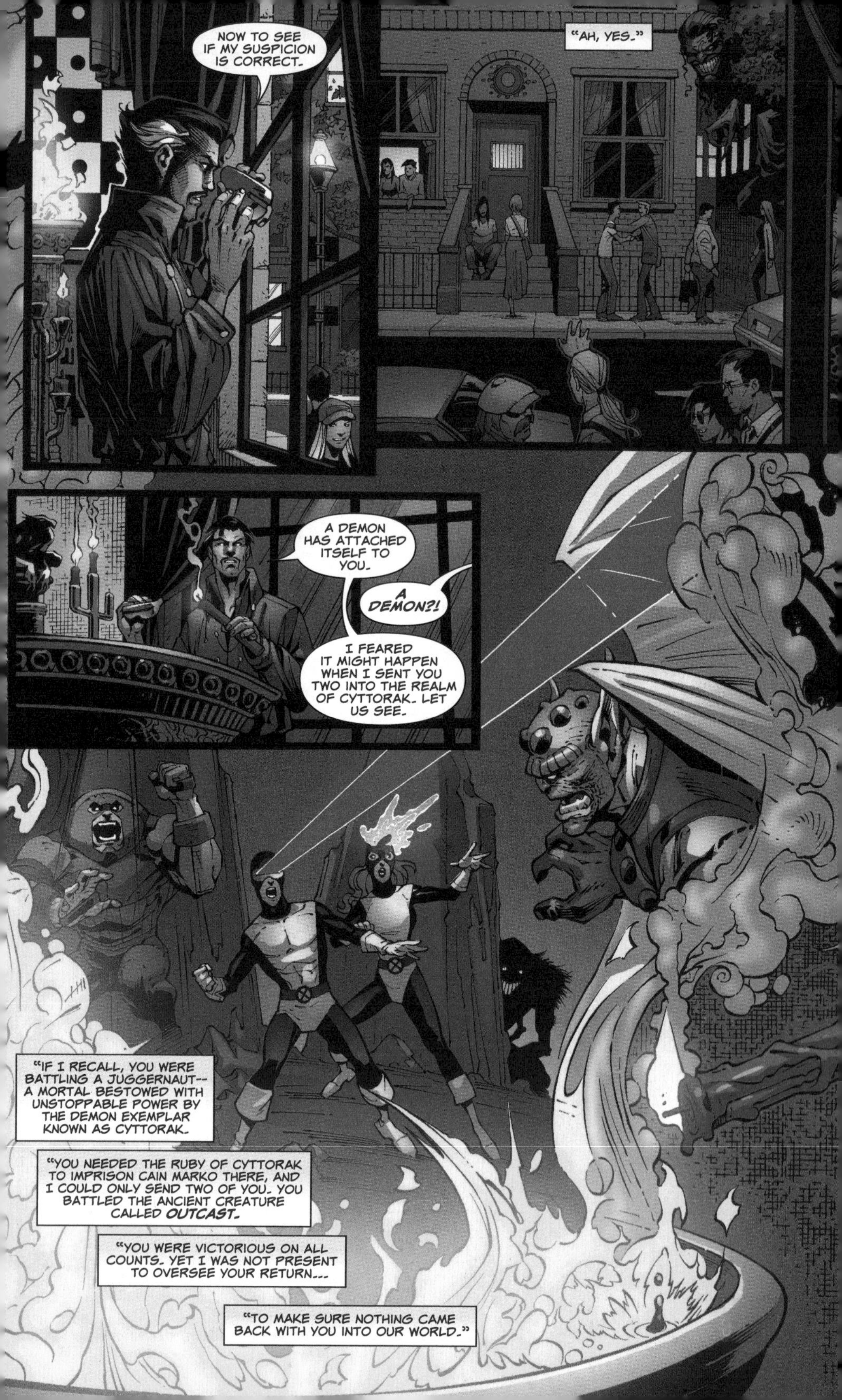
NOW TO SEE IF MY SUSPICION IS CORRECT.
"AH, YES."
A DEMON HAS ATTACHED ITSELF TO YOU.
A DEMON?!
I FEARED IT MIGHT HAPPEN WHEN I SENT YOU TWO INTO THE REALM OF CYTTORAK. LET US SEE.
"IF I RECALL, YOU WERE BATTLING A JUGGERNAUT-- A MORTAL BESTOWED WITH UNSTOPPABLE POWER BY THE DEMON EXEMPLAR KNOWN AS CYTTORAK.
"YOU NEEDED THE RUBY OF CYTTORAK TO IMPRISON CAIN MARKO THERE, AND I COULD ONLY SEND TWO OF YOU. YOU BATTLED THE ANCIENT CREATURE CALLED OUTCAST.
"YOU WERE VICTORIOUS ON ALL COUNTS. YET I WAS NOT PRESENT TO OVERSEE YOUR RETURN...
"TO MAKE SURE NOTHING CAME BACK WITH YOU INTO OUR WORLD."

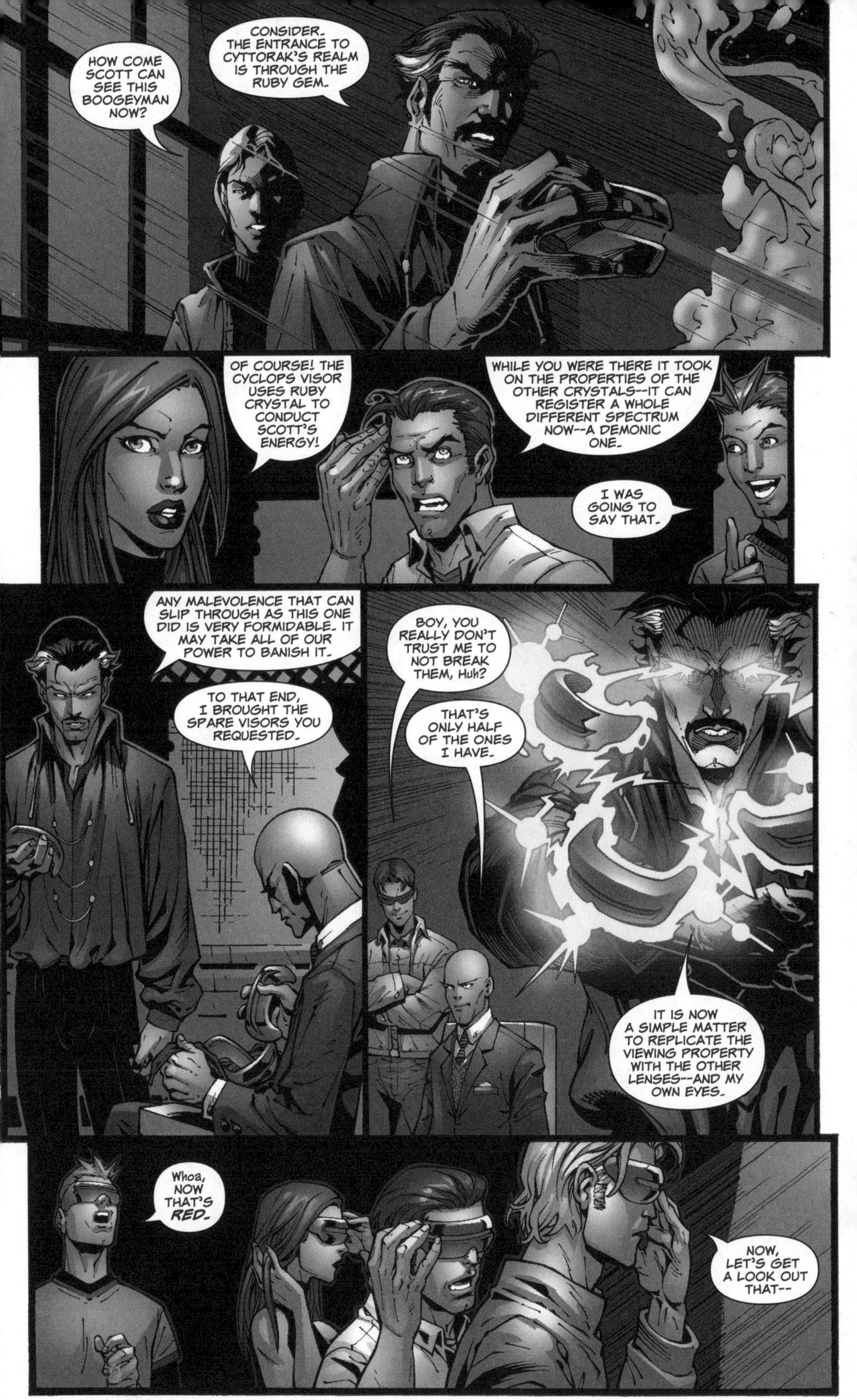
HOW COME SCOTT CAN SEE THIS BOOGEYMAN NOW?
CONSIDER. THE ENTRANCE TO CYTTORAK'S REALM IS THROUGH THE RUBY GEM.
OF COURSE! THE CYCLOPS VISOR USES RUBY CRYSTAL TO CONDUCT SCOTT'S ENERGY!
WHILE YOU WERE THERE IT TOOK ON THE PROPERTIES OF THE OTHER CRYSTALS--IT CAN REGISTER A WHOLE DIFFERENT SPECTRUM NOW--A DEMONIC ONE.
I WAS GOING TO SAY THAT.
ANY MALEVOLENCE THAT CAN SLIP THROUGH AS THIS ONE DID IS VERY FORMIDABLE. IT MAY TAKE ALL OF OUR POWER TO BANISH IT.
TO THAT END, I BROUGHT THE SPARE VISORS YOU REQUESTED.
BOY, YOU REALLY DON'T TRUST ME TO NOT BREAK THEM, Huh?
THAT'S ONLY HALF OF THE ONES I HAVE.
IT IS NOW A SIMPLE MATTER TO REPLICATE THE VIEWING PROPERTY WITH THE OTHER LENSES--AND MY OWN EYES.
Whoa, NOW THAT'S RED.
NOW, LET'S GET A LOOK OUT THAT--

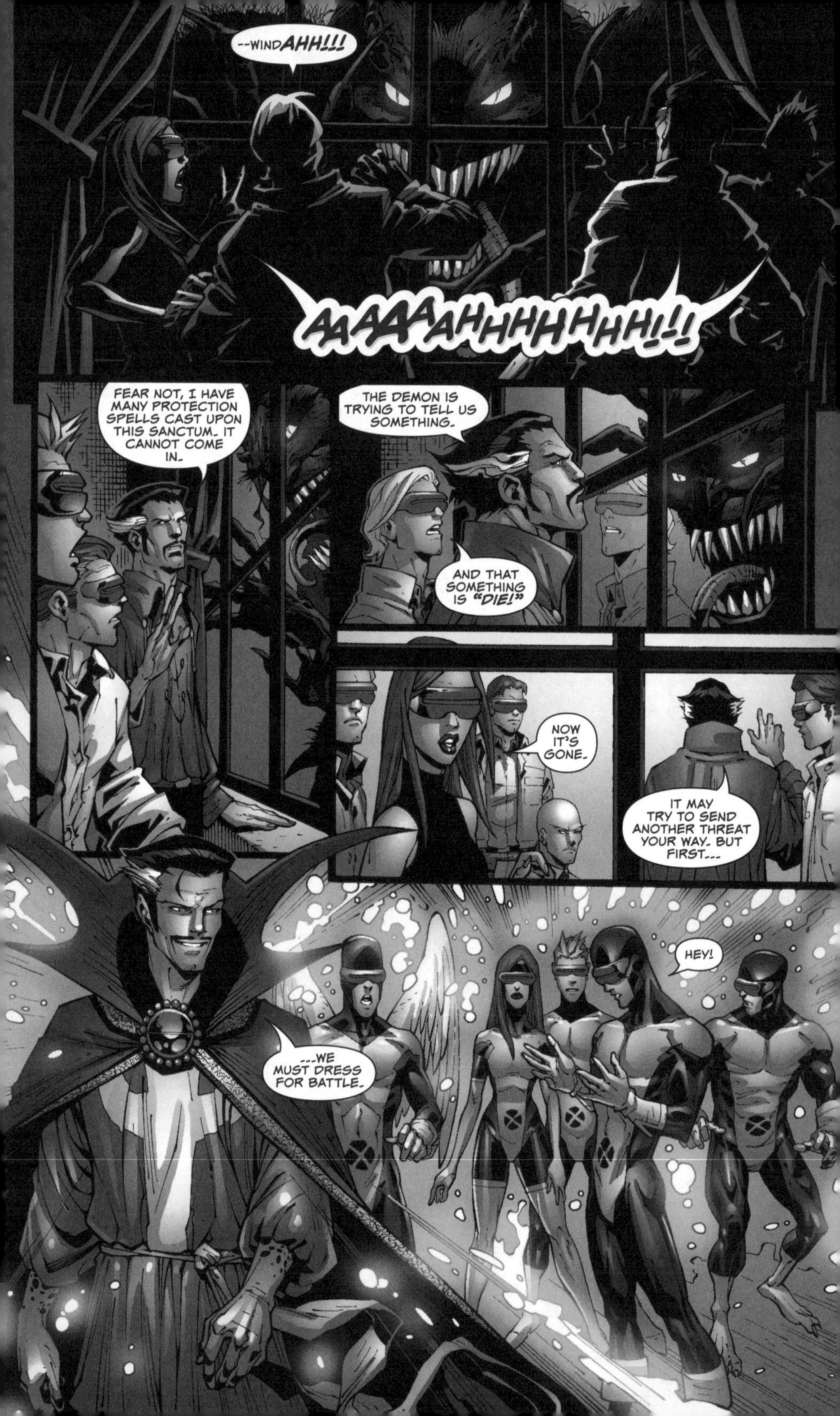
--WINDAHH!!!
AAAAAAHHHHHHH!!!
FEAR NOT, I HAVE MANY PROTECTION SPELLS CAST UPON THIS SANCTUM. IT CANNOT COME IN.
THE DEMON IS TRYING TO TELL US SOMETHING.
AND THAT SOMETHING IS "DIE!"
NOW IT'S GONE.
IT MAY TRY TO SEND ANOTHER THREAT YOUR WAY. BUT FIRST---
---WE MUST DRESS FOR BATTLE.
HEY!

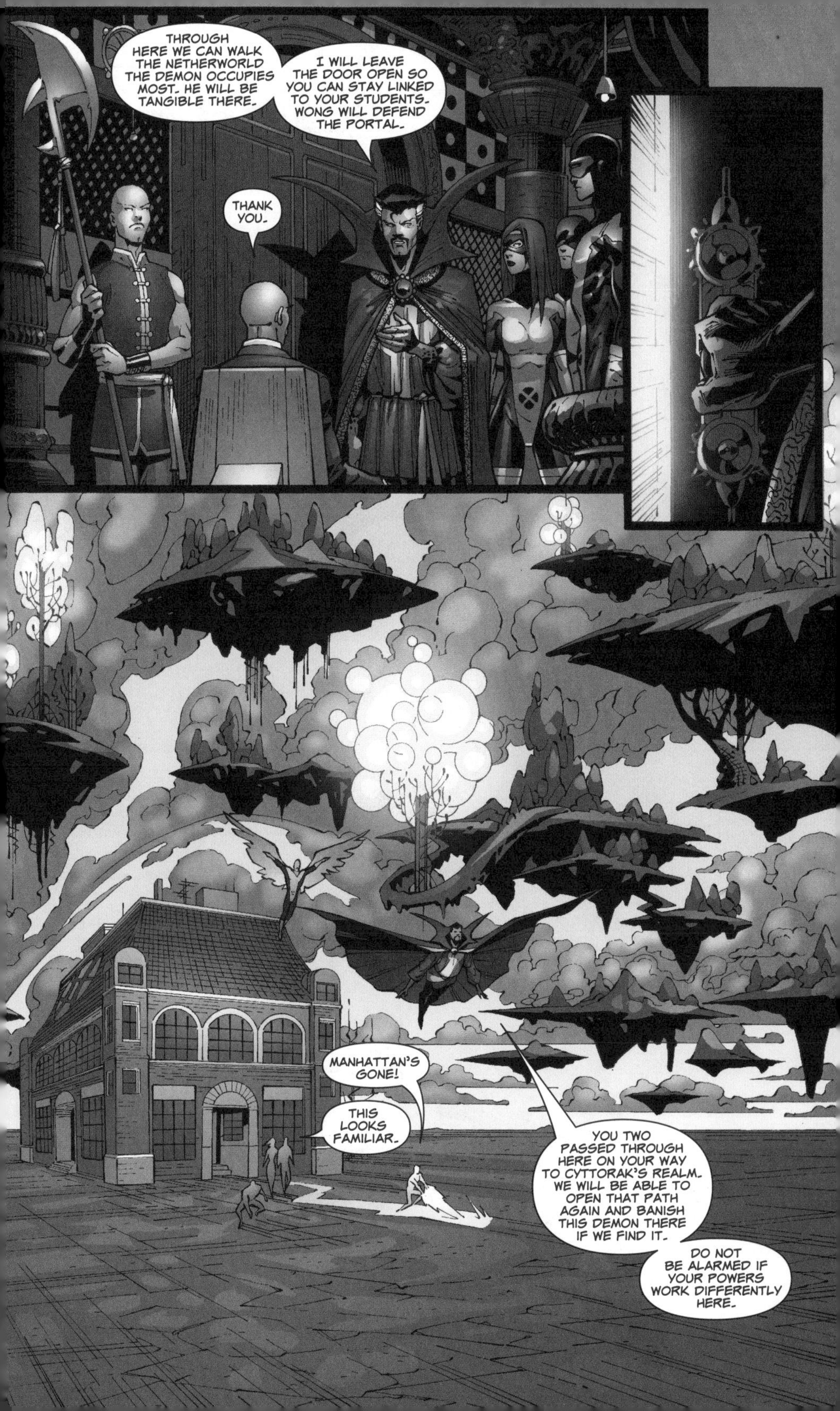
THROUGH HERE WE CAN WALK THE NETHERWORLD THE DEMON OCCUPIES MOST. HE WILL BE TANGIBLE THERE.
I WILL LEAVE THE DOOR OPEN SO YOU CAN STAY LINKED TO YOUR STUDENTS. WONG WILL DEFEND THE PORTAL.
THANK YOU.
MANHATTAN'S GONE!
THIS LOOKS FAMILIAR.
YOU TWO PASSED THROUGH HERE ON YOUR WAY TO CYTTORAK'S REALM. WE WILL BE ABLE TO OPEN THAT PATH AGAIN AND BANISH THIS DEMON THERE IF WE FIND IT.
DO NOT BE ALARMED IF YOUR POWERS WORK DIFFERENTLY HERE.

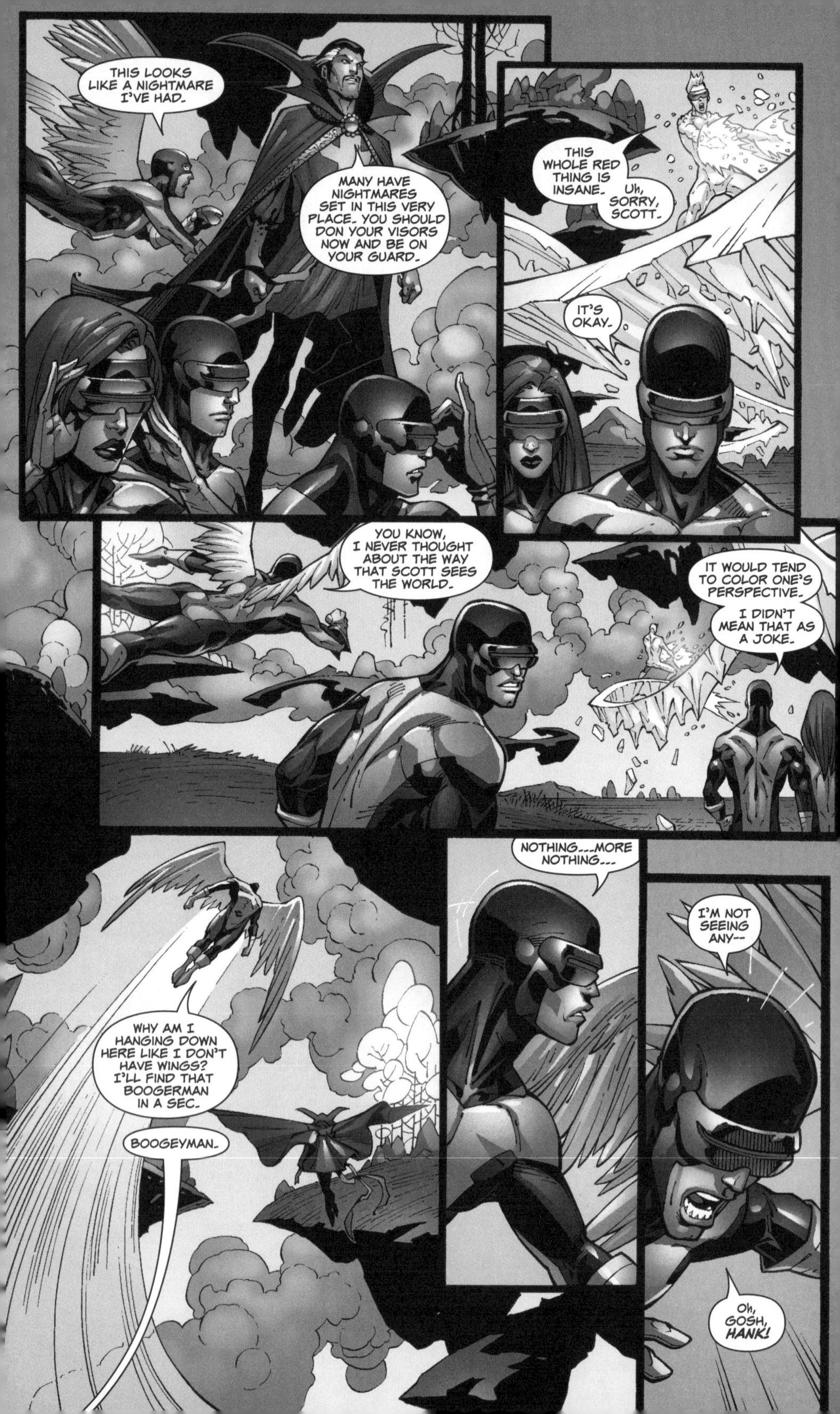
THIS LOOKS LIKE A NIGHTMARE I'VE HAD.
MANY HAVE NIGHTMARES SET IN THIS VERY PLACE. YOU SHOULD DON YOUR VISORS NOW AND BE ON YOUR GUARD.
THIS WHOLE RED THING IS INSANE.
Uh, SORRY, SCOTT.
IT'S OKAY.
YOU KNOW, I NEVER THOUGHT ABOUT THE WAY THAT SCOTT SEES THE WORLD.
IT WOULD TEND TO COLOR ONE'S PERSPECTIVE.
I DIDN'T MEAN THAT AS A JOKE.
WHY AM I HANGING DOWN HERE LIKE I DON'T HAVE WINGS? I'LL FIND THAT BOOGERMAN IN A SEC.
BOOGEYMAN.
NOTHING...MORE NOTHING...
I'M NOT SEEING ANY--
Oh, GOSH, HANK!

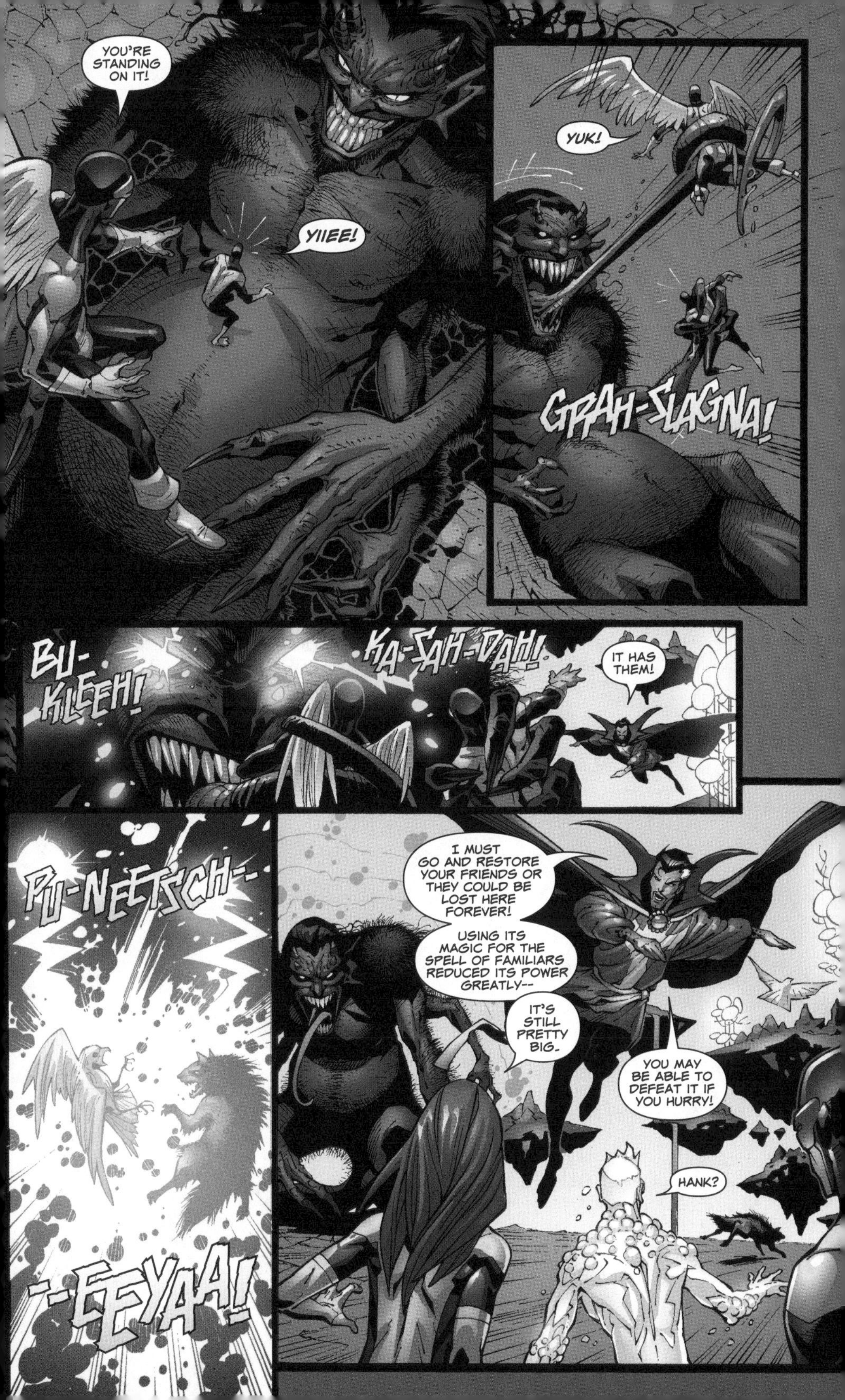

YOU'RE STANDING ON IT!
YIIEE!
YUK!
GRAH-SLAGNA!
BU-KLEEH!
KA-SAH-DAH!
IT HAS THEM!
PU-NEETSCH--
--EEYAA!
I MUST GO AND RESTORE YOUR FRIENDS OR THEY COULD BE LOST HERE FOREVER!
USING ITS MAGIC FOR THE SPELL OF FAMILIARS REDUCED ITS POWER GREATLY--
IT'S STILL PRETTY BIG.
YOU MAY BE ABLE TO DEFEAT IT IF YOU HURRY!
HANK?

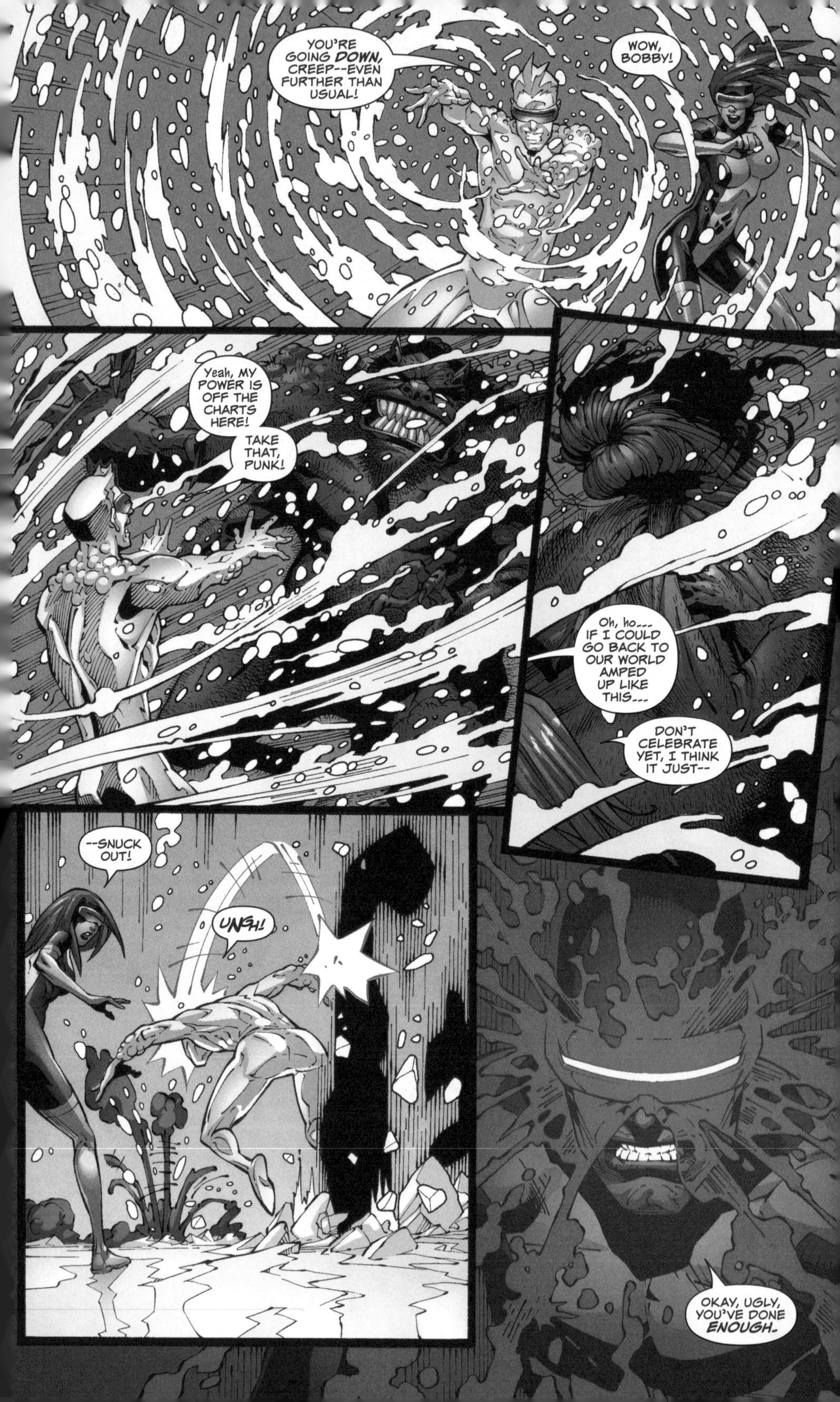

YOU'RE GOING DOWN, CREEP--EVEN FURTHER THAN USUAL!
WOW, BOBBY!
Yeah, MY POWER IS OFF THE CHARTS HERE!
TAKE THAT, PUNK!
Oh, ho--- IF I COULD GO BACK TO OUR WORLD AMPED UP LIKE THIS---
DON'T CELEBRATE YET, I THINK IT JUST--
--SNUCK OUT!
UNGH!
OKAY, UGLY, YOU'VE DONE ENOUGH.

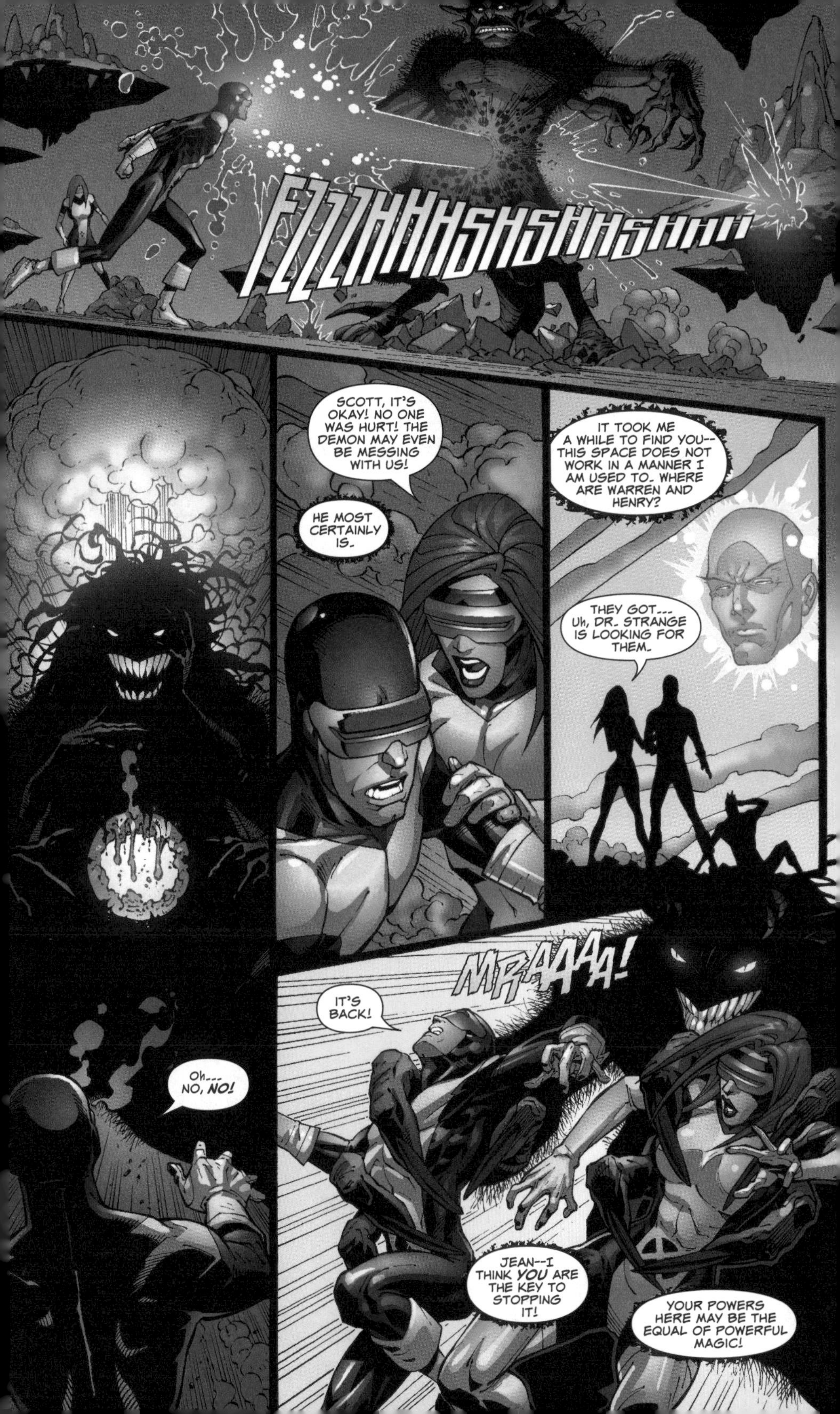

FZZZHHHHSHSHHSHHH
SCOTT, IT'S OKAY! NO ONE WAS HURT! THE DEMON MAY EVEN BE MESSING WITH US!
HE MOST CERTAINLY IS.
IT TOOK ME A WHILE TO FIND YOU-- THIS SPACE DOES NOT WORK IN A MANNER I AM USED TO. WHERE ARE WARREN AND HENRY?
THEY GOT... Uh, DR. STRANGE IS LOOKING FOR THEM.
MRAAAA!
IT'S BACK!
Oh... NO, NO!
JEAN--I THINK YOU ARE THE KEY TO STOPPING IT!
YOUR POWERS HERE MAY BE THE EQUAL OF POWERFUL MAGIC!

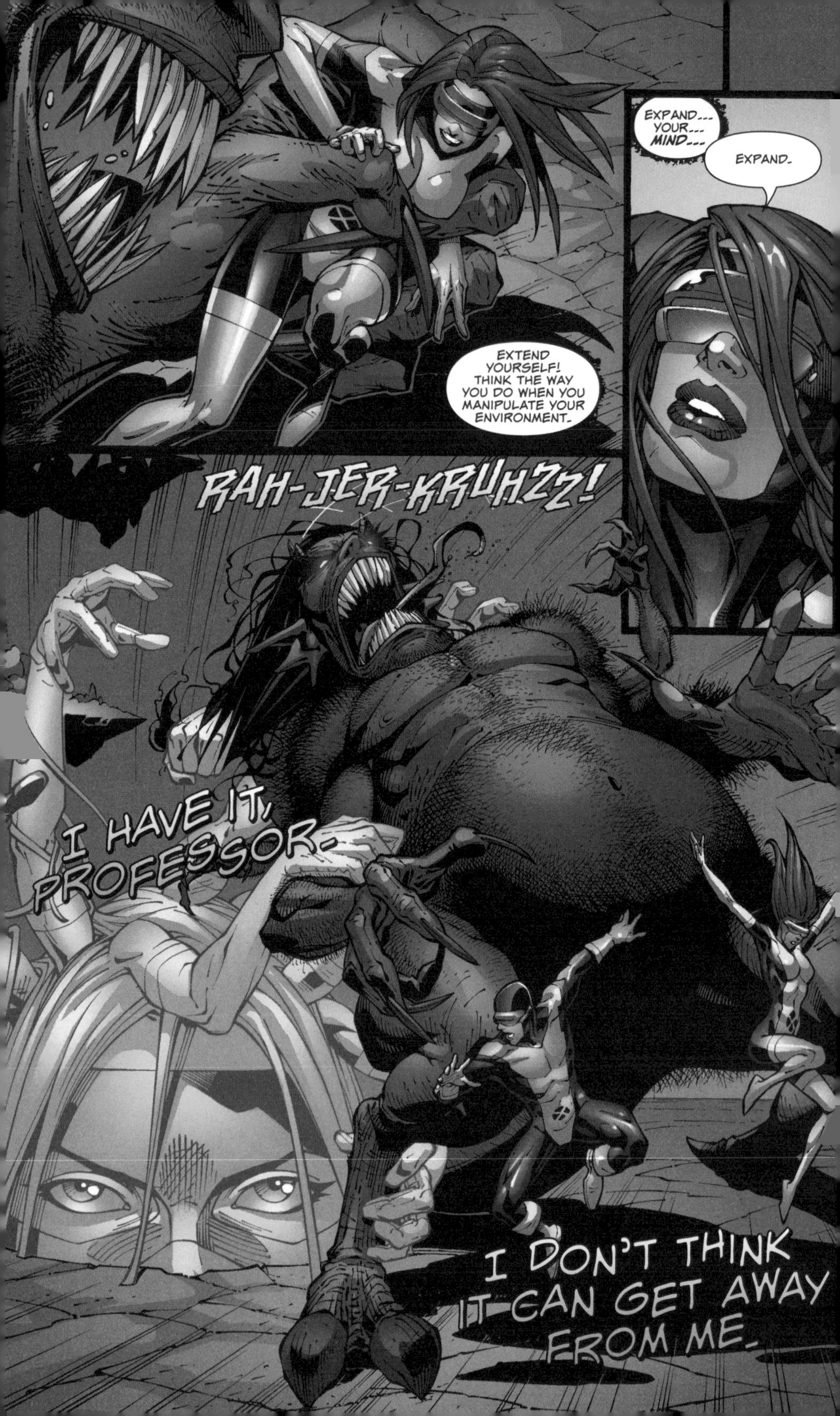
EXTEND YOURSELF! THINK THE WAY YOU DO WHEN YOU MANIPULATE YOUR ENVIRONMENT.
EXPAND... YOUR... MIND...
EXPAND.
RAH-JER-KRUHZZ!
I HAVE IT, PROFESSOR.
I DON'T THINK IT CAN GET AWAY FROM ME.

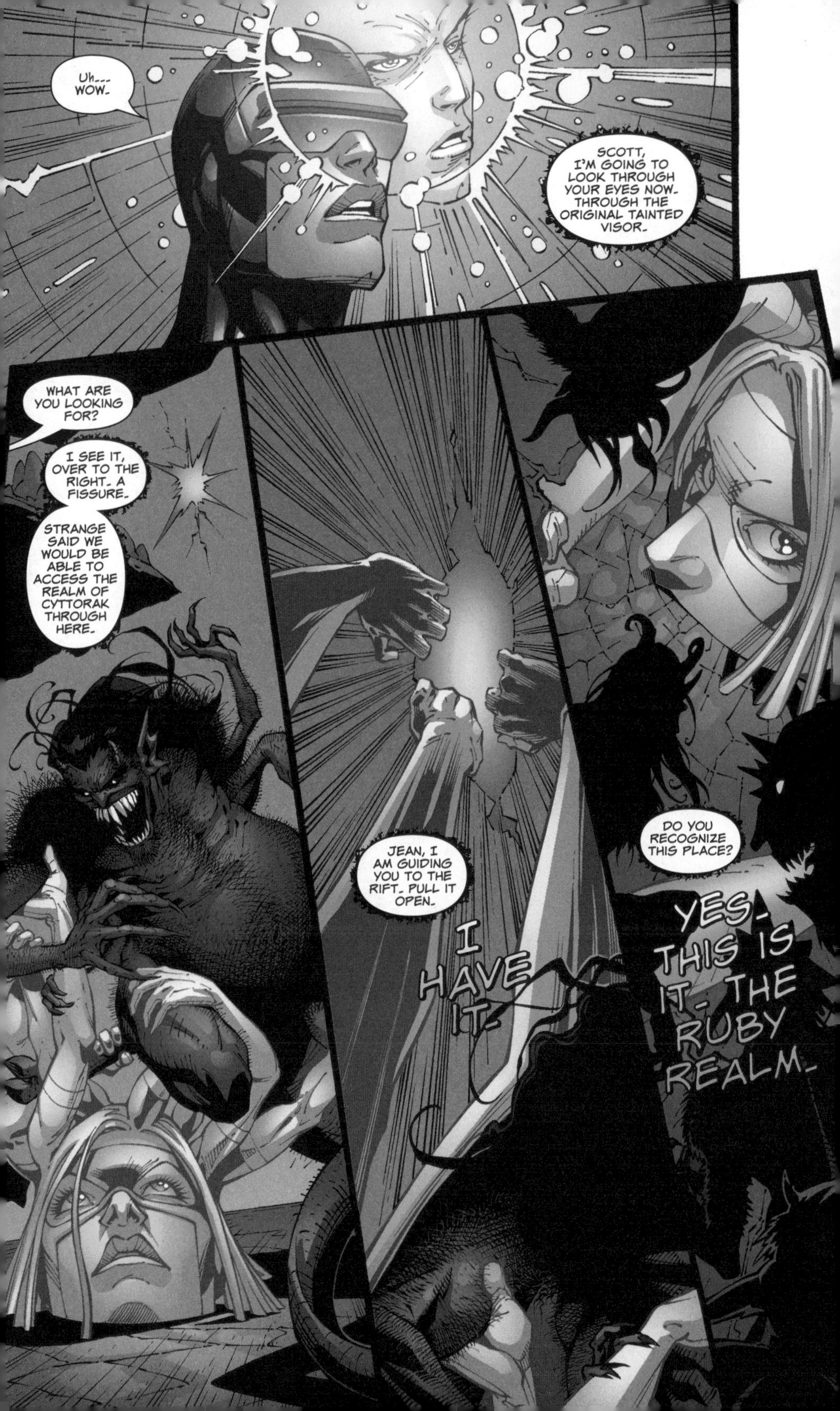

Uh... WOW.
SCOTT, I'M GOING TO LOOK THROUGH YOUR EYES NOW. THROUGH THE ORIGINAL TAINTED VISOR.
WHAT ARE YOU LOOKING FOR?
I SEE IT, OVER TO THE RIGHT. A FISSURE.
STRANGE SAID WE WOULD BE ABLE TO ACCESS THE REALM OF CYTTORAK THROUGH HERE.
JEAN, I AM GUIDING YOU TO THE RIFT. PULL IT OPEN.
I HAVE IT.
DO YOU RECOGNIZE THIS PLACE?
YES. THIS IS IT. THE RUBY REALM.

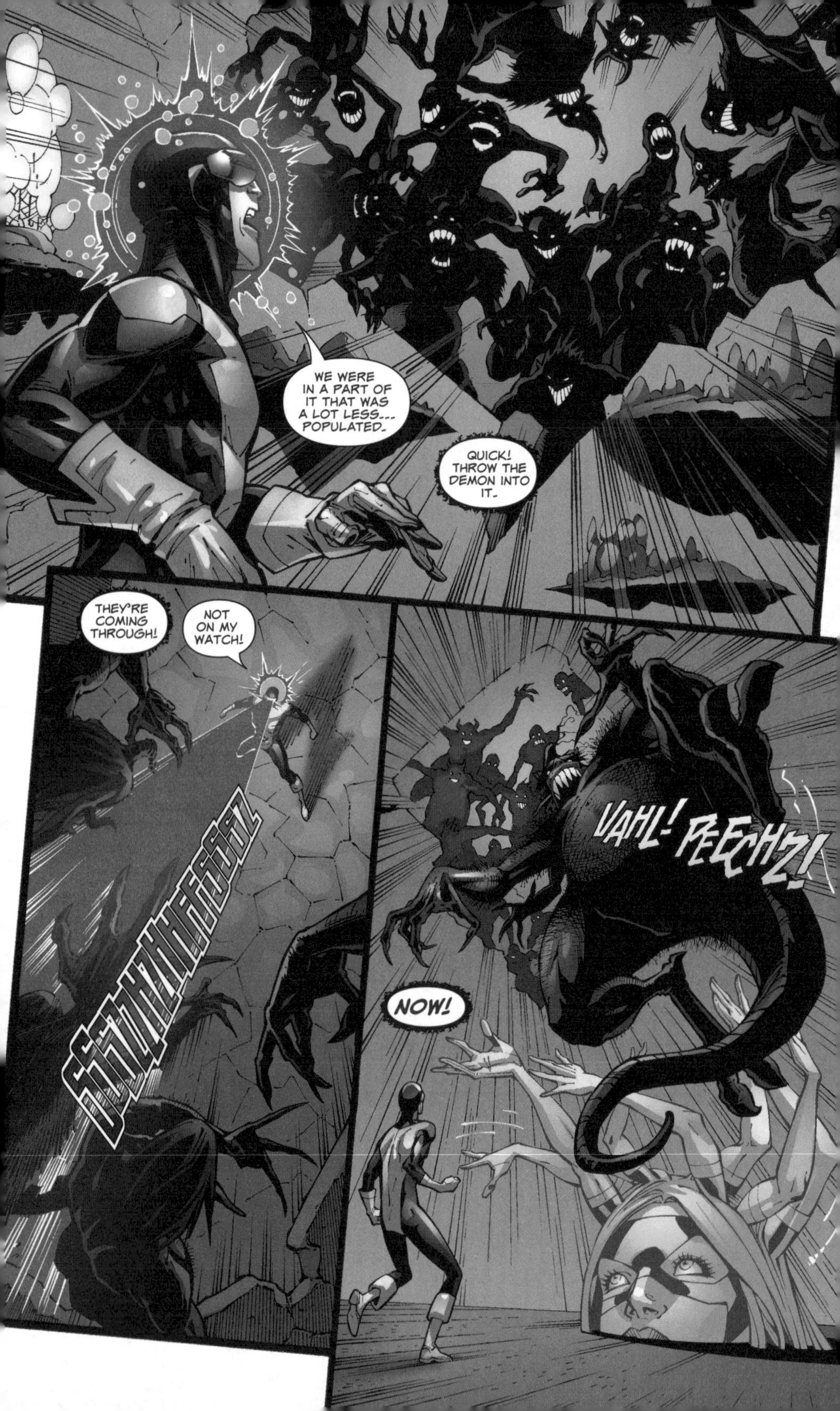
WE WERE IN A PART OF IT THAT WAS A LOT LESS... POPULATED.
QUICK! THROW THE DEMON INTO IT.
THEY'RE COMING THROUGH!
NOT ON MY WATCH!
SSSHHHSSSSZ
VAHL! PEECHZ!
NOW!

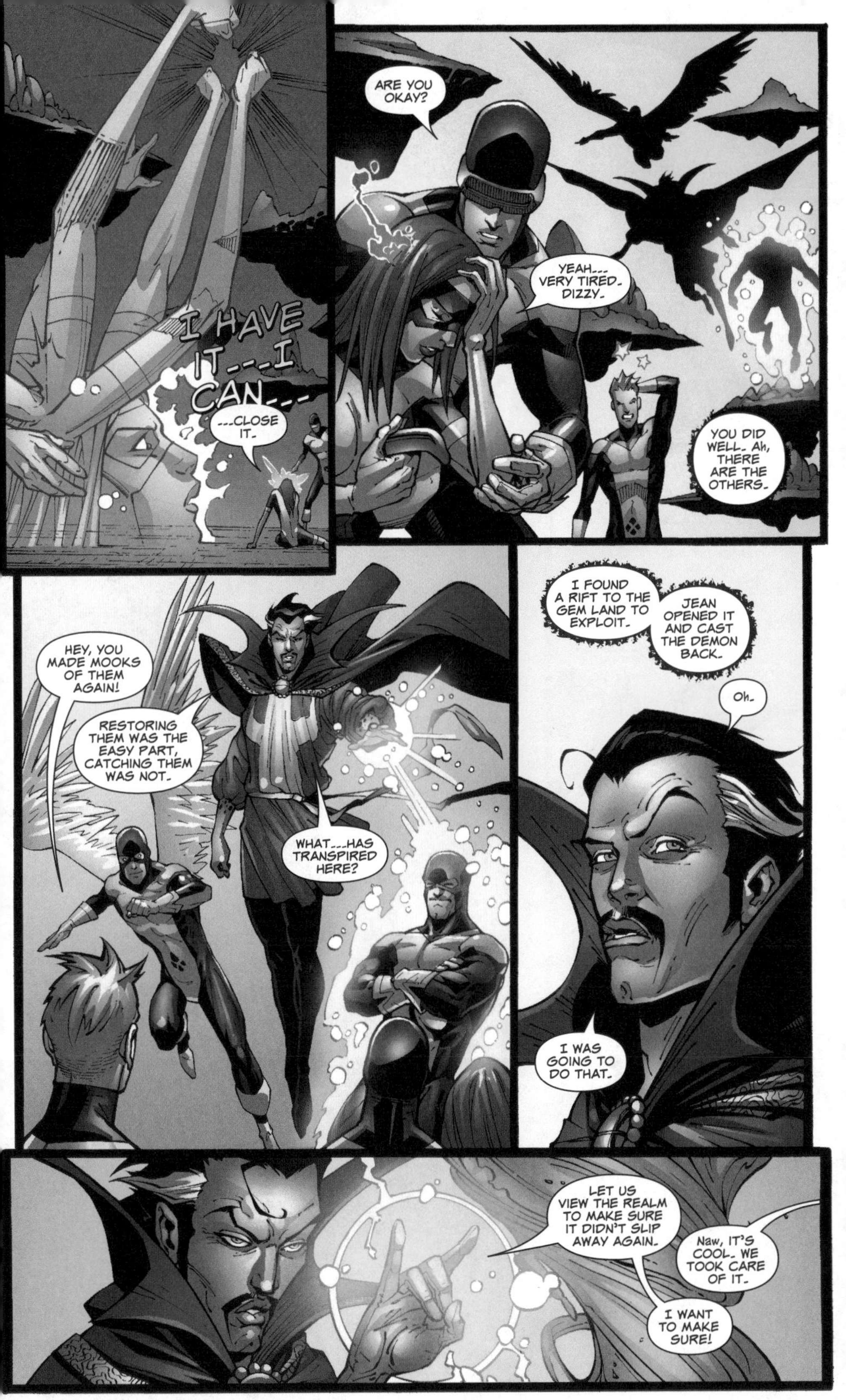
I HAVE IT---I CAN---
---CLOSE IT.
ARE YOU OKAY?
YEAH--- VERY TIRED. DIZZY.
YOU DID WELL. Ah, THERE ARE THE OTHERS.
HEY, YOU MADE MOOKS OF THEM AGAIN!
RESTORING THEM WAS THE EASY PART, CATCHING THEM WAS NOT.
WHAT---HAS TRANSPIRED HERE?
I FOUND A RIFT TO THE GEM LAND TO EXPLOIT.
JEAN OPENED IT AND CAST THE DEMON BACK.
Oh.
I WAS GOING TO DO THAT.
LET US VIEW THE REALM TO MAKE SURE IT DIDN'T SLIP AWAY AGAIN.
Naw, IT'S COOL. WE TOOK CARE OF IT.
I WANT TO MAKE SURE!

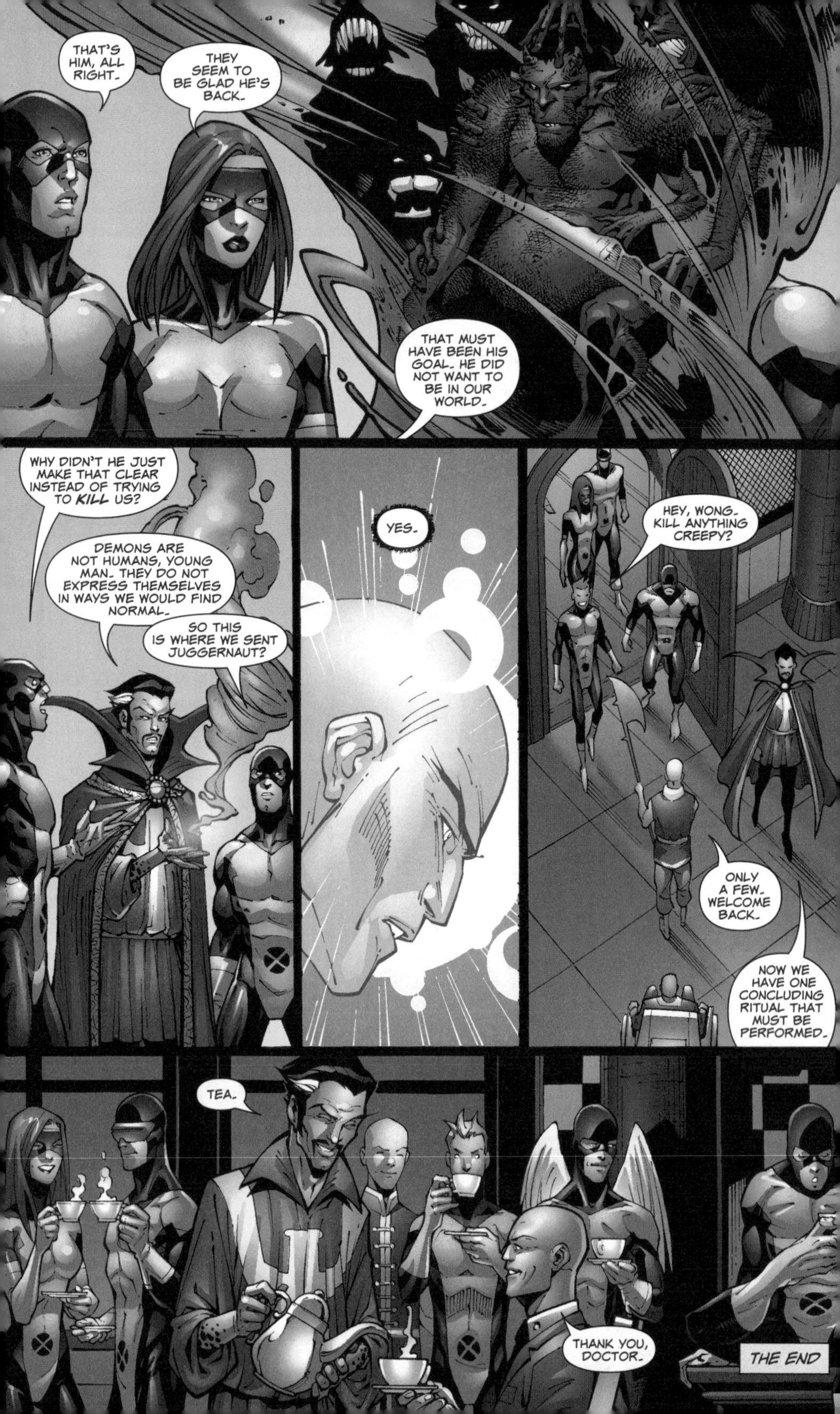
THAT'S HIM, ALL RIGHT.
THEY SEEM TO BE GLAD HE'S BACK.
THAT MUST HAVE BEEN HIS GOAL. HE DID NOT WANT TO BE IN OUR WORLD.
WHY DIDN'T HE JUST MAKE THAT CLEAR INSTEAD OF TRYING TO KILL US?
DEMONS ARE NOT HUMANS, YOUNG MAN. THEY DO NOT EXPRESS THEMSELVES IN WAYS WE WOULD FIND NORMAL.
SO THIS IS WHERE WE SENT JUGGERNAUT?
YES.
HEY, WONG. KILL ANYTHING CREEPY?
ONLY A FEW. WELCOME BACK.
NOW WE HAVE ONE CONCLUDING RITUAL THAT MUST BE PERFORMED.
TEA.
THANK YOU, DOCTOR.
THE END

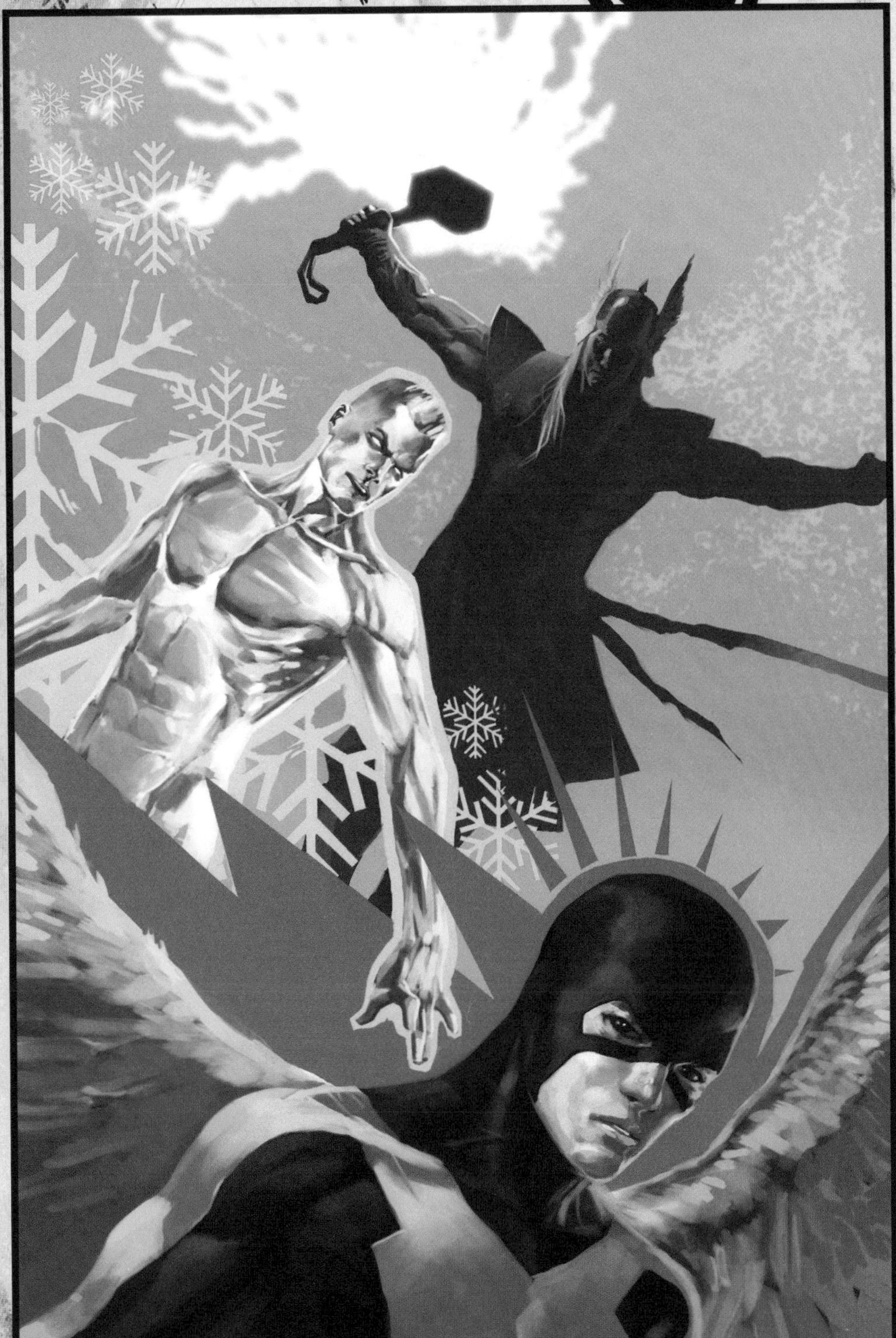

X-Men: First Class (2006) **#5**

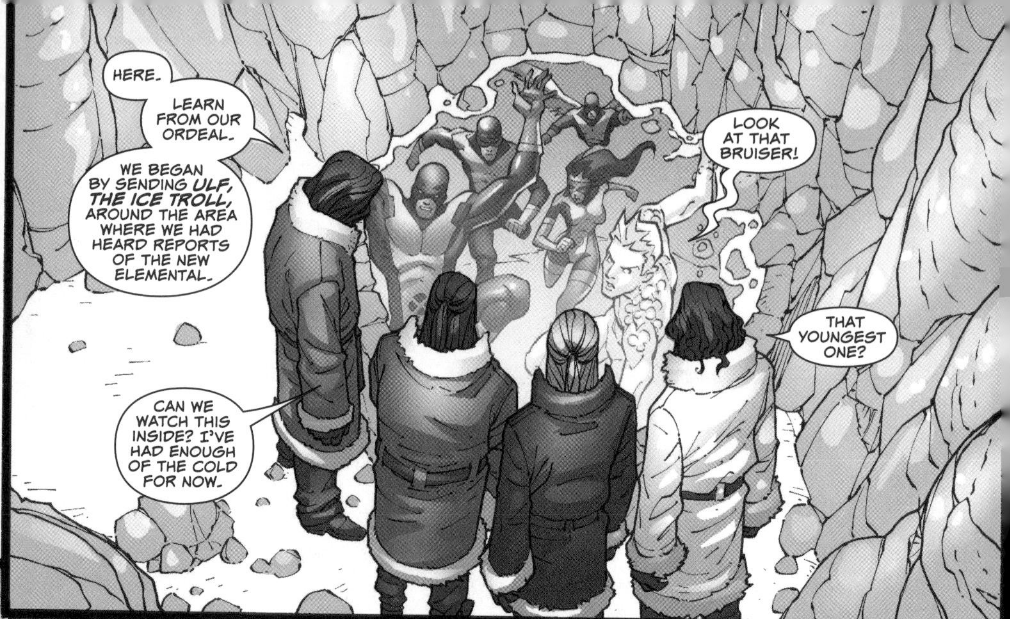
HERE.
LEARN FROM OUR ORDEAL.
WE BEGAN BY SENDING ULF, THE ICE TROLL, AROUND THE AREA WHERE WE HAD HEARD REPORTS OF THE NEW ELEMENTAL.
LOOK AT THAT BRUISER!
THAT YOUNGEST ONE?
CAN WE WATCH THIS INSIDE? I'VE HAD ENOUGH OF THE COLD FOR NOW.

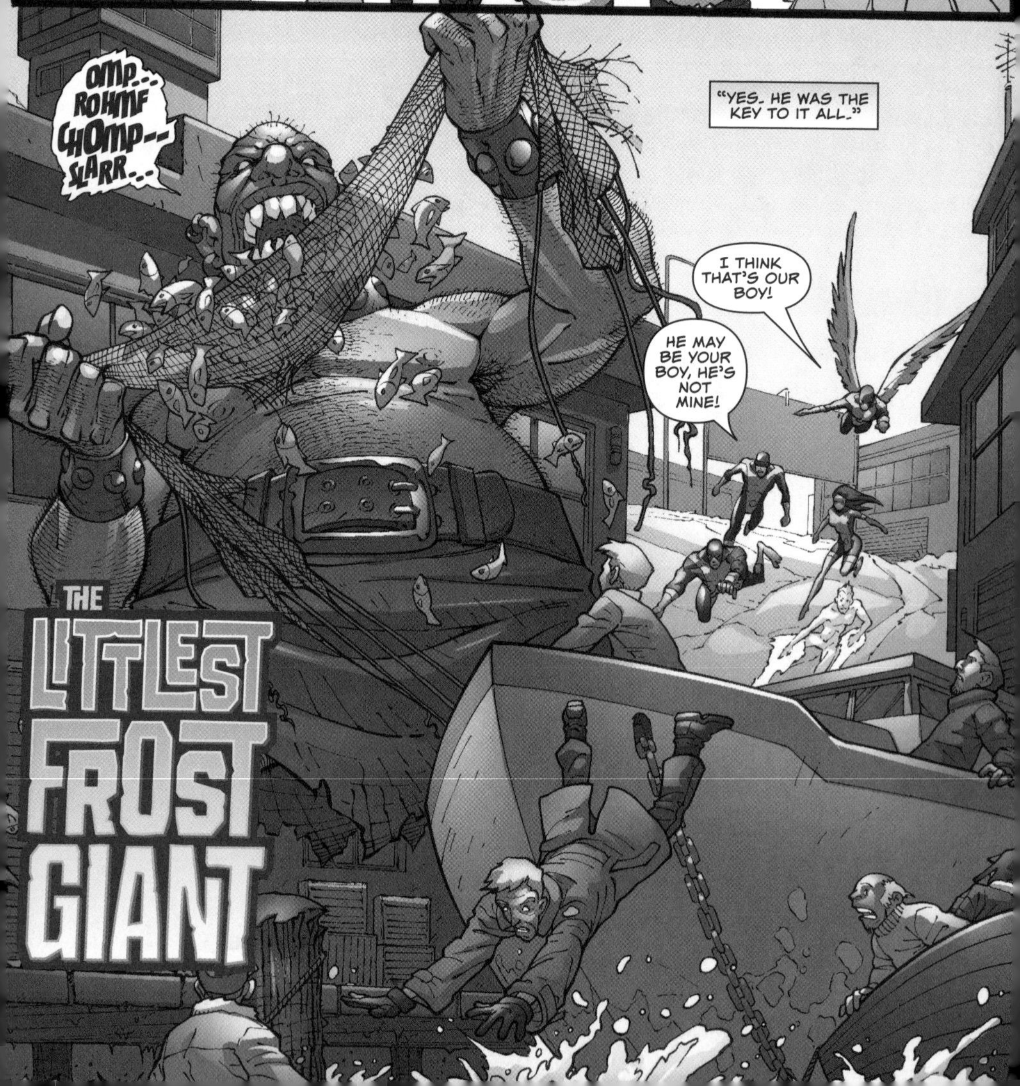
OMP... ROHMF CHOMP... SLARR...
"YES. HE WAS THE KEY TO IT ALL."
I THINK THAT'S OUR BOY!
HE MAY BE YOUR BOY, HE'S NOT MINE!
THE LITTLEST FROST GIANT

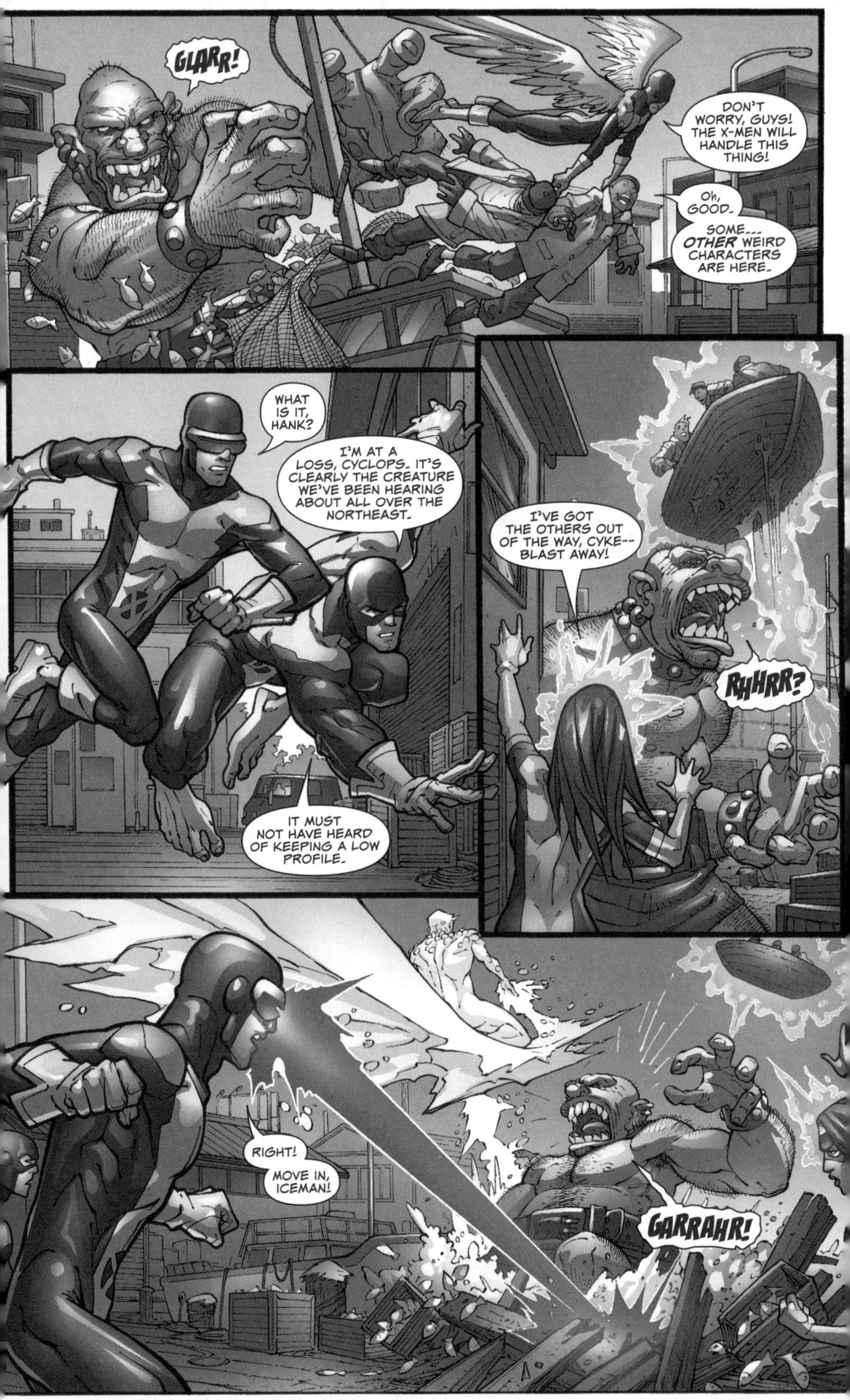
GLARR!
DON'T WORRY, GUYS! THE X-MEN WILL HANDLE THIS THING!
Oh, GOOD.
SOME... OTHER WEIRD CHARACTERS ARE HERE.
WHAT IS IT, HANK?
I'M AT A LOSS, CYCLOPS. IT'S CLEARLY THE CREATURE WE'VE BEEN HEARING ABOUT ALL OVER THE NORTHEAST.
IT MUST NOT HAVE HEARD OF KEEPING A LOW PROFILE.
I'VE GOT THE OTHERS OUT OF THE WAY, CYKE-- BLAST AWAY!
RHHRR?
RIGHT!
MOVE IN, ICEMAN!
GARRAHR!

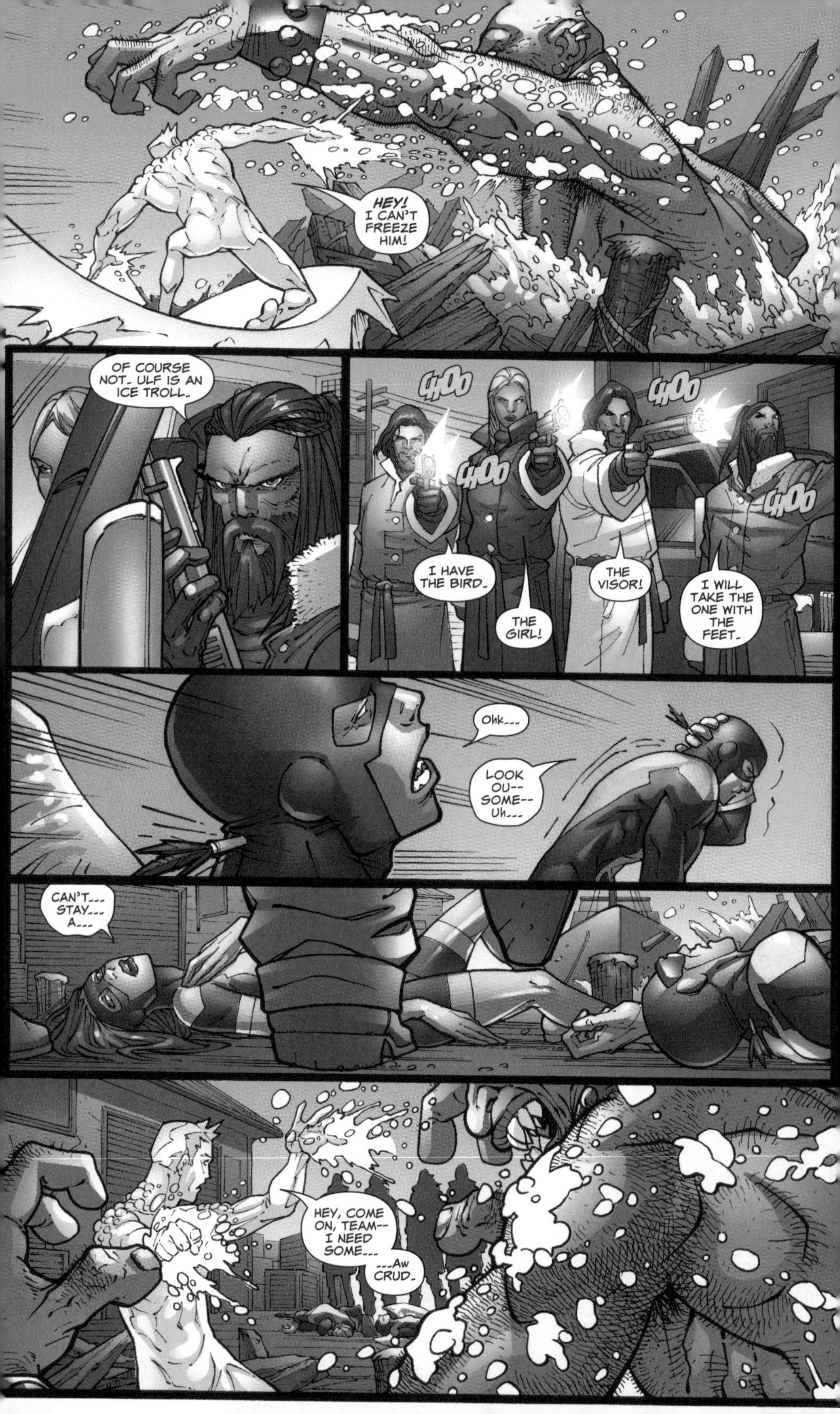
HEY! I CAN'T FREEZE HIM!
OF COURSE NOT. ULF IS AN ICE TROLL.
CHOO
CHOO
CHOO
CHOO
I HAVE THE BIRD.
THE GIRL!
THE VISOR!
I WILL TAKE THE ONE WITH THE FEET.
Ohk...
LOOK OU-- SOME-- Uh...
CAN'T... STAY... A...
HEY, COME ON, TEAM-- I NEED SOME...
...Aw CRUD.

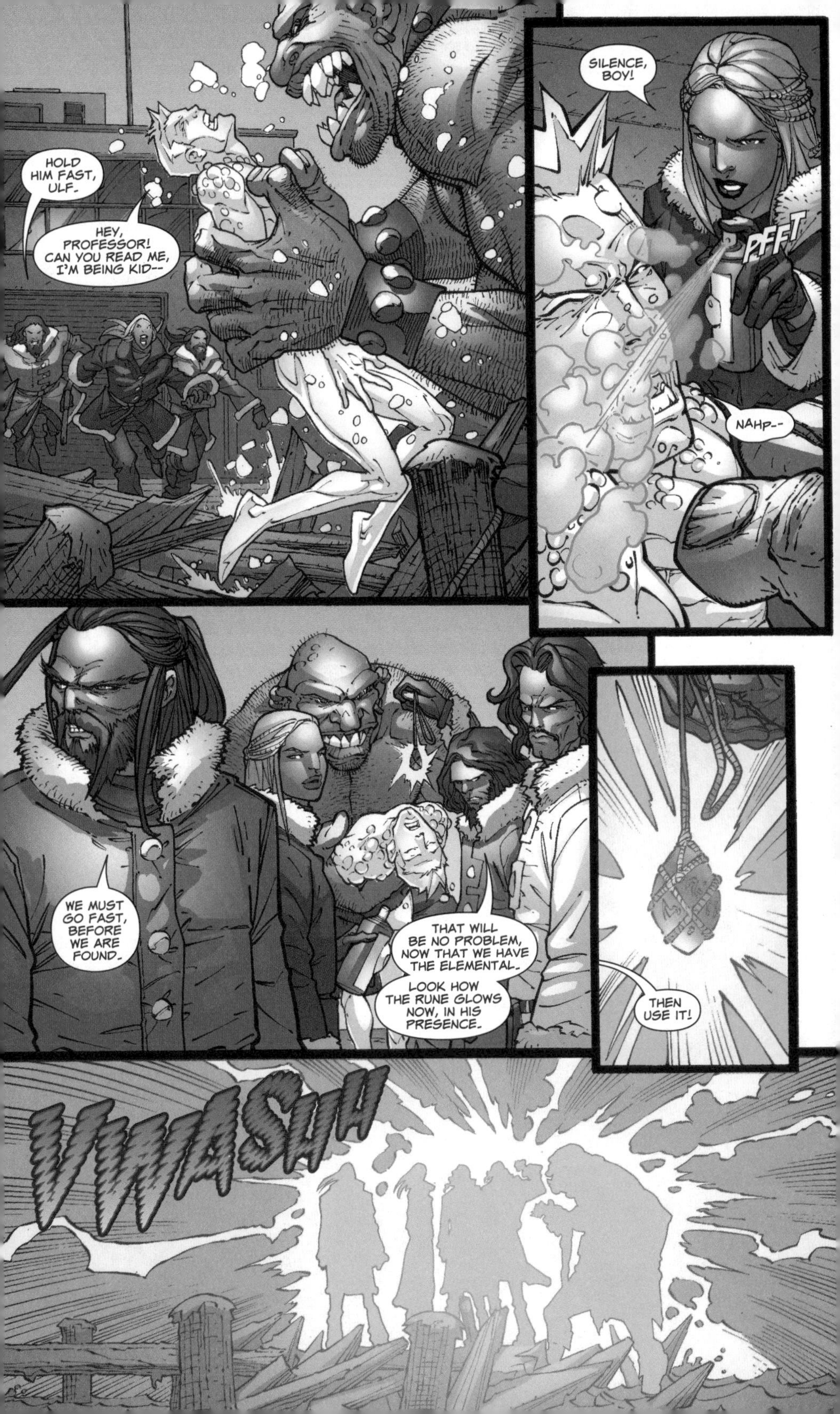
HOLD HIM FAST, ULF.
HEY, PROFESSOR! CAN YOU READ ME, I'M BEING KID--
SILENCE, BOY!
PFFT
NAHP--
WE MUST GO FAST, BEFORE WE ARE FOUND.
THAT WILL BE NO PROBLEM, NOW THAT WE HAVE THE ELEMENTAL.
LOOK HOW THE RUNE GLOWS NOW, IN HIS PRESENCE.
THEN USE IT!
VMASH

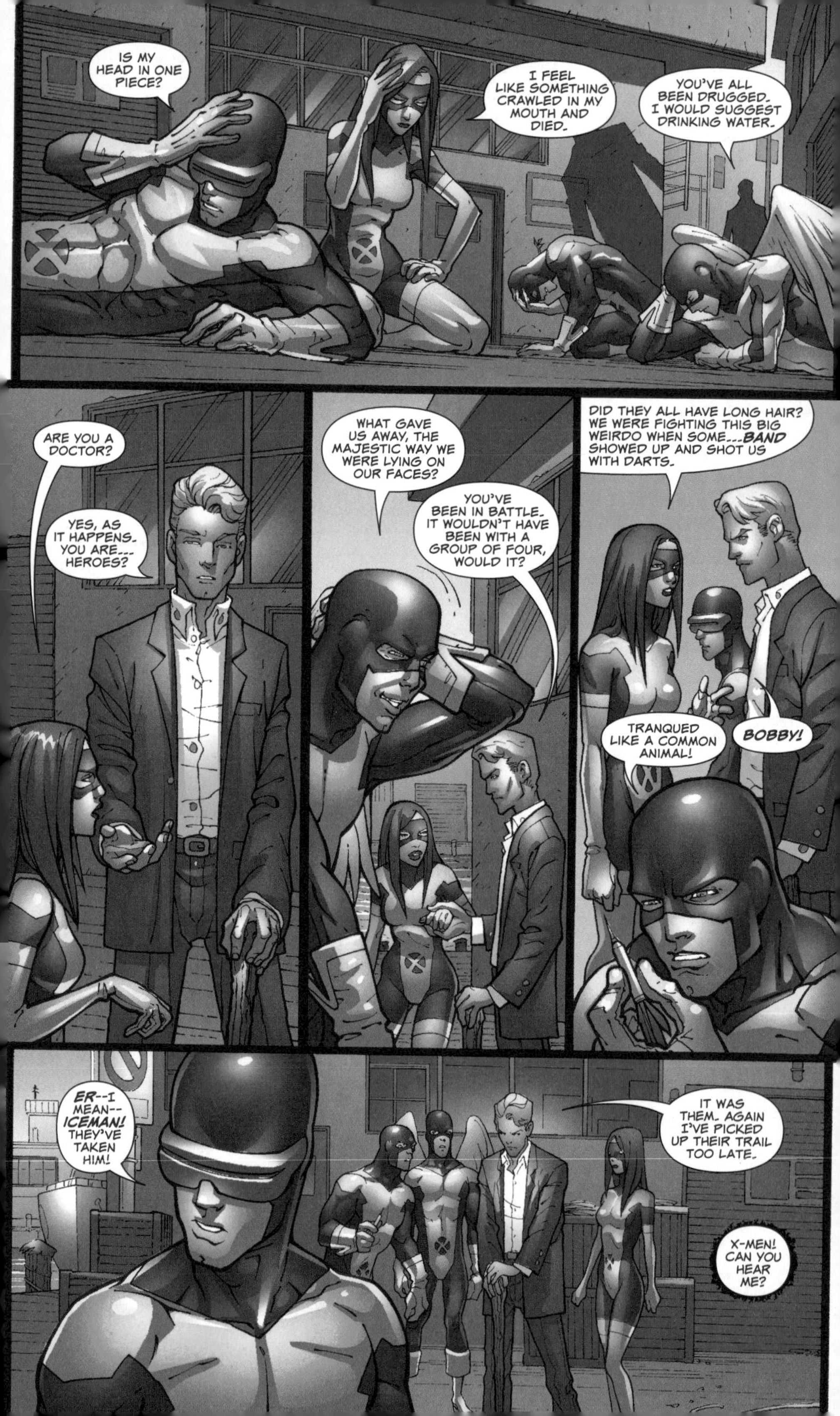
IS MY HEAD IN ONE PIECE?
I FEEL LIKE SOMETHING CRAWLED IN MY MOUTH AND DIED.
YOU'VE ALL BEEN DRUGGED. I WOULD SUGGEST DRINKING WATER.
ARE YOU A DOCTOR?
YES, AS IT HAPPENS. YOU ARE... HEROES?
WHAT GAVE US AWAY, THE MAJESTIC WAY WE WERE LYING ON OUR FACES?
YOU'VE BEEN IN BATTLE. IT WOULDN'T HAVE BEEN WITH A GROUP OF FOUR, WOULD IT?
DID THEY ALL HAVE LONG HAIR? WE WERE FIGHTING THIS BIG WEIRDO WHEN SOME... BAND SHOWED UP AND SHOT US WITH DARTS.
TRANQUED LIKE A COMMON ANIMAL!
BOBBY!
ER--I MEAN-- ICEMAN! THEY'VE TAKEN HIM!
IT WAS THEM. AGAIN I'VE PICKED UP THEIR TRAIL TOO LATE.
X-MEN! CAN YOU HEAR ME?

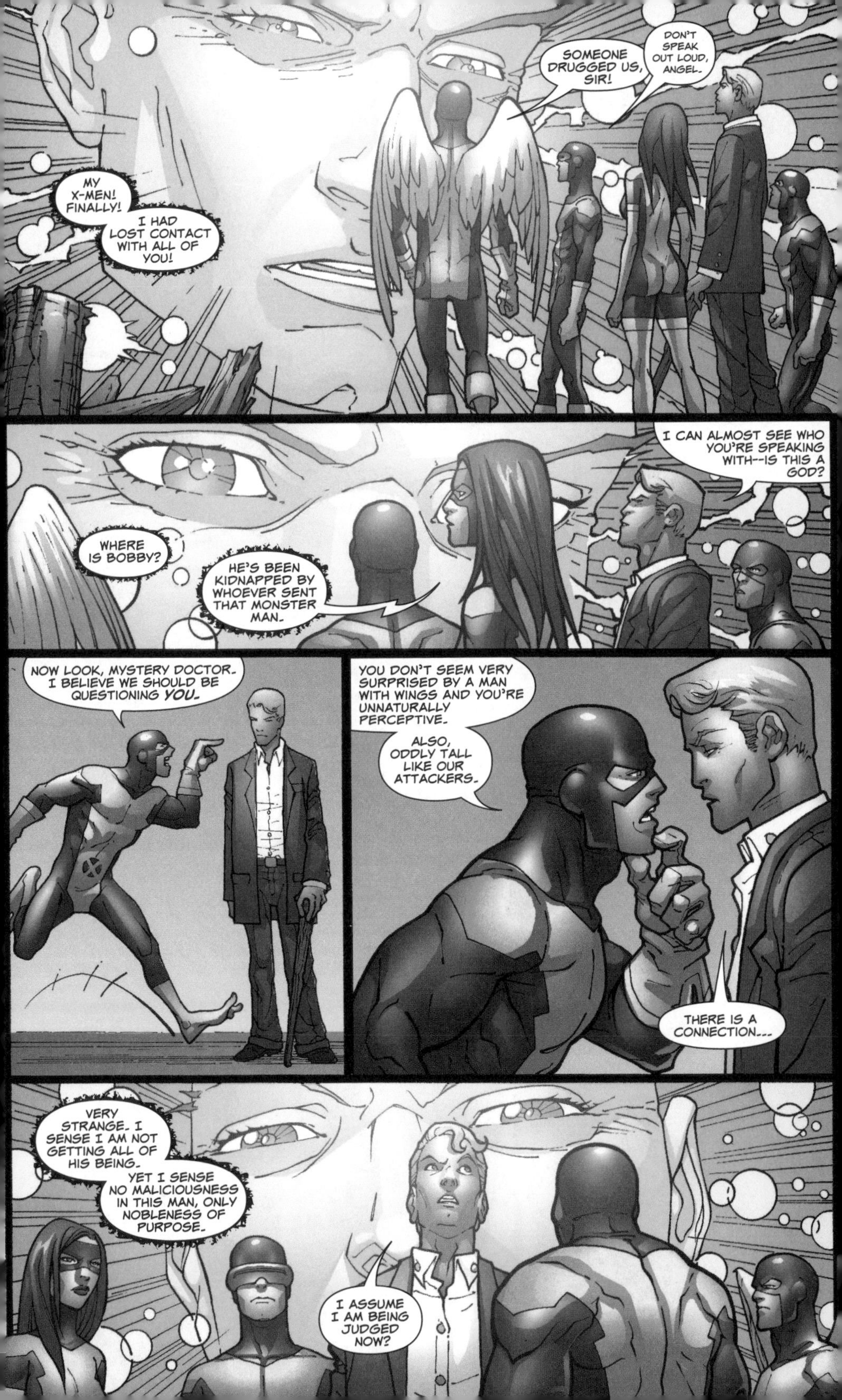

SOMEONE DRUGGED US, SIR!
DON'T SPEAK OUT LOUD, ANGEL.
MY X-MEN! FINALLY!
I HAD LOST CONTACT WITH ALL OF YOU!
I CAN ALMOST SEE WHO YOU'RE SPEAKING WITH--IS THIS A GOD?
WHERE IS BOBBY?
HE'S BEEN KIDNAPPED BY WHOEVER SENT THAT MONSTER MAN.
NOW LOOK, MYSTERY DOCTOR. I BELIEVE WE SHOULD BE QUESTIONING YOU.
YOU DON'T SEEM VERY SURPRISED BY A MAN WITH WINGS AND YOU'RE UNNATURALLY PERCEPTIVE.
ALSO, ODDLY TALL LIKE OUR ATTACKERS.
THERE IS A CONNECTION...
VERY STRANGE. I SENSE I AM NOT GETTING ALL OF HIS BEING.
YET I SENSE NO MALICIOUSNESS IN THIS MAN, ONLY NOBLENESS OF PURPOSE.
I ASSUME I AM BEING JUDGED NOW?

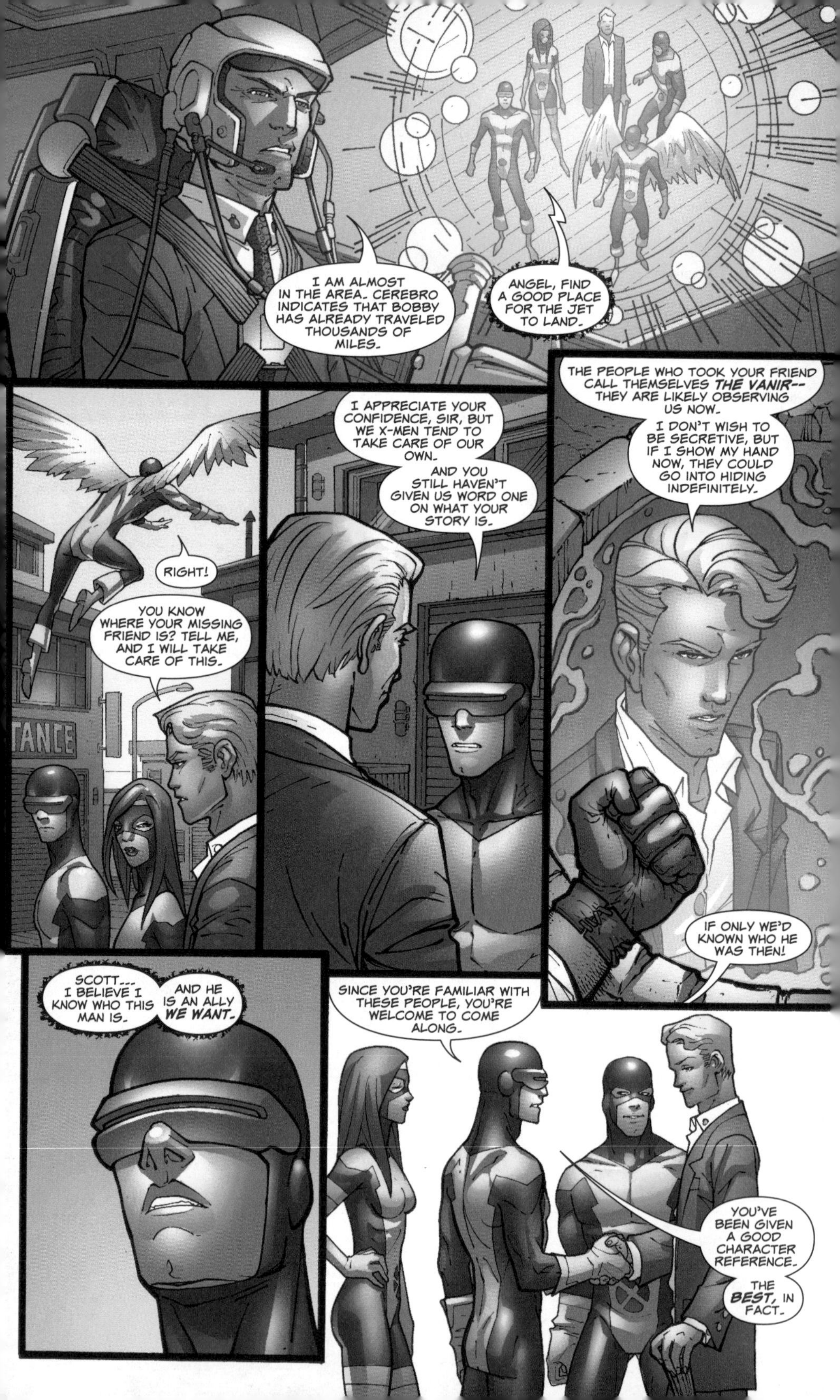

I AM ALMOST IN THE AREA. CEREBRO INDICATES THAT BOBBY HAS ALREADY TRAVELED THOUSANDS OF MILES.
ANGEL, FIND A GOOD PLACE FOR THE JET TO LAND.
RIGHT!
YOU KNOW WHERE YOUR MISSING FRIEND IS? TELL ME, AND I WILL TAKE CARE OF THIS.
TANCE
I APPRECIATE YOUR CONFIDENCE, SIR, BUT WE X-MEN TEND TO TAKE CARE OF OUR OWN.
AND YOU STILL HAVEN'T GIVEN US WORD ONE ON WHAT YOUR STORY IS.
THE PEOPLE WHO TOOK YOUR FRIEND CALL THEMSELVES THE VANIR-- THEY ARE LIKELY OBSERVING US NOW.
I DON'T WISH TO BE SECRETIVE, BUT IF I SHOW MY HAND NOW, THEY COULD GO INTO HIDING INDEFINITELY.
IF ONLY WE'D KNOWN WHO HE WAS THEN!
SCOTT... I BELIEVE I KNOW WHO THIS MAN IS.
AND HE IS AN ALLY WE WANT.
SINCE YOU'RE FAMILIAR WITH THESE PEOPLE, YOU'RE WELCOME TO COME ALONG.
YOU'VE BEEN GIVEN A GOOD CHARACTER REFERENCE.
THE BEST, IN FACT.

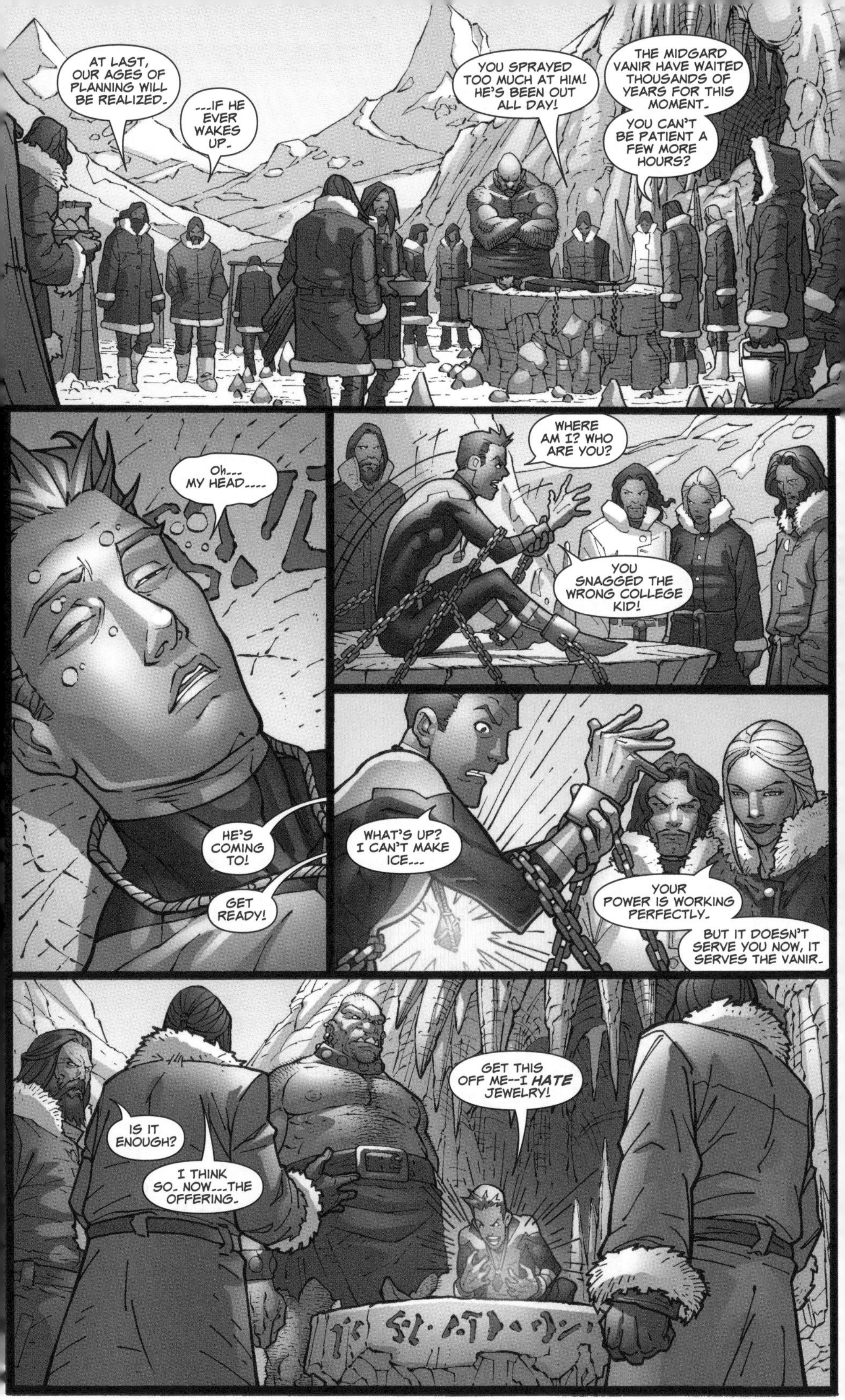
AT LAST, OUR AGES OF PLANNING WILL BE REALIZED.
...IF HE EVER WAKES UP.
YOU SPRAYED TOO MUCH AT HIM! HE'S BEEN OUT ALL DAY!
THE MIDGARD VANIR HAVE WAITED THOUSANDS OF YEARS FOR THIS MOMENT.
YOU CAN'T BE PATIENT A FEW MORE HOURS?
Oh... MY HEAD....
HE'S COMING TO!
GET READY!
WHERE AM I? WHO ARE YOU?
YOU SNAGGED THE WRONG COLLEGE KID!
WHAT'S UP? I CAN'T MAKE ICE...
YOUR POWER IS WORKING PERFECTLY.
BUT IT DOESN'T SERVE YOU NOW, IT SERVES THE VANIR.
IS IT ENOUGH?
I THINK SO. NOW...THE OFFERING.
GET THIS OFF ME--I *HATE* JEWELRY!

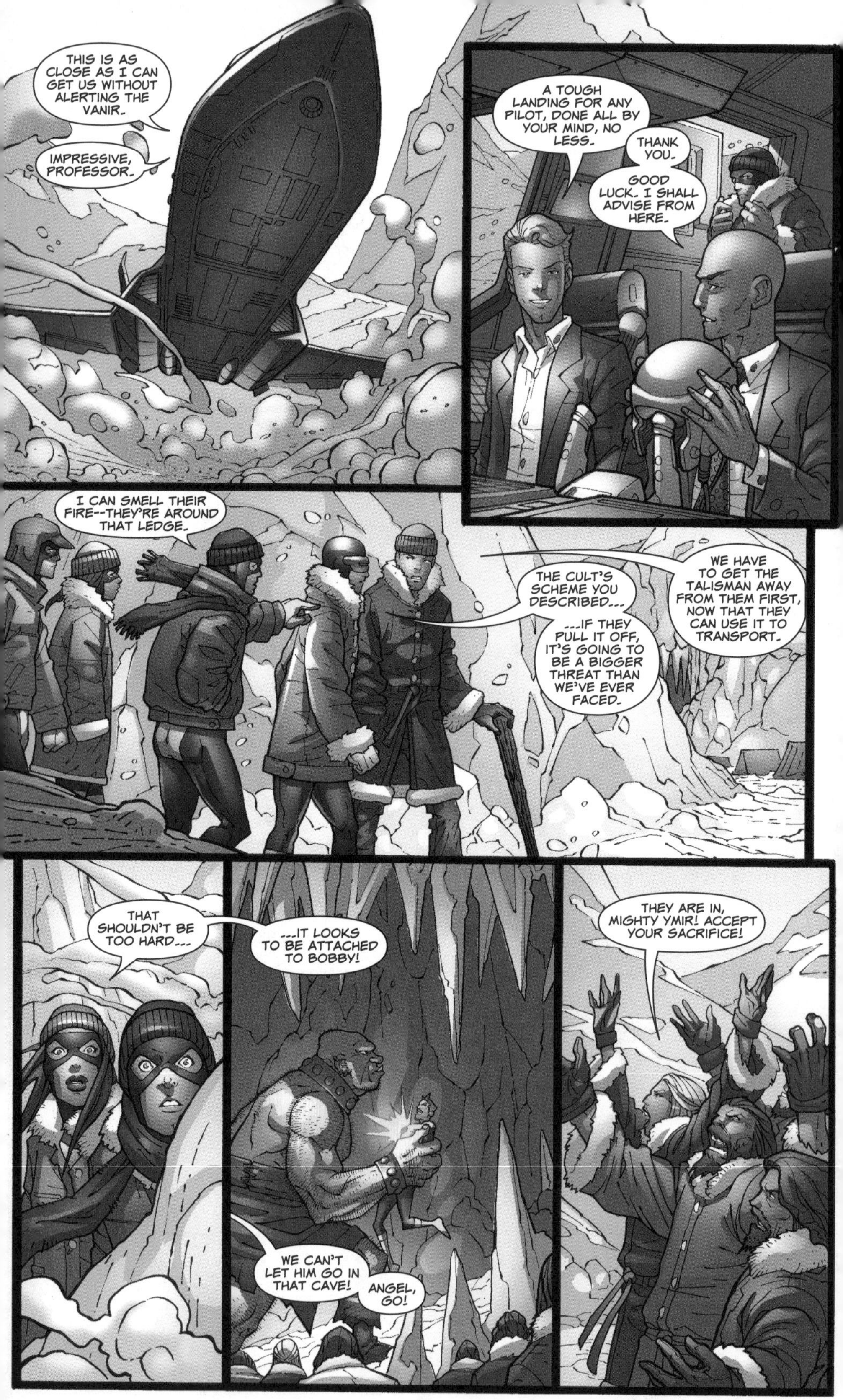

THIS IS AS CLOSE AS I CAN GET US WITHOUT ALERTING THE VANIR.
IMPRESSIVE, PROFESSOR.
A TOUGH LANDING FOR ANY PILOT, DONE ALL BY YOUR MIND, NO LESS.
THANK YOU.
GOOD LUCK. I SHALL ADVISE FROM HERE.
I CAN SMELL THEIR FIRE--THEY'RE AROUND THAT LEDGE.
THE CULT'S SCHEME YOU DESCRIBED...
...IF THEY PULL IT OFF, IT'S GOING TO BE A BIGGER THREAT THAN WE'VE EVER FACED.
WE HAVE TO GET THE TALISMAN AWAY FROM THEM FIRST, NOW THAT THEY CAN USE IT TO TRANSPORT.
THAT SHOULDN'T BE TOO HARD...
...IT LOOKS TO BE ATTACHED TO BOBBY!
WE CAN'T LET HIM GO IN THAT CAVE!
ANGEL, GO!
THEY ARE IN, MIGHTY YMIR! ACCEPT YOUR SACRIFICE!

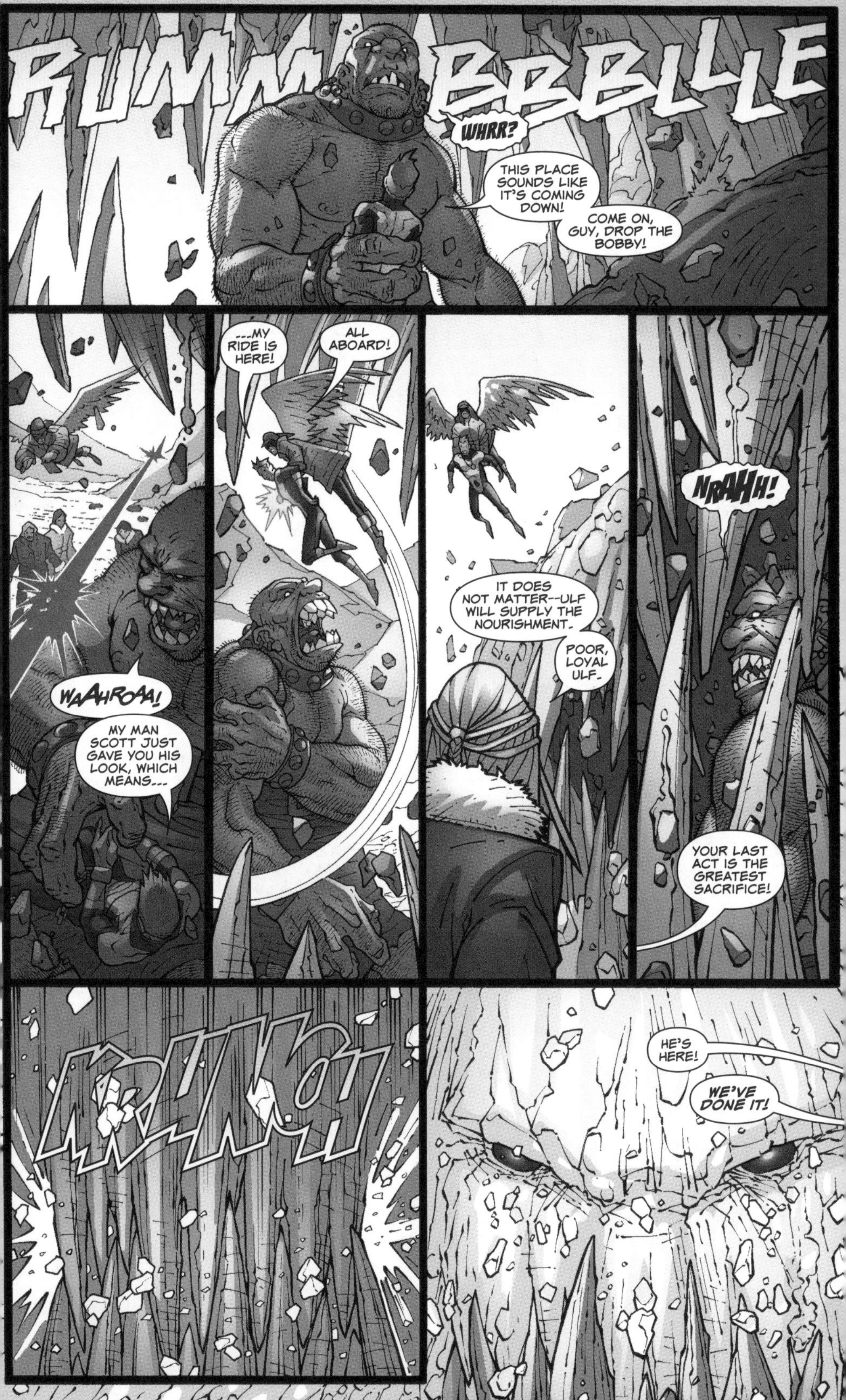
RUMMMBBBLLE
WHRR?
THIS PLACE SOUNDS LIKE IT'S COMING DOWN!
COME ON, GUY, DROP THE BOBBY!
WAAHROAA!
MY MAN SCOTT JUST GAVE YOU HIS LOOK, WHICH MEANS...
...MY RIDE IS HERE!
ALL ABOARD!
IT DOES NOT MATTER--ULF WILL SUPPLY THE NOURISHMENT.
POOR, LOYAL ULF.
NRAHH!
YOUR LAST ACT IS THE GREATEST SACRIFICE!
HE'S HERE!
WE'VE DONE IT!

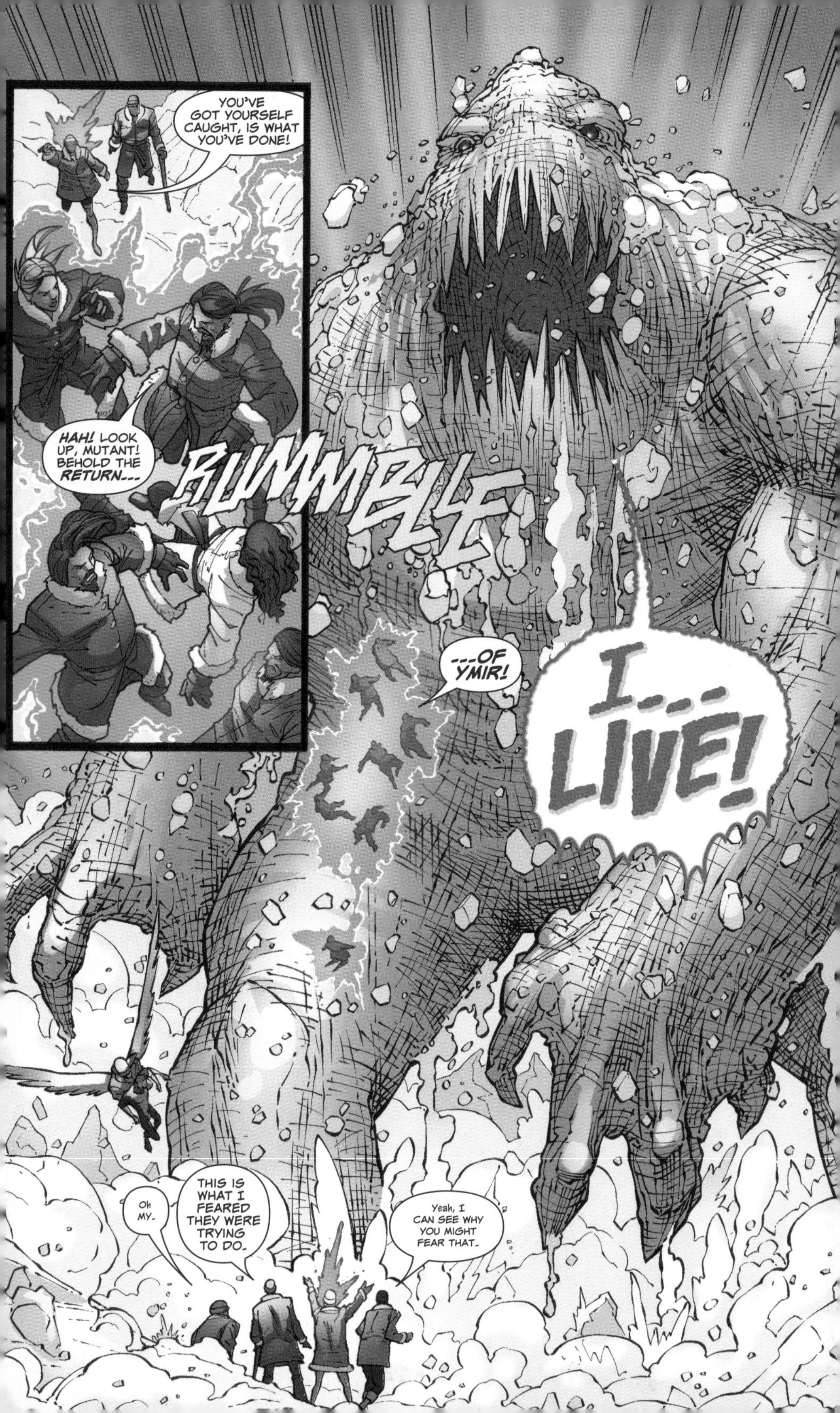
YOU'VE GOT YOURSELF CAUGHT, IS WHAT YOU'VE DONE!
HAH! LOOK UP, MUTANT! BEHOLD THE RETURN---
RUMMBLE
---OF YMIR!
I... LIVE!
Oh my.
THIS IS WHAT I FEARED THEY WERE TRYING TO DO.
Yeah, I can see why you might fear that.

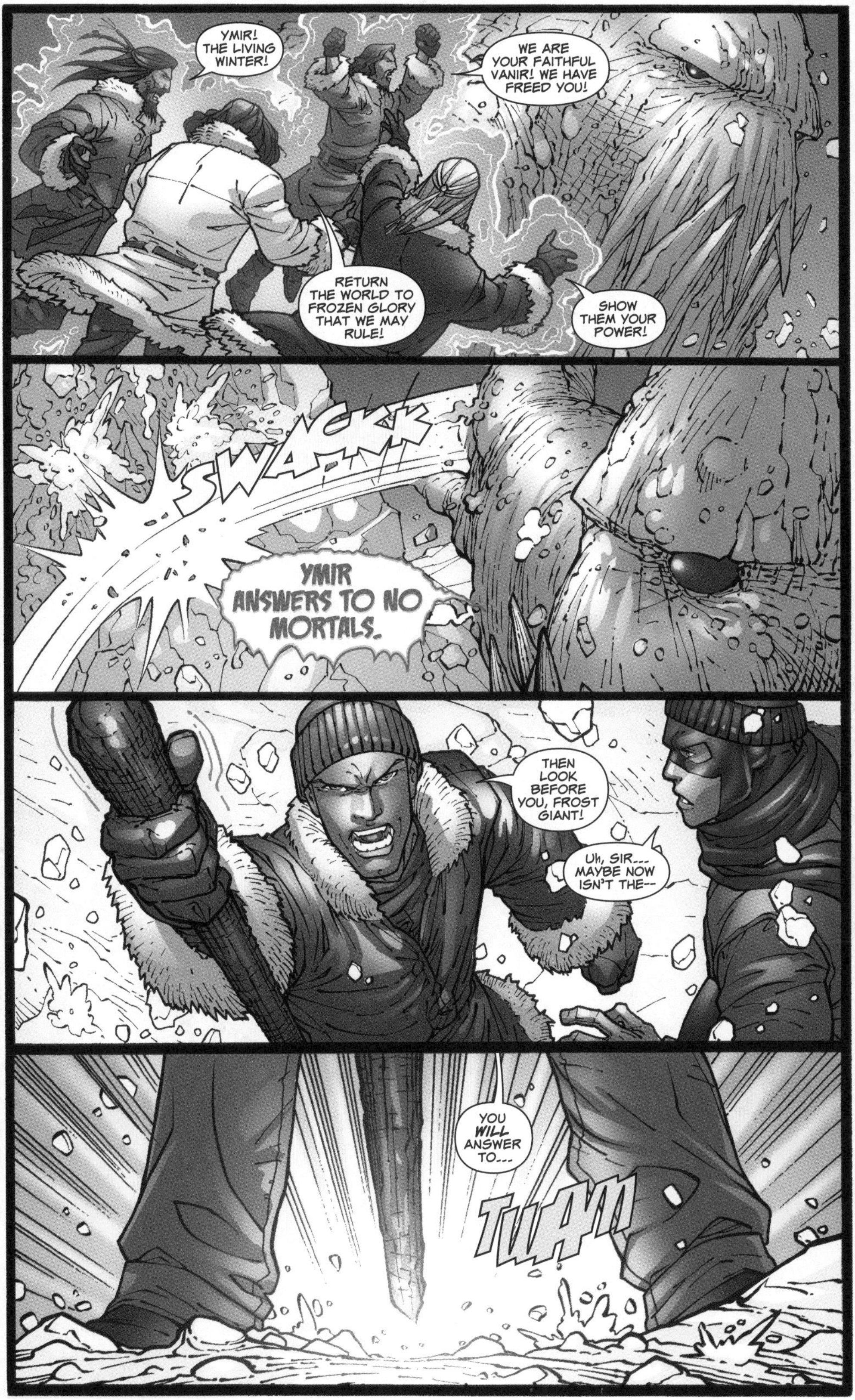
YMIR! THE LIVING WINTER!
WE ARE YOUR FAITHFUL VANIR! WE HAVE FREED YOU!
RETURN THE WORLD TO FROZEN GLORY THAT WE MAY RULE!
SHOW THEM YOUR POWER!
SWACKK
YMIR ANSWERS TO NO MORTALS.
THEN LOOK BEFORE YOU, FROST GIANT!
Uh, SIR... MAYBE NOW ISN'T THE--
YOU WILL ANSWER TO...
TUAM

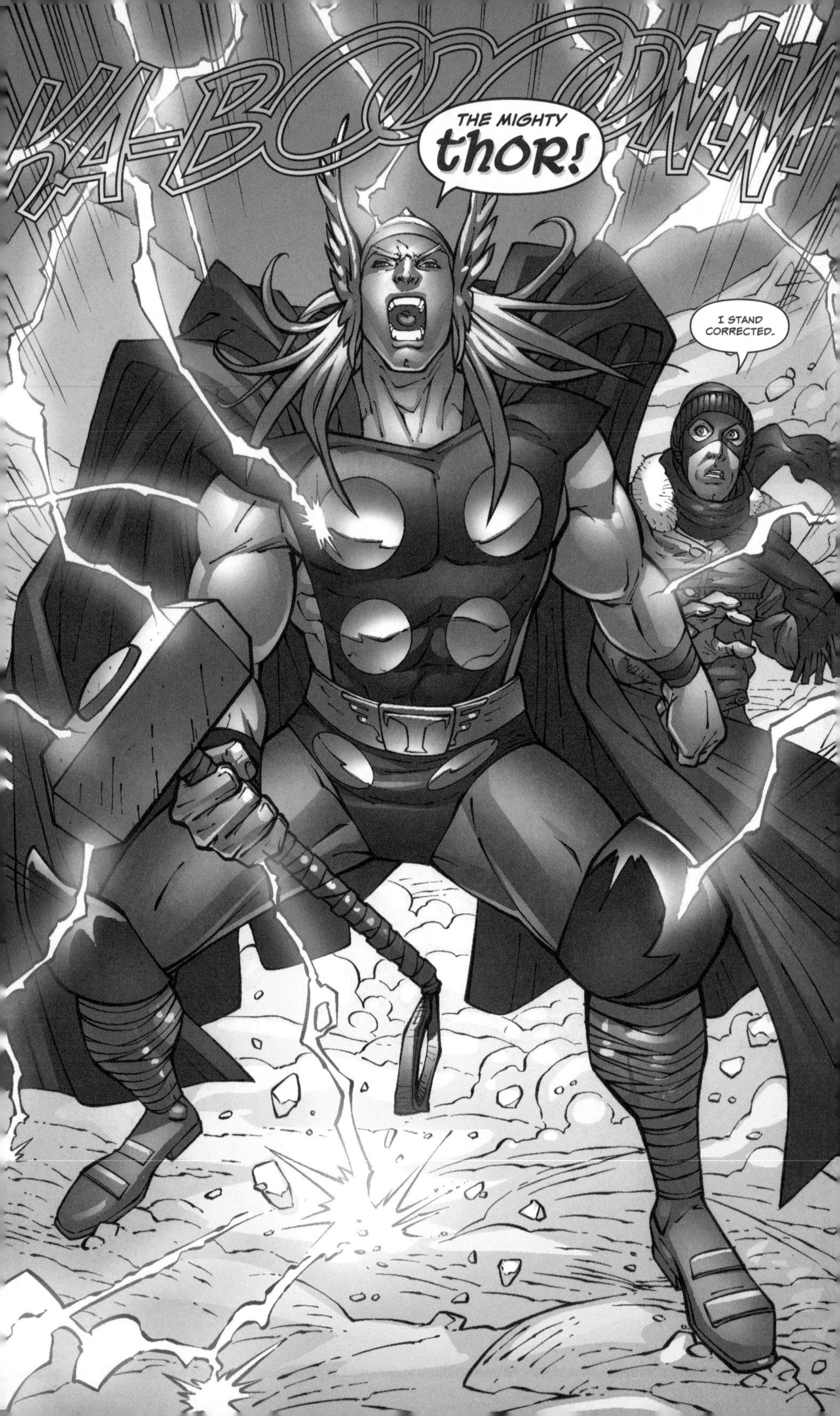
KA-BOOOOOMM
THE MIGHTY thor!
I STAND CORRECTED.

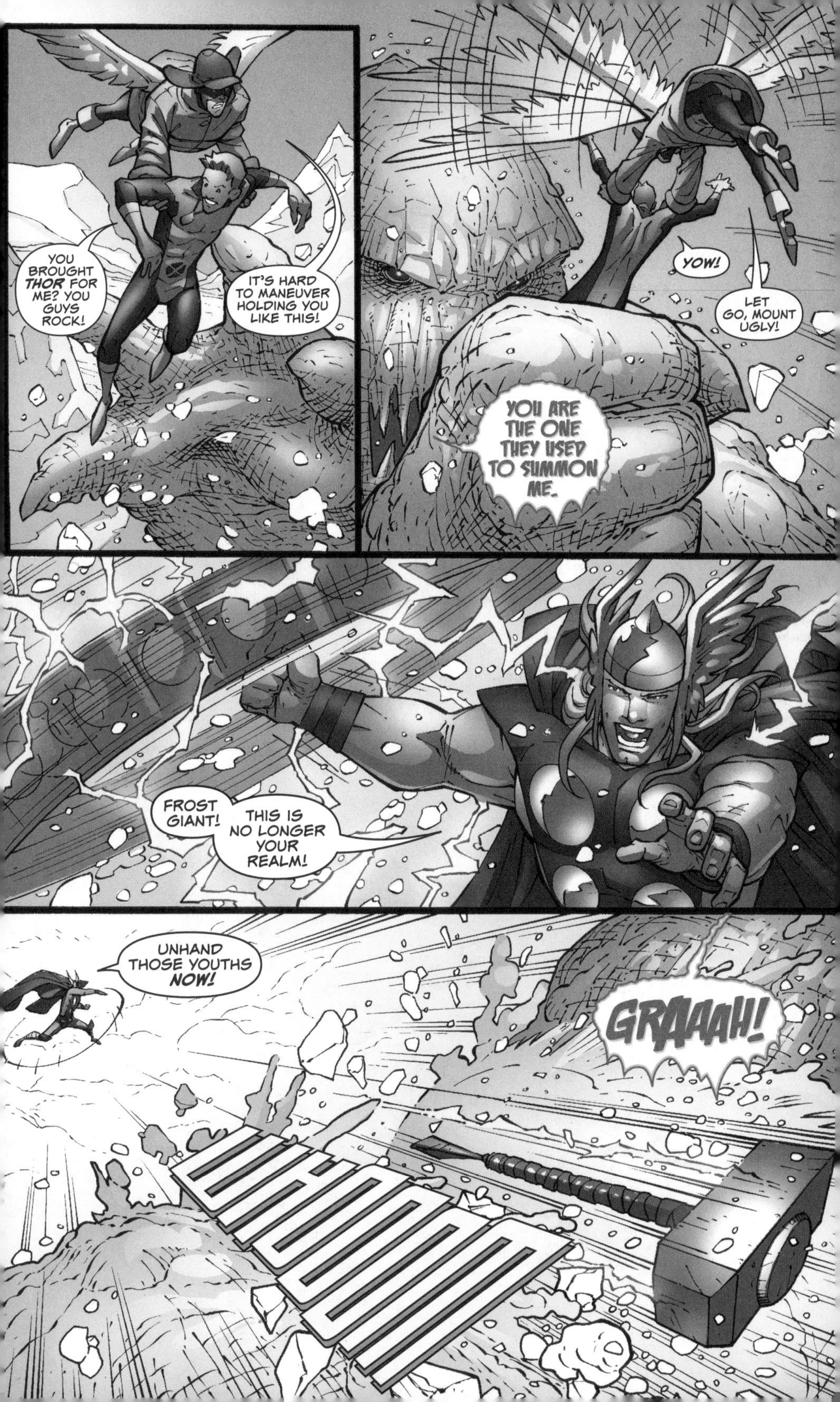

YOU BROUGHT THOR FOR ME? YOU GUYS ROCK!
IT'S HARD TO MANEUVER HOLDING YOU LIKE THIS!
YOW!
LET GO, MOUNT UGLY!
YOU ARE THE ONE THEY USED TO SUMMON ME.
FROST GIANT!
THIS IS NO LONGER YOUR REALM!
UNHAND THOSE YOUTHS NOW!
GRAAAH!

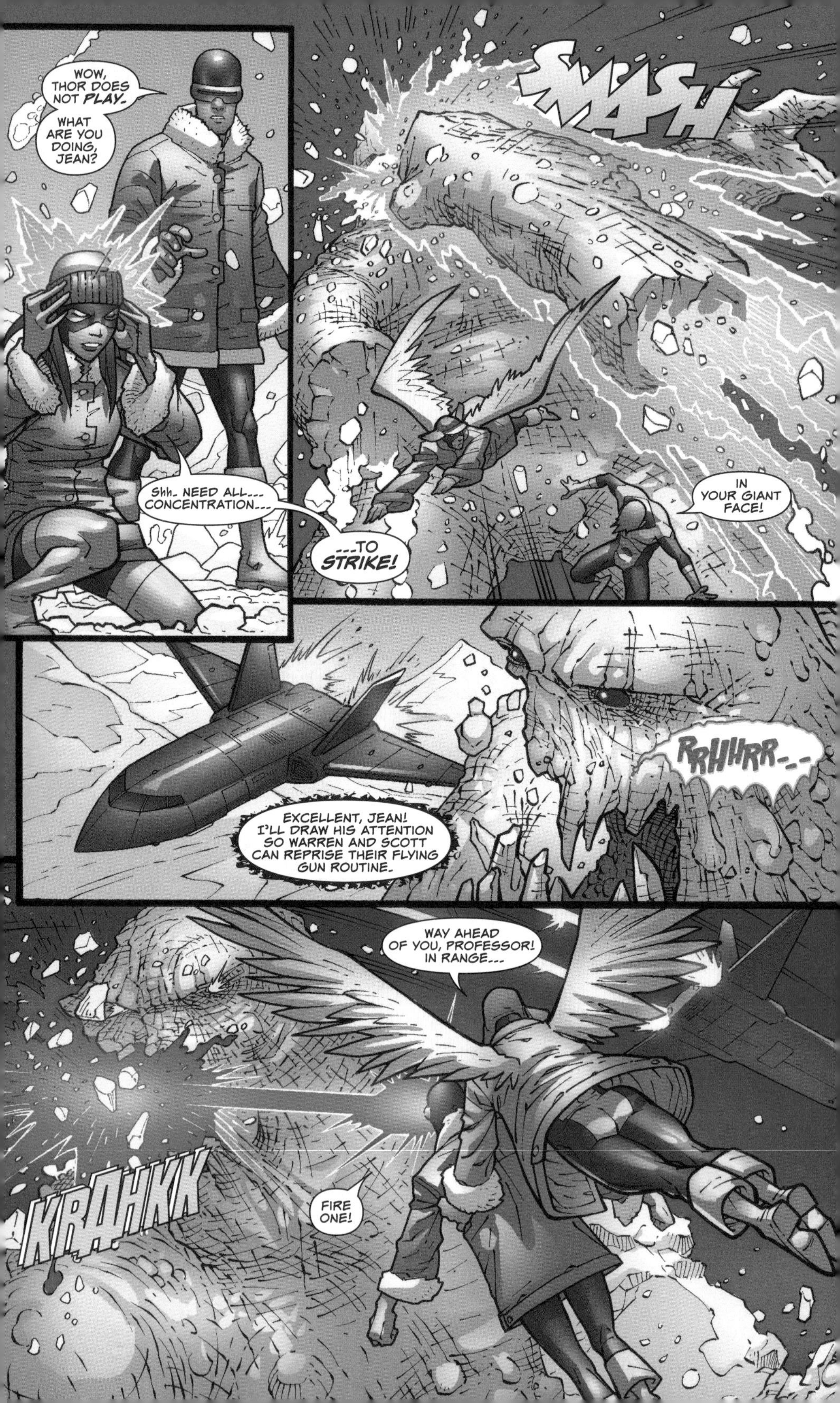
WOW, THOR DOES NOT PLAY.
WHAT ARE YOU DOING, JEAN?
SHH. NEED ALL... CONCENTRATION...
...TO STRIKE!
SMASH
IN YOUR GIANT FACE!
RRHHRR...
EXCELLENT, JEAN! I'LL DRAW HIS ATTENTION SO WARREN AND SCOTT CAN REPRISE THEIR FLYING GUN ROUTINE.
WAY AHEAD OF YOU, PROFESSOR! IN RANGE...
KRAHKK
FIRE ONE!

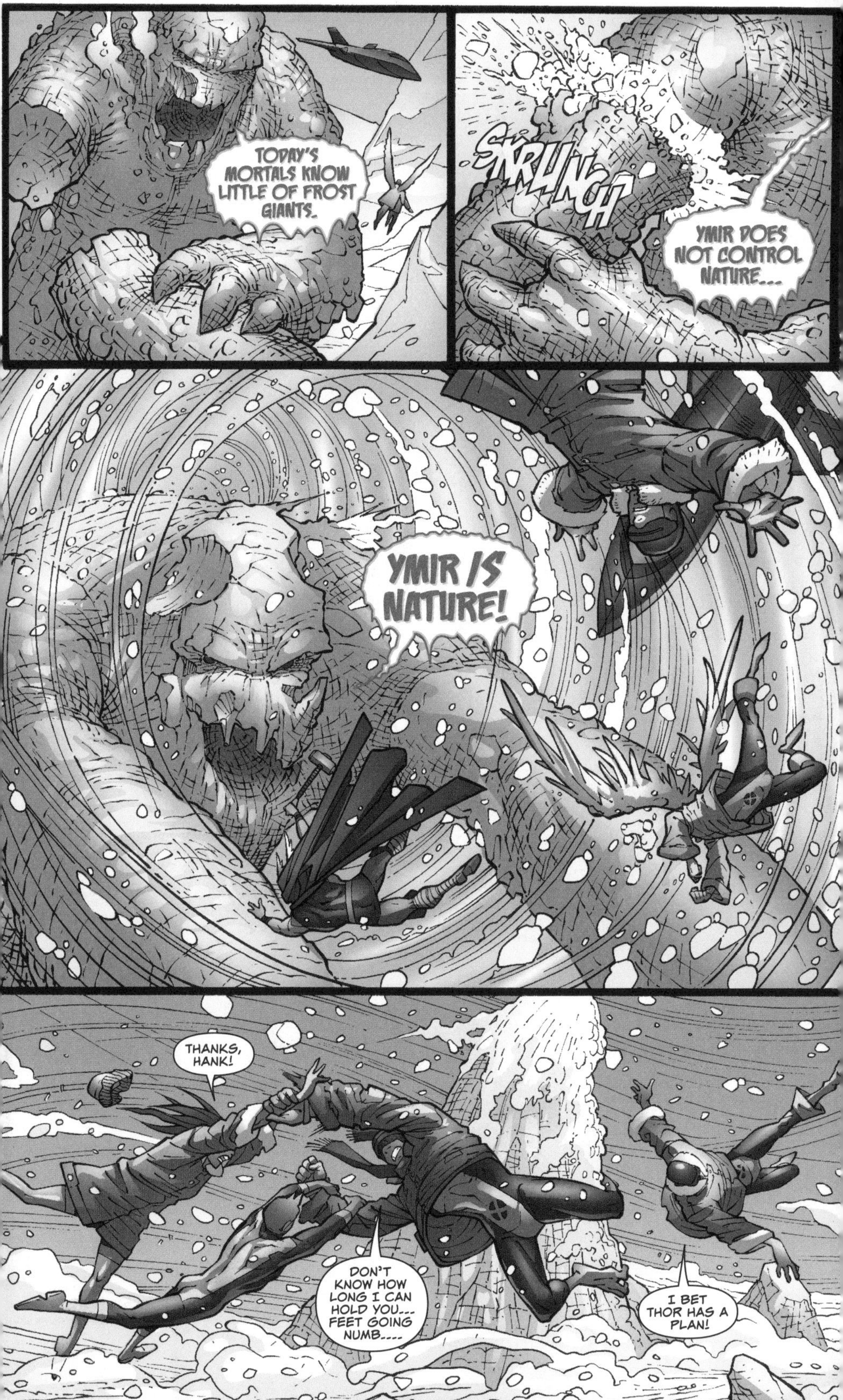
TODAY'S MORTALS KNOW LITTLE OF FROST GIANTS.
SKRUNCH
YMIR DOES NOT CONTROL NATURE...
YMIR IS NATURE!
THANKS, HANK!
DON'T KNOW HOW LONG I CAN HOLD YOU... FEET GOING NUMB....
I BET THOR HAS A PLAN!

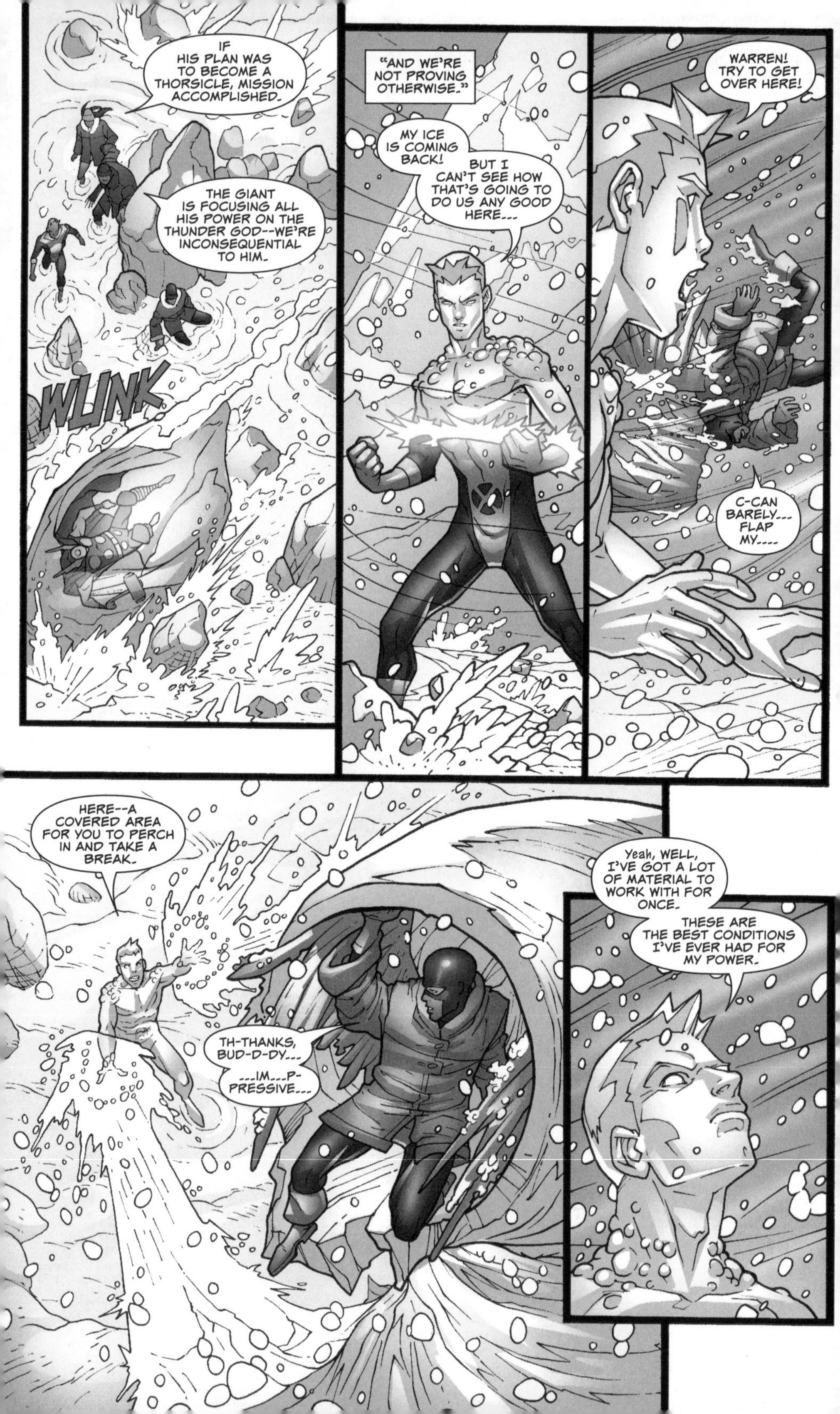
IF HIS PLAN WAS TO BECOME A THORSICLE, MISSION ACCOMPLISHED.
THE GIANT IS FOCUSING ALL HIS POWER ON THE THUNDER GOD--WE'RE INCONSEQUENTIAL TO HIM.
WUNK
"AND WE'RE NOT PROVING OTHERWISE."
MY ICE IS COMING BACK!
BUT I CAN'T SEE HOW THAT'S GOING TO DO US ANY GOOD HERE...
WARREN! TRY TO GET OVER HERE!
C-CAN BARELY... FLAP MY....
HERE--A COVERED AREA FOR YOU TO PERCH IN AND TAKE A BREAK.
TH-THANKS, BUD-D-DY...
...IM...P-PRESSIVE...
Yeah, WELL, I'VE GOT A LOT OF MATERIAL TO WORK WITH FOR ONCE.
THESE ARE THE BEST CONDITIONS I'VE EVER HAD FOR MY POWER.

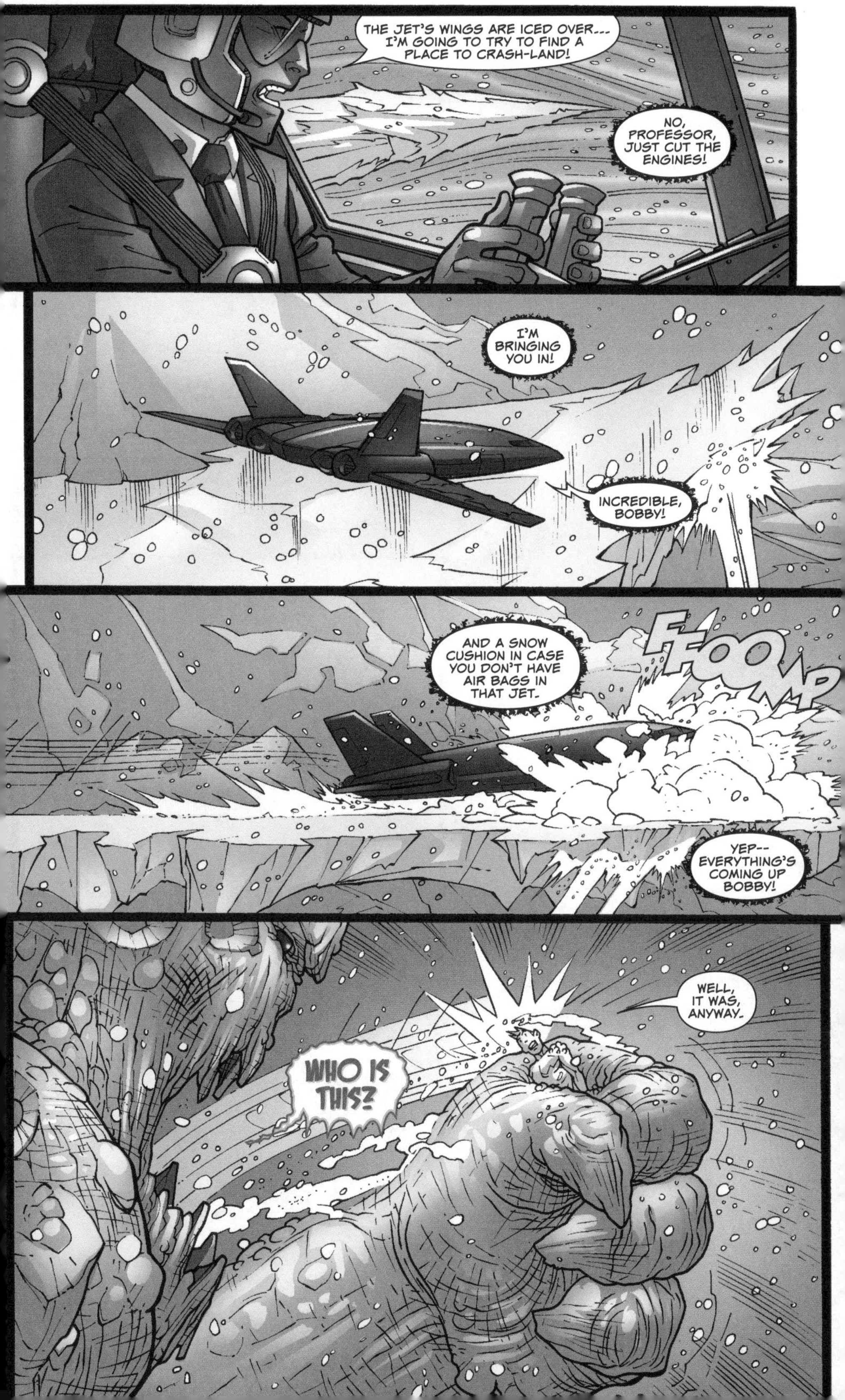
THE JET'S WINGS ARE ICED OVER... I'M GOING TO TRY TO FIND A PLACE TO CRASH-LAND!
NO, PROFESSOR, JUST CUT THE ENGINES!
I'M BRINGING YOU IN!
INCREDIBLE, BOBBY!
AND A SNOW CUSHION IN CASE YOU DON'T HAVE AIR BAGS IN THAT JET.
FFOOMP
YEP-- EVERYTHING'S COMING UP BOBBY!
WELL, IT WAS, ANYWAY.
WHO IS THIS?

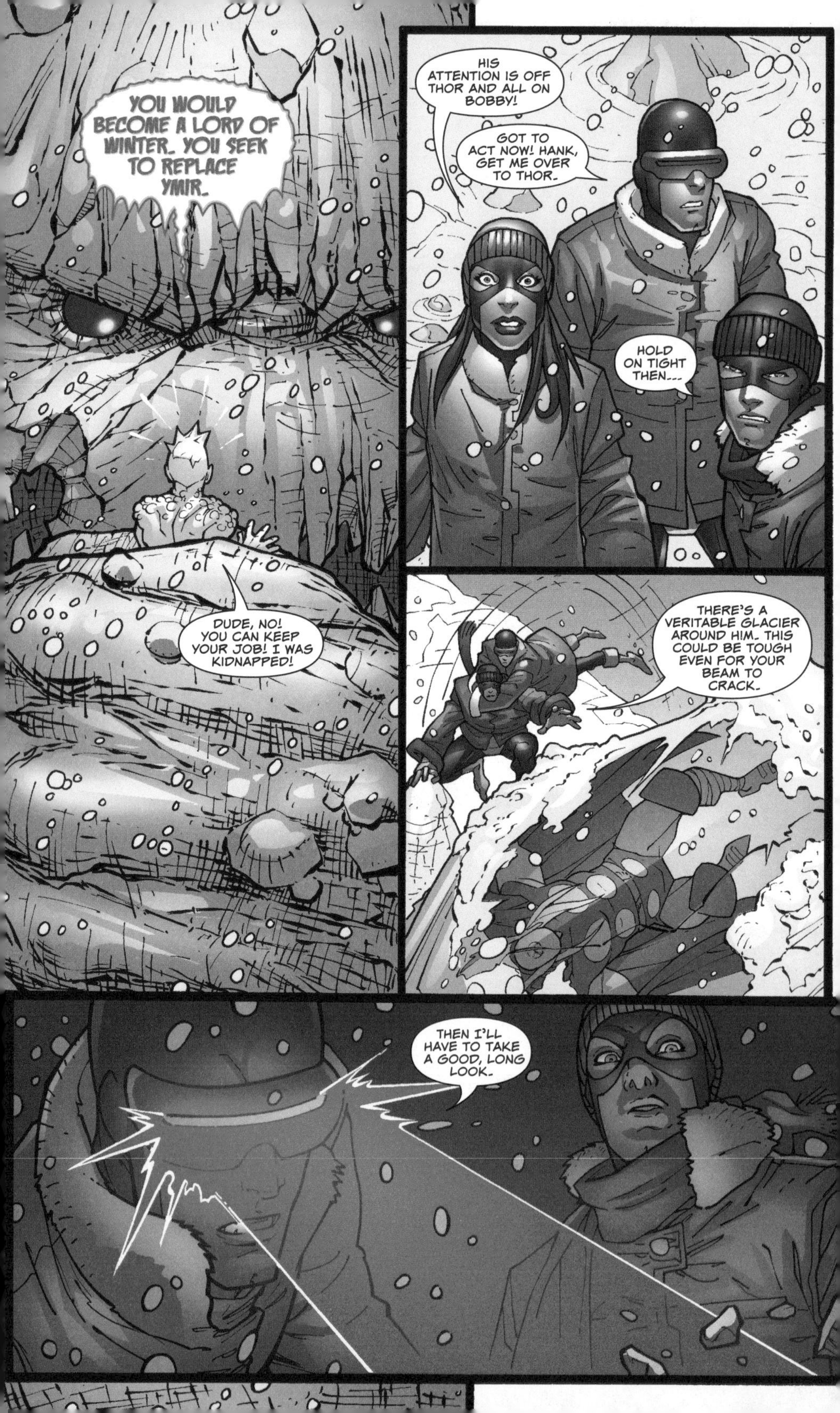
YOU WOULD BECOME A LORD OF WINTER. YOU SEEK TO REPLACE YMIR.
HIS ATTENTION IS OFF THOR AND ALL ON BOBBY!
GOT TO ACT NOW! HANK, GET ME OVER TO THOR.
HOLD ON TIGHT THEN...
DUDE, NO! YOU CAN KEEP YOUR JOB! I WAS KIDNAPPED!
THERE'S A VERITABLE GLACIER AROUND HIM. THIS COULD BE TOUGH EVEN FOR YOUR BEAM TO CRACK.
THEN I'LL HAVE TO TAKE A GOOD, LONG LOOK.

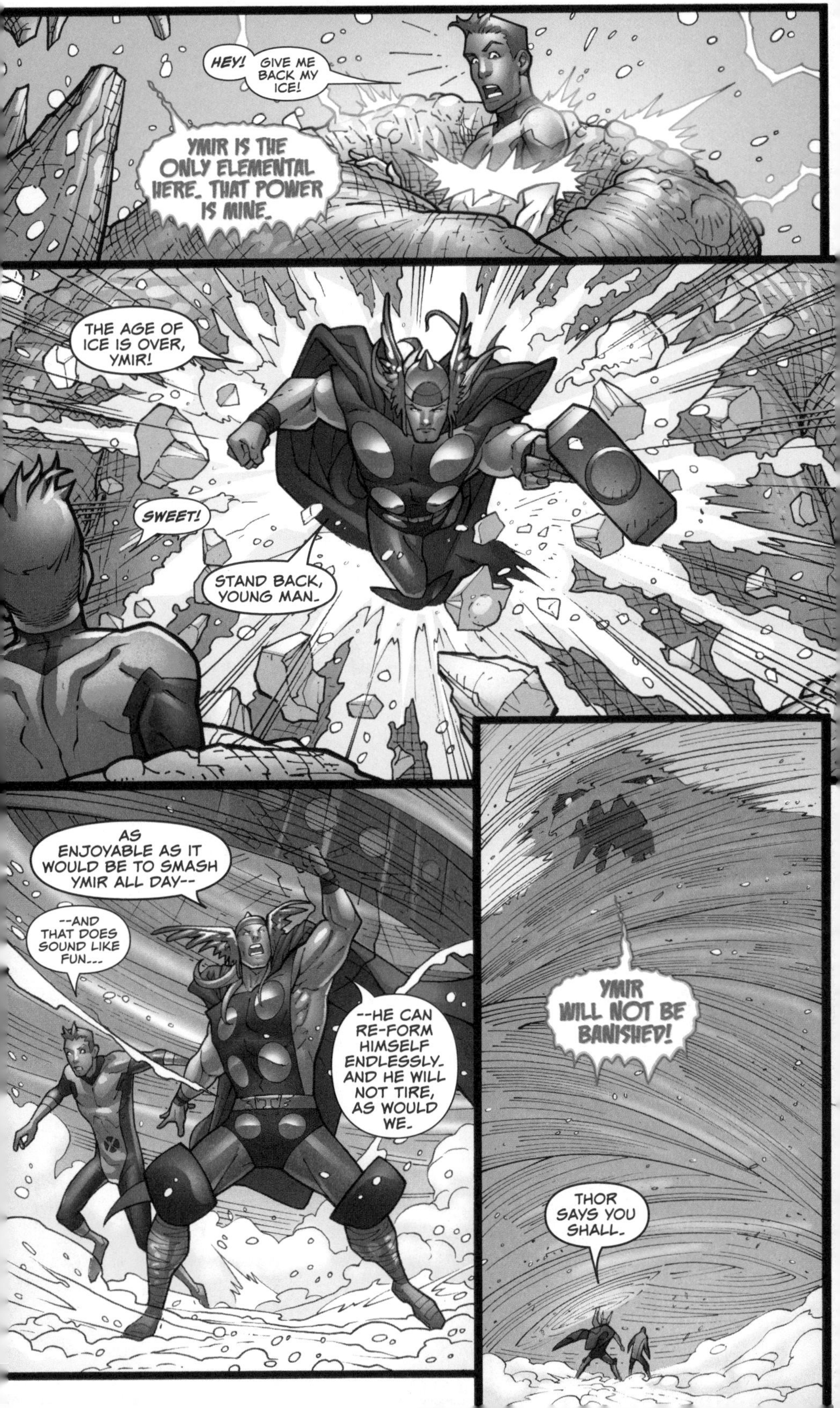
HEY! GIVE ME BACK MY ICE!
YMIR IS THE ONLY ELEMENTAL HERE. THAT POWER IS MINE.
THE AGE OF ICE IS OVER, YMIR!
SWEET!
STAND BACK, YOUNG MAN.
YMIR WILL NOT BE BANISHED!
THOR SAYS YOU SHALL.
AS ENJOYABLE AS IT WOULD BE TO SMASH YMIR ALL DAY--
--AND THAT DOES SOUND LIKE FUN...
--HE CAN RE-FORM HIMSELF ENDLESSLY. AND HE WILL NOT TIRE, AS WOULD WE.

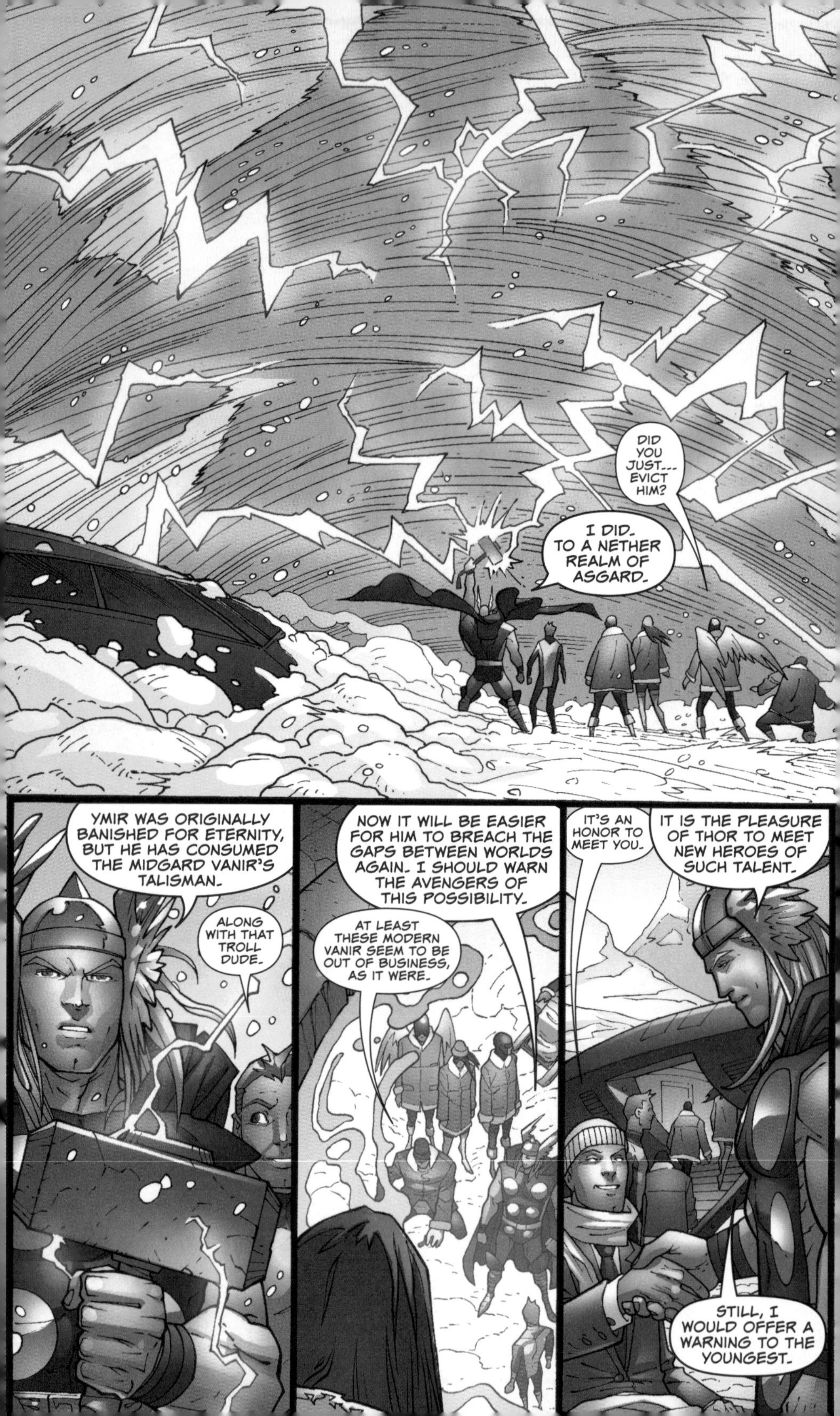
DID YOU JUST--- EVICT HIM?
I DID. TO A NETHER REALM OF ASGARD.
YMIR WAS ORIGINALLY BANISHED FOR ETERNITY, BUT HE HAS CONSUMED THE MIDGARD VANIR'S TALISMAN.
ALONG WITH THAT TROLL DUDE.
NOW IT WILL BE EASIER FOR HIM TO BREACH THE GAPS BETWEEN WORLDS AGAIN. I SHOULD WARN THE AVENGERS OF THIS POSSIBILITY.
AT LEAST THESE MODERN VANIR SEEM TO BE OUT OF BUSINESS, AS IT WERE.
IT'S AN HONOR TO MEET YOU.
IT IS THE PLEASURE OF THOR TO MEET NEW HEROES OF SUCH TALENT.
STILL, I WOULD OFFER A WARNING TO THE YOUNGEST.

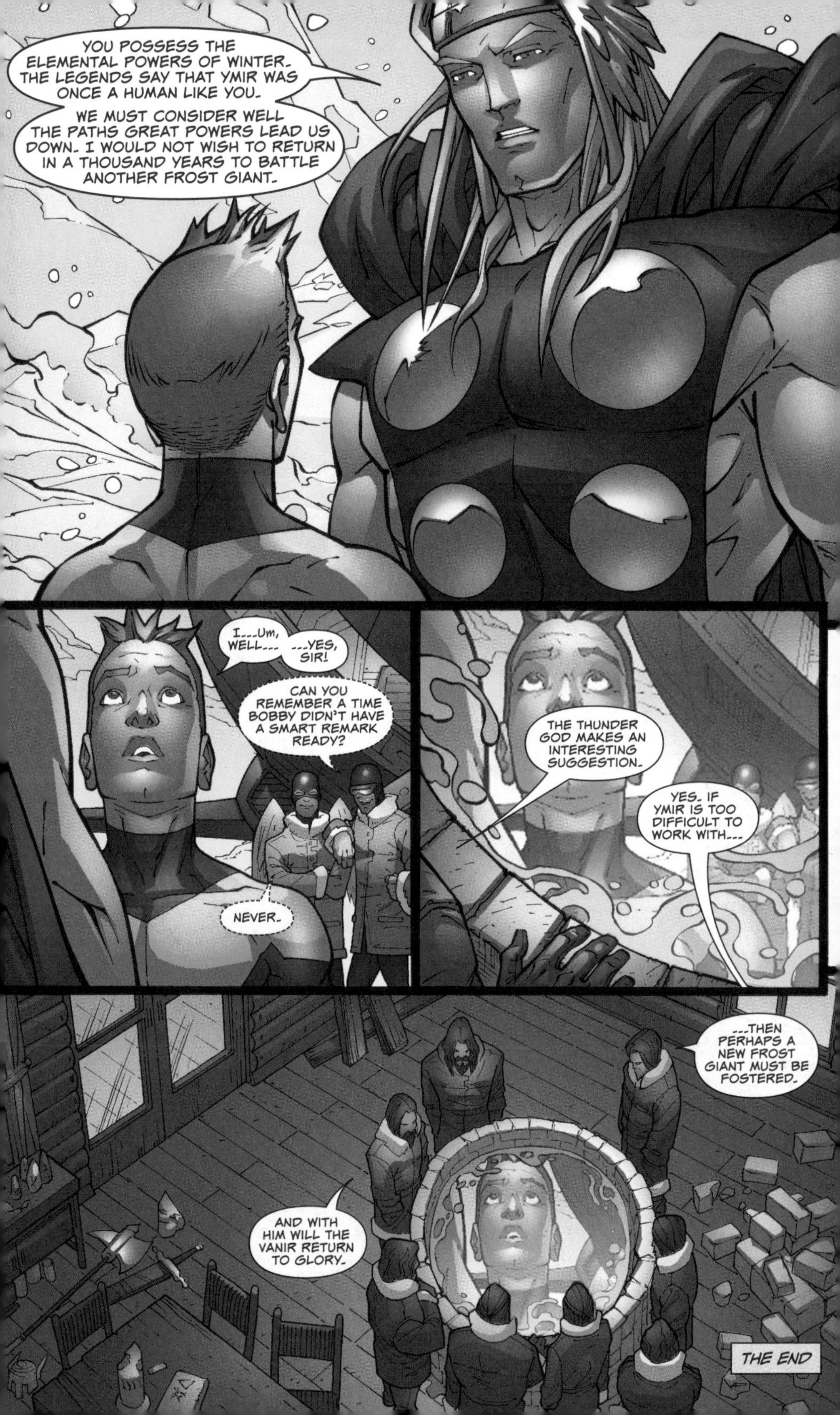
YOU POSSESS THE ELEMENTAL POWERS OF WINTER. THE LEGENDS SAY THAT YMIR WAS ONCE A HUMAN LIKE YOU.
WE MUST CONSIDER WELL THE PATHS GREAT POWERS LEAD US DOWN. I WOULD NOT WISH TO RETURN IN A THOUSAND YEARS TO BATTLE ANOTHER FROST GIANT.
I...Um, WELL...
...YES, SIR!
CAN YOU REMEMBER A TIME BOBBY DIDN'T HAVE A SMART REMARK READY?
NEVER.
THE THUNDER GOD MAKES AN INTERESTING SUGGESTION.
YES. IF YMIR IS TOO DIFFICULT TO WORK WITH...
...THEN PERHAPS A NEW FROST GIANT MUST BE FOSTERED.
AND WITH HIM WILL THE VANIR RETURN TO GLORY.
THE END

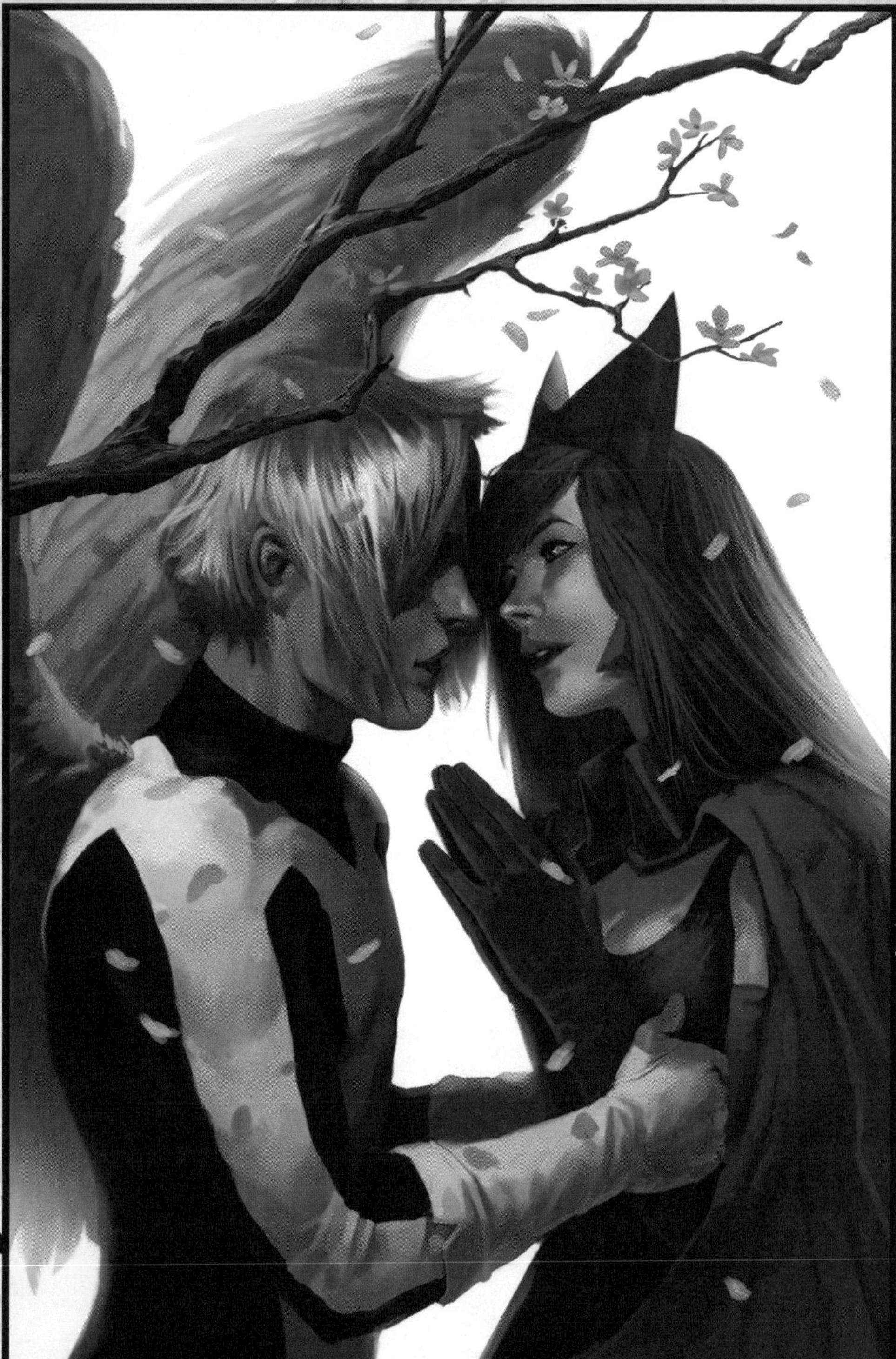

X-Men: First Class (2006) **#7**

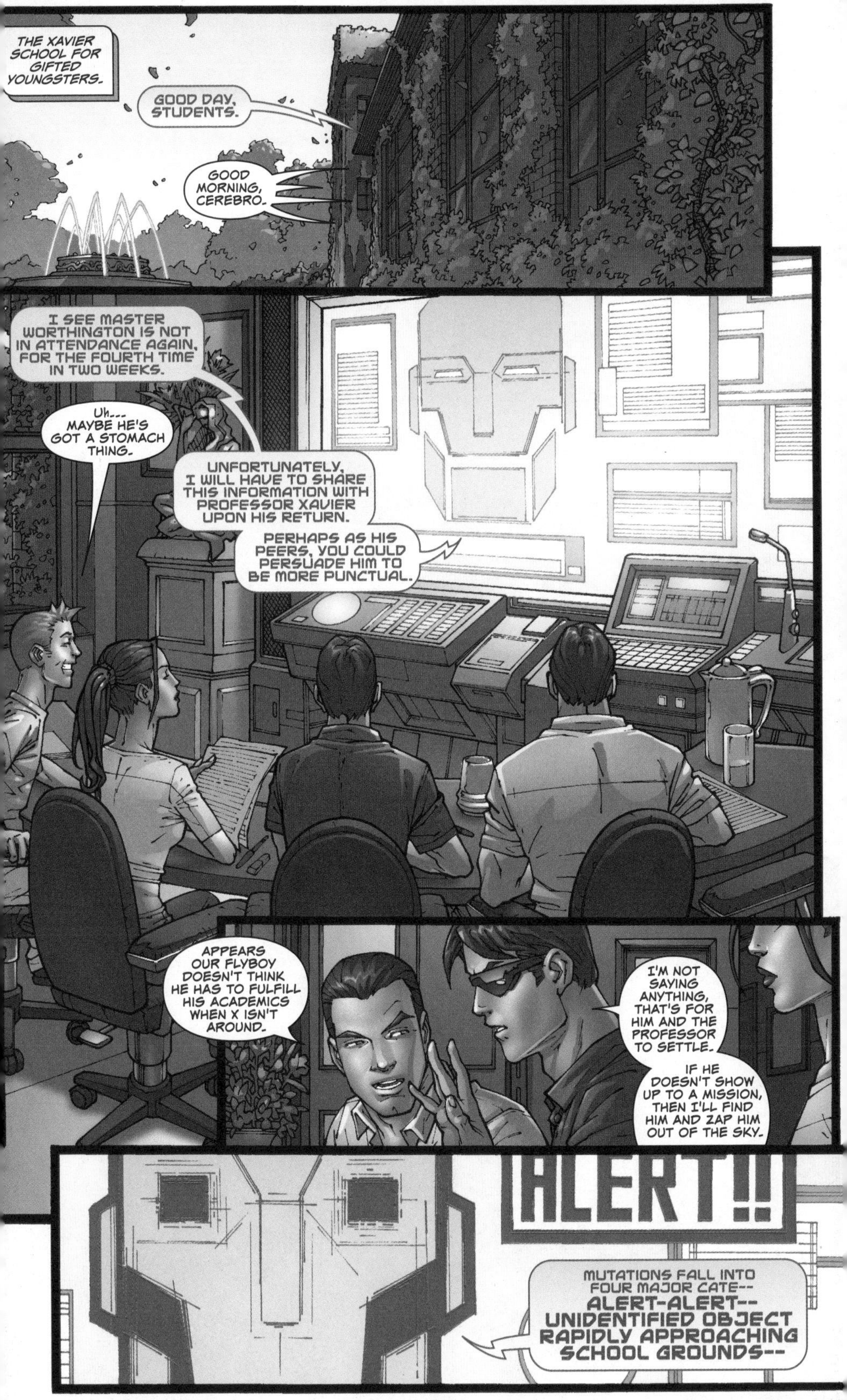
THE XAVIER SCHOOL FOR GIFTED YOUNGSTERS.
GOOD DAY, STUDENTS.
GOOD MORNING, CEREBRO.
I SEE MASTER WORTHINGTON IS NOT IN ATTENDANCE AGAIN. FOR THE FOURTH TIME IN TWO WEEKS.
Uh... MAYBE HE'S GOT A STOMACH THING.
UNFORTUNATELY, I WILL HAVE TO SHARE THIS INFORMATION WITH PROFESSOR XAVIER UPON HIS RETURN.
PERHAPS AS HIS PEERS, YOU COULD PERSUADE HIM TO BE MORE PUNCTUAL.
APPEARS OUR FLYBOY DOESN'T THINK HE HAS TO FULFILL HIS ACADEMICS WHEN X ISN'T AROUND.
I'M NOT SAYING ANYTHING, THAT'S FOR HIM AND THE PROFESSOR TO SETTLE.
IF HE DOESN'T SHOW UP TO A MISSION, THEN I'LL FIND HIM AND ZAP HIM OUT OF THE SKY.
ALERT!!
MUTATIONS FALL INTO FOUR MAJOR CATE-- ALERT-ALERT-- UNIDENTIFIED OBJECT RAPIDLY APPROACHING SCHOOL GROUNDS--

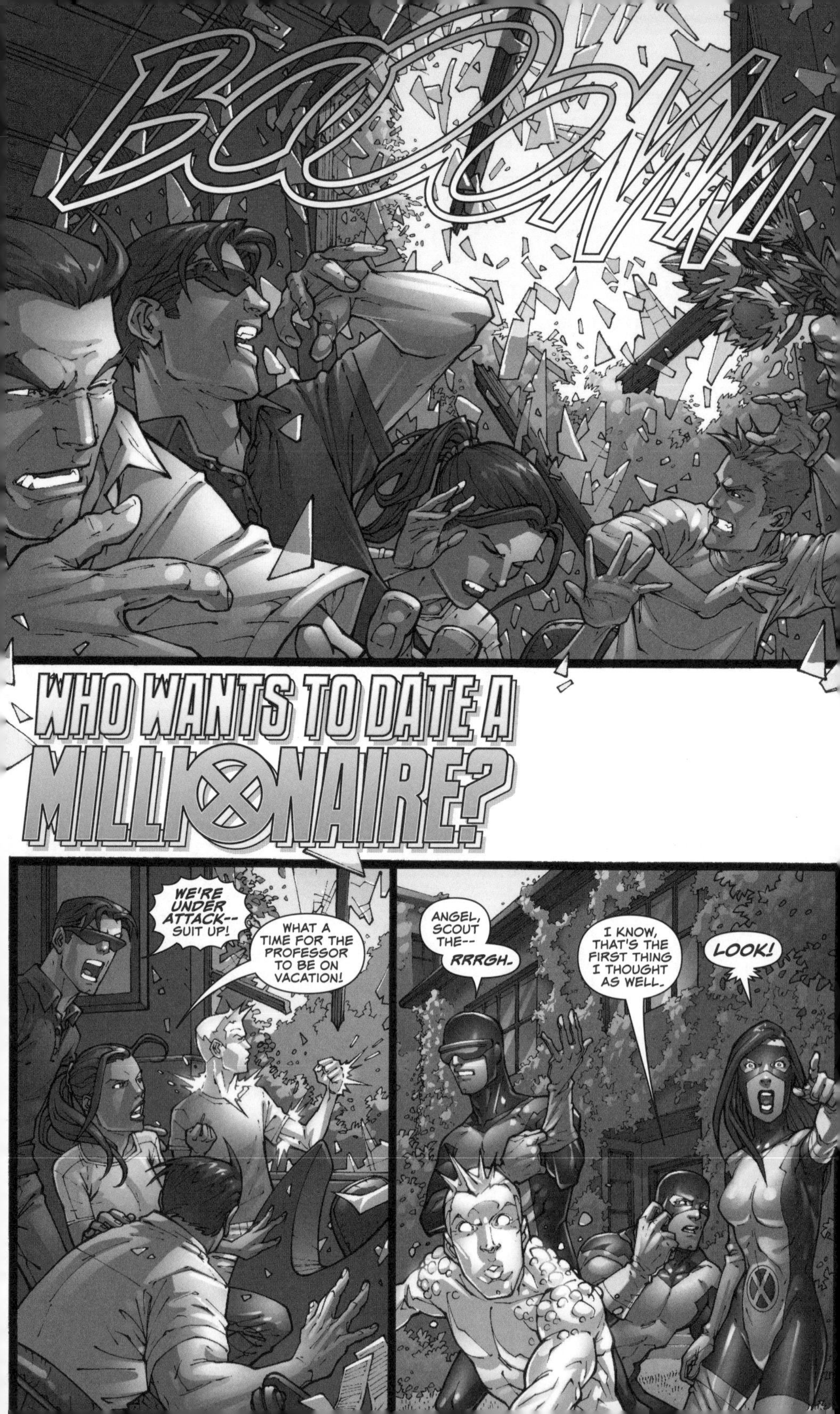
BOOOM
WHO WANTS TO DATE A MILLIONAIRE?
WE'RE UNDER ATTACK-- SUIT UP!
WHAT A TIME FOR THE PROFESSOR TO BE ON VACATION!
ANGEL, SCOUT THE-- RRRGH.
I KNOW, THAT'S THE FIRST THING I THOUGHT AS WELL.
LOOK!

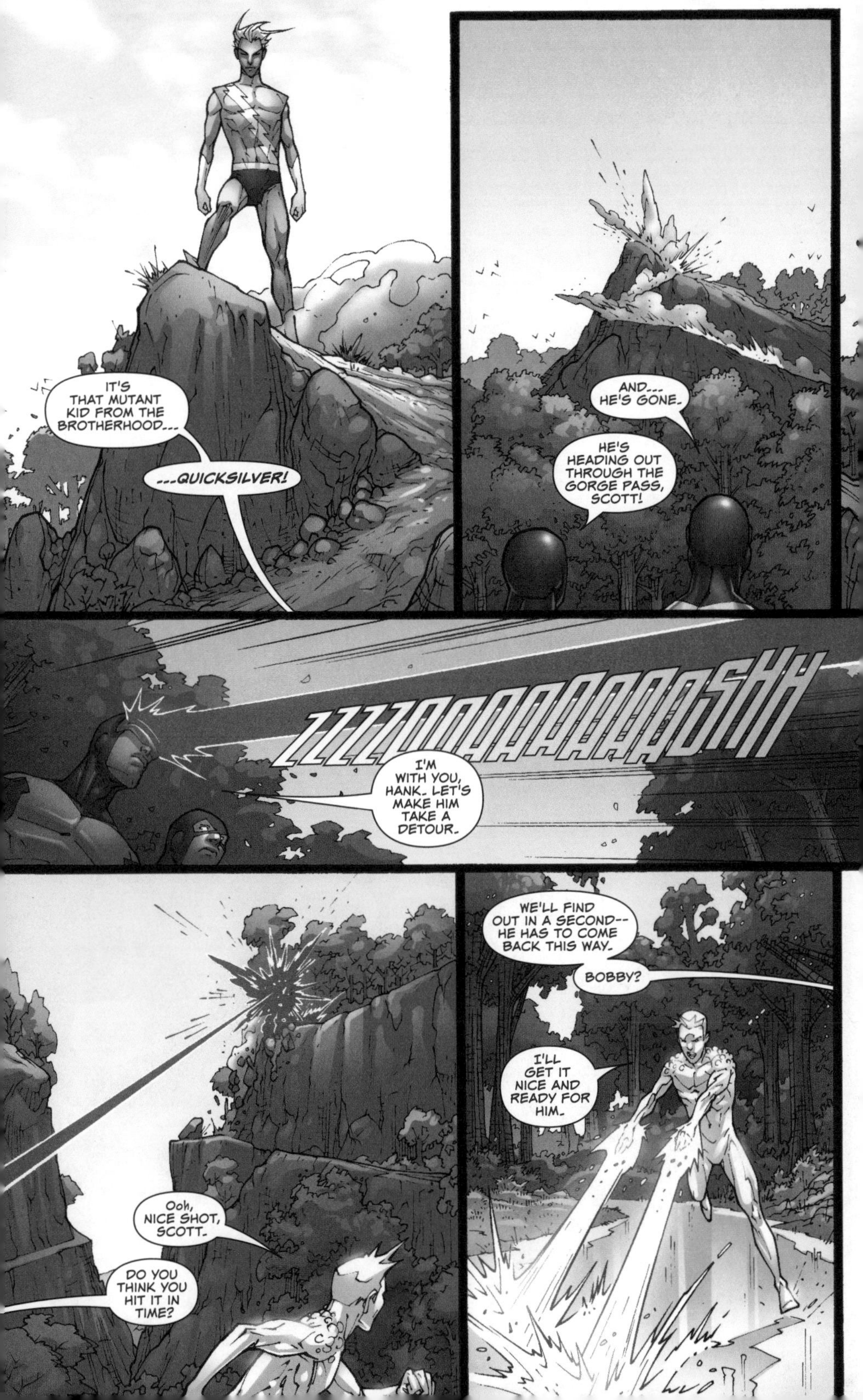
IT'S THAT MUTANT KID FROM THE BROTHERHOOD...
...QUICKSILVER!
AND... HE'S GONE.
HE'S HEADING OUT THROUGH THE GORGE PASS, SCOTT!
ZZZZOOOOAAAAAAOOSHH
I'M WITH YOU, HANK. LET'S MAKE HIM TAKE A DETOUR.
Ooh, NICE SHOT, SCOTT.
DO YOU THINK YOU HIT IT IN TIME?
WE'LL FIND OUT IN A SECOND-- HE HAS TO COME BACK THIS WAY.
BOBBY?
I'LL GET IT NICE AND READY FOR HIM.

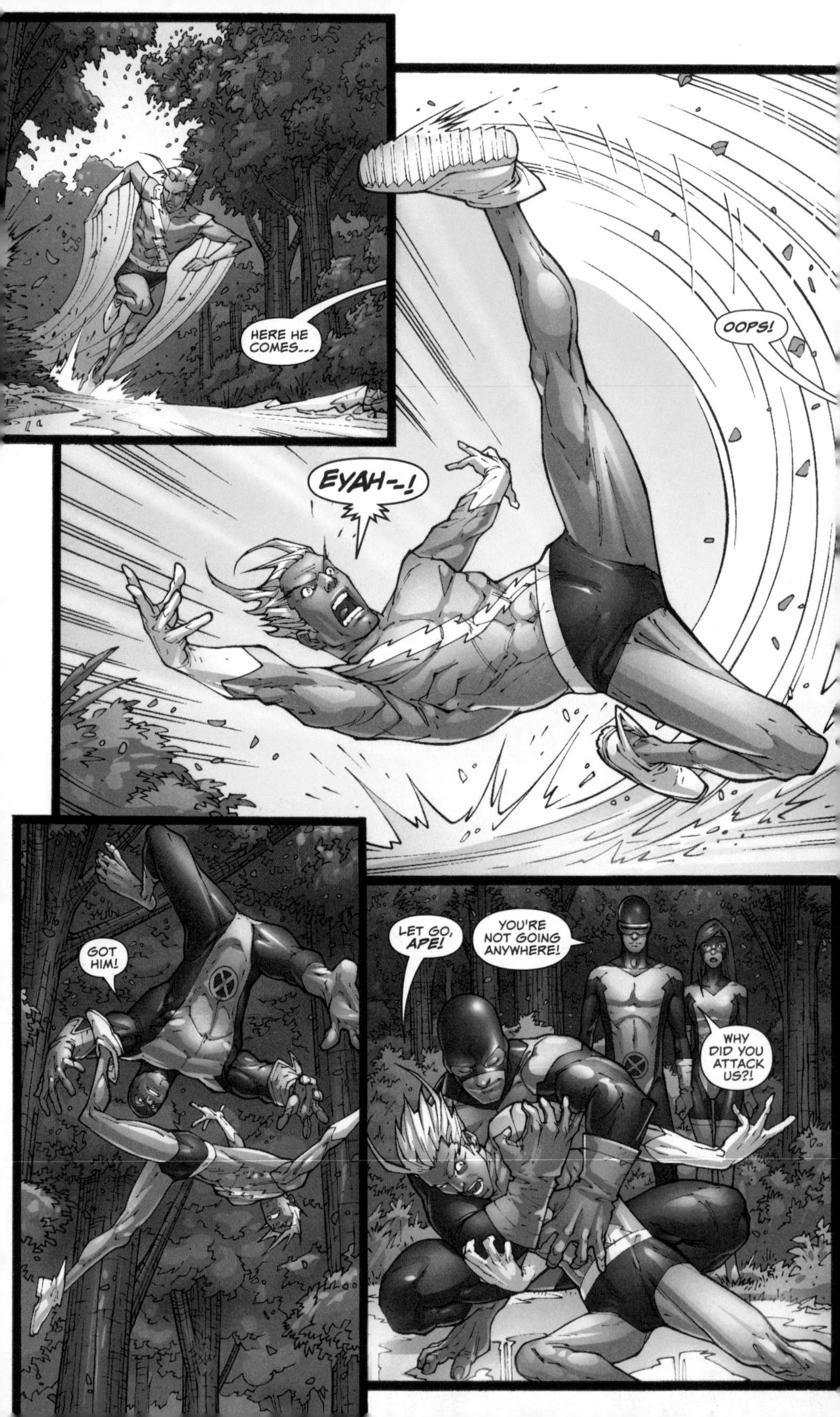
HERE HE COMES...
OOPS!
EYAH--!
GOT HIM!
LET GO, APE!
YOU'RE NOT GOING ANYWHERE!
WHY DID YOU ATTACK US?!

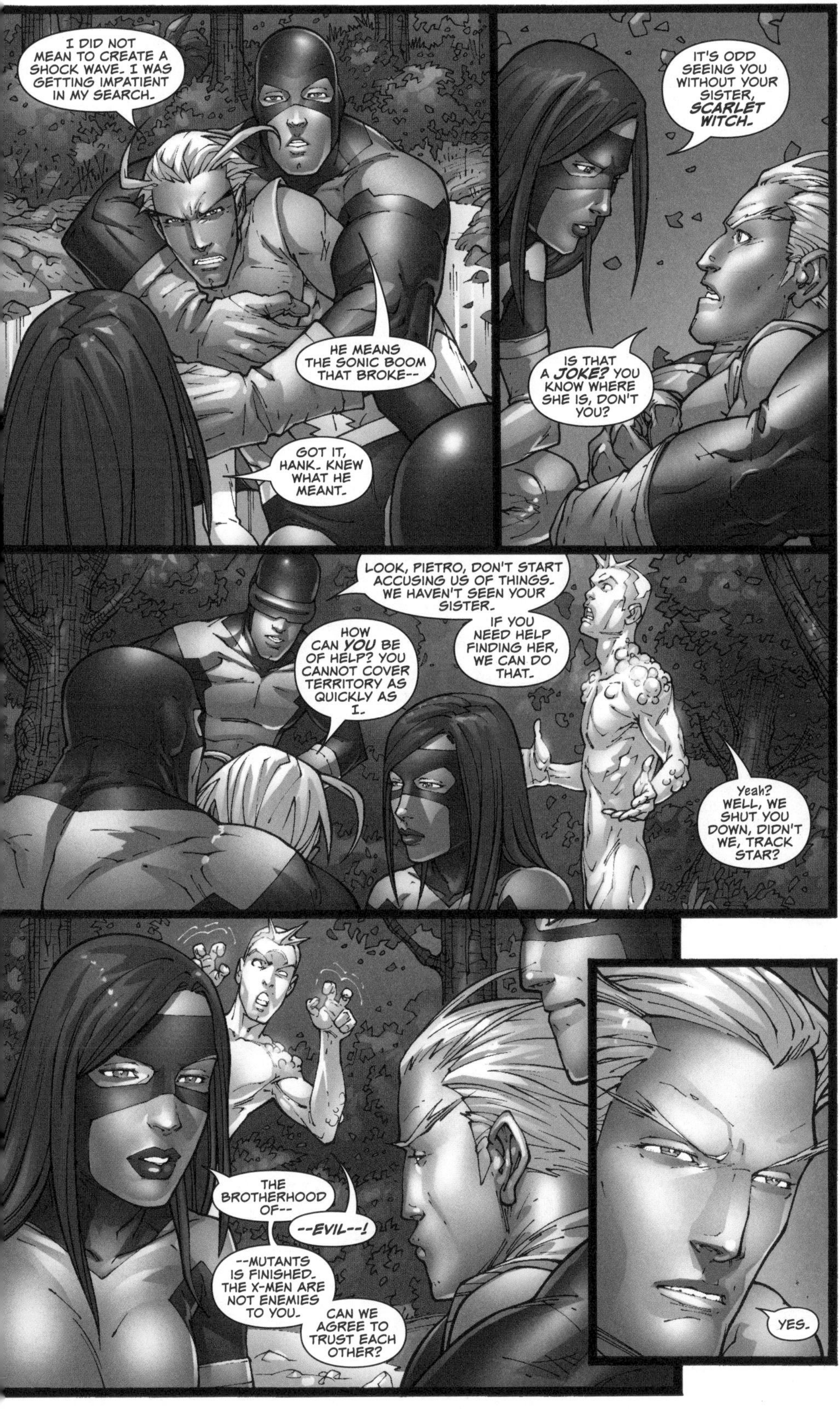
I DID NOT MEAN TO CREATE A SHOCK WAVE. I WAS GETTING IMPATIENT IN MY SEARCH.
HE MEANS THE SONIC BOOM THAT BROKE--
GOT IT, HANK. KNEW WHAT HE MEANT.
IT'S ODD SEEING YOU WITHOUT YOUR SISTER, SCARLET WITCH.
IS THAT A JOKE? YOU KNOW WHERE SHE IS, DON'T YOU?
LOOK, PIETRO, DON'T START ACCUSING US OF THINGS. WE HAVEN'T SEEN YOUR SISTER.
IF YOU NEED HELP FINDING HER, WE CAN DO THAT.
HOW CAN YOU BE OF HELP? YOU CANNOT COVER TERRITORY AS QUICKLY AS I.
Yeah? WELL, WE SHUT YOU DOWN, DIDN'T WE, TRACK STAR?
THE BROTHERHOOD OF--
--EVIL--!
--MUTANTS IS FINISHED. THE X-MEN ARE NOT ENEMIES TO YOU.
CAN WE AGREE TO TRUST EACH OTHER?
YES.

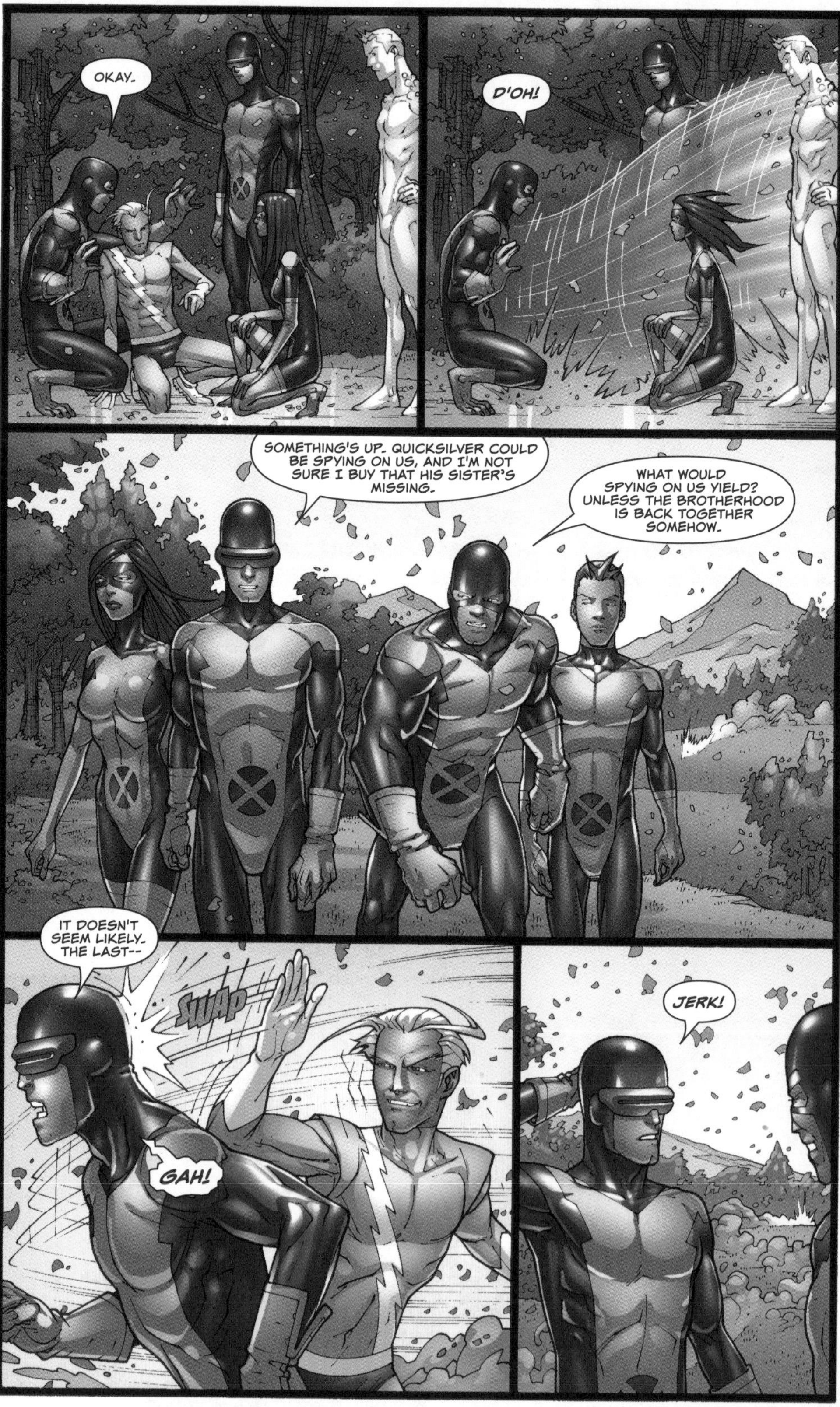
OKAY.
D'OH!
SOMETHING'S UP. QUICKSILVER COULD BE SPYING ON US, AND I'M NOT SURE I BUY THAT HIS SISTER'S MISSING.
WHAT WOULD SPYING ON US YIELD? UNLESS THE BROTHERHOOD IS BACK TOGETHER SOMEHOW.
IT DOESN'T SEEM LIKELY. THE LAST--
SWAP
GAH!
JERK!

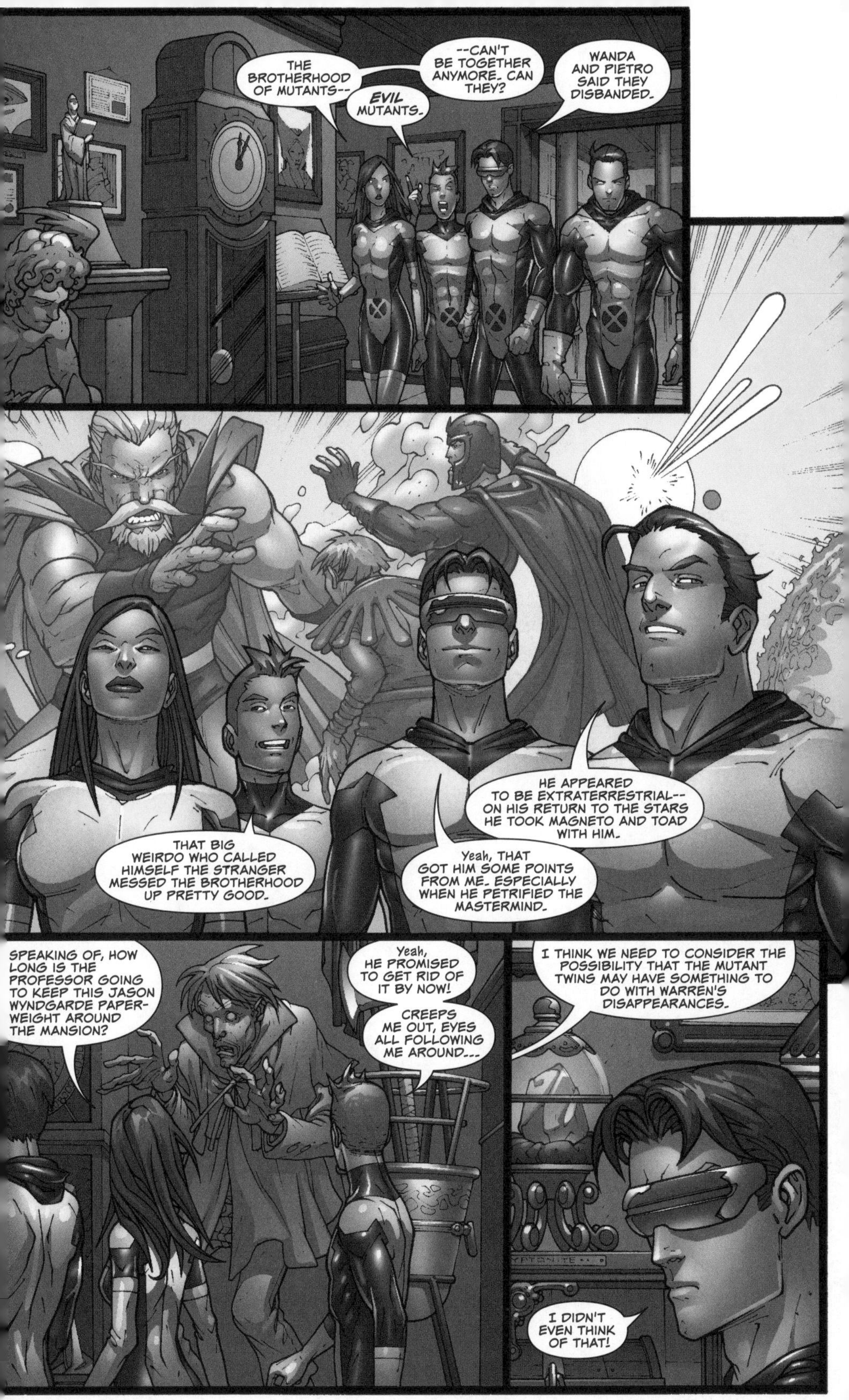

THE BROTHERHOOD OF MUTANTS--
EVIL MUTANTS.
--CAN'T BE TOGETHER ANYMORE. CAN THEY?
WANDA AND PIETRO SAID THEY DISBANDED.
THAT BIG WEIRDO WHO CALLED HIMSELF THE STRANGER MESSED THE BROTHERHOOD UP PRETTY GOOD.
Yeah, THAT GOT HIM SOME POINTS FROM ME. ESPECIALLY WHEN HE PETRIFIED THE MASTERMIND.
HE APPEARED TO BE EXTRATERRESTRIAL-- ON HIS RETURN TO THE STARS HE TOOK MAGNETO AND TOAD WITH HIM.
SPEAKING OF, HOW LONG IS THE PROFESSOR GOING TO KEEP THIS JASON WYNDGARDE PAPER-WEIGHT AROUND THE MANSION?
Yeah, HE PROMISED TO GET RID OF IT BY NOW!
CREEPS ME OUT, EYES ALL FOLLOWING ME AROUND...
I THINK WE NEED TO CONSIDER THE POSSIBILITY THAT THE MUTANT TWINS MAY HAVE SOMETHING TO DO WITH WARREN'S DISAPPEARANCES.
I DIDN'T EVEN THINK OF THAT!

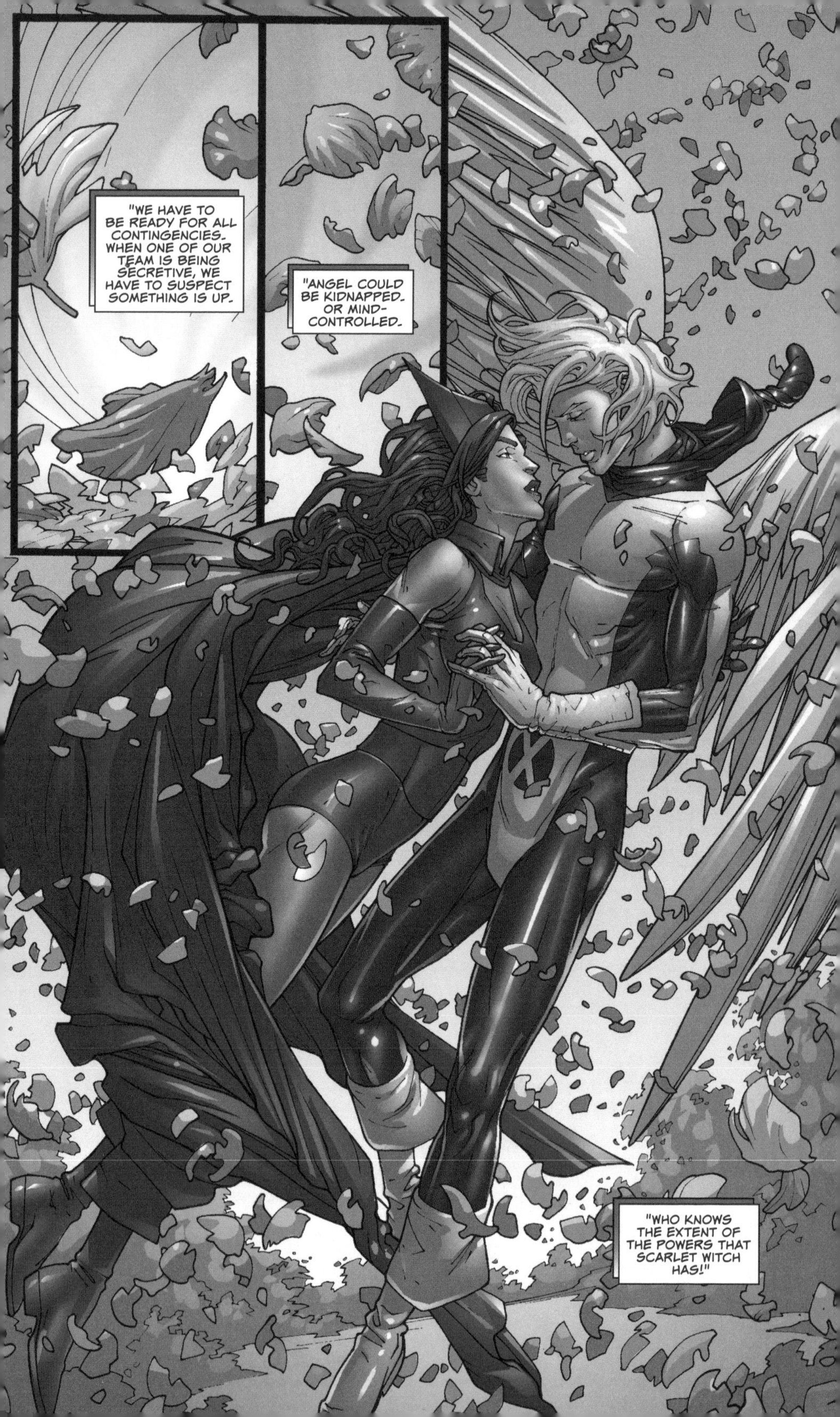
"WE HAVE TO BE READY FOR ALL CONTINGENCIES. WHEN ONE OF OUR TEAM IS BEING SECRETIVE, WE HAVE TO SUSPECT SOMETHING IS UP.
"ANGEL COULD BE KIDNAPPED. OR MIND-CONTROLLED.
"WHO KNOWS THE EXTENT OF THE POWERS THAT SCARLET WITCH HAS!"

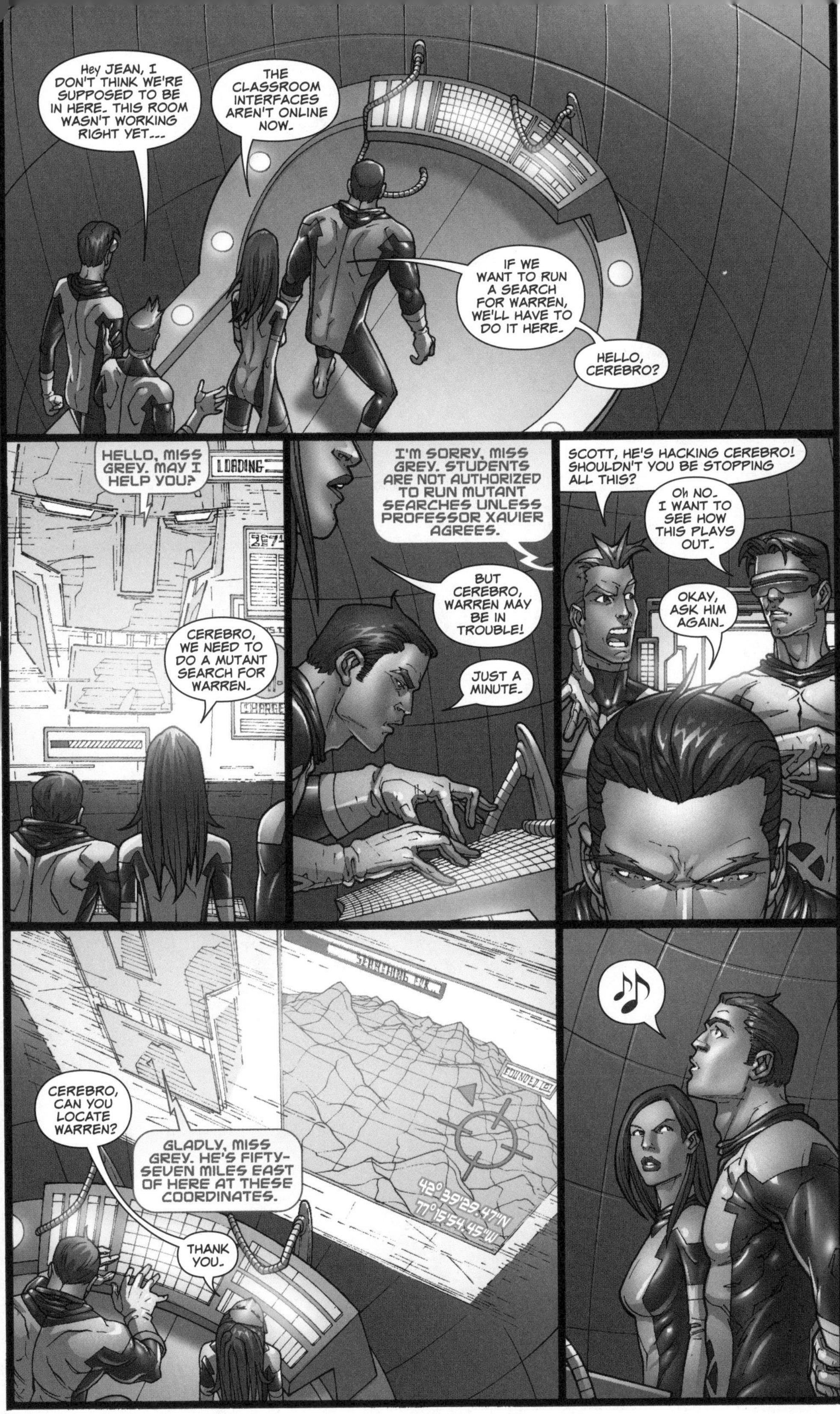
Hey JEAN, I DON'T THINK WE'RE SUPPOSED TO BE IN HERE. THIS ROOM WASN'T WORKING RIGHT YET...
THE CLASSROOM INTERFACES AREN'T ONLINE NOW.
IF WE WANT TO RUN A SEARCH FOR WARREN, WE'LL HAVE TO DO IT HERE.
HELLO, CEREBRO?
HELLO, MISS GREY. MAY I HELP YOU?
LOADING
CEREBRO, WE NEED TO DO A MUTANT SEARCH FOR WARREN.
I'M SORRY, MISS GREY. STUDENTS ARE NOT AUTHORIZED TO RUN MUTANT SEARCHES UNLESS PROFESSOR XAVIER AGREES.
BUT CEREBRO, WARREN MAY BE IN TROUBLE!
JUST A MINUTE.
SCOTT, HE'S HACKING CEREBRO! SHOULDN'T YOU BE STOPPING ALL THIS?
Oh NO. I WANT TO SEE HOW THIS PLAYS OUT.
OKAY, ASK HIM AGAIN.
CEREBRO, CAN YOU LOCATE WARREN?
GLADLY, MISS GREY. HE'S FIFTY-SEVEN MILES EAST OF HERE AT THESE COORDINATES.
42°39'29.47"N
77°15'54.45"W
THANK YOU.
♫

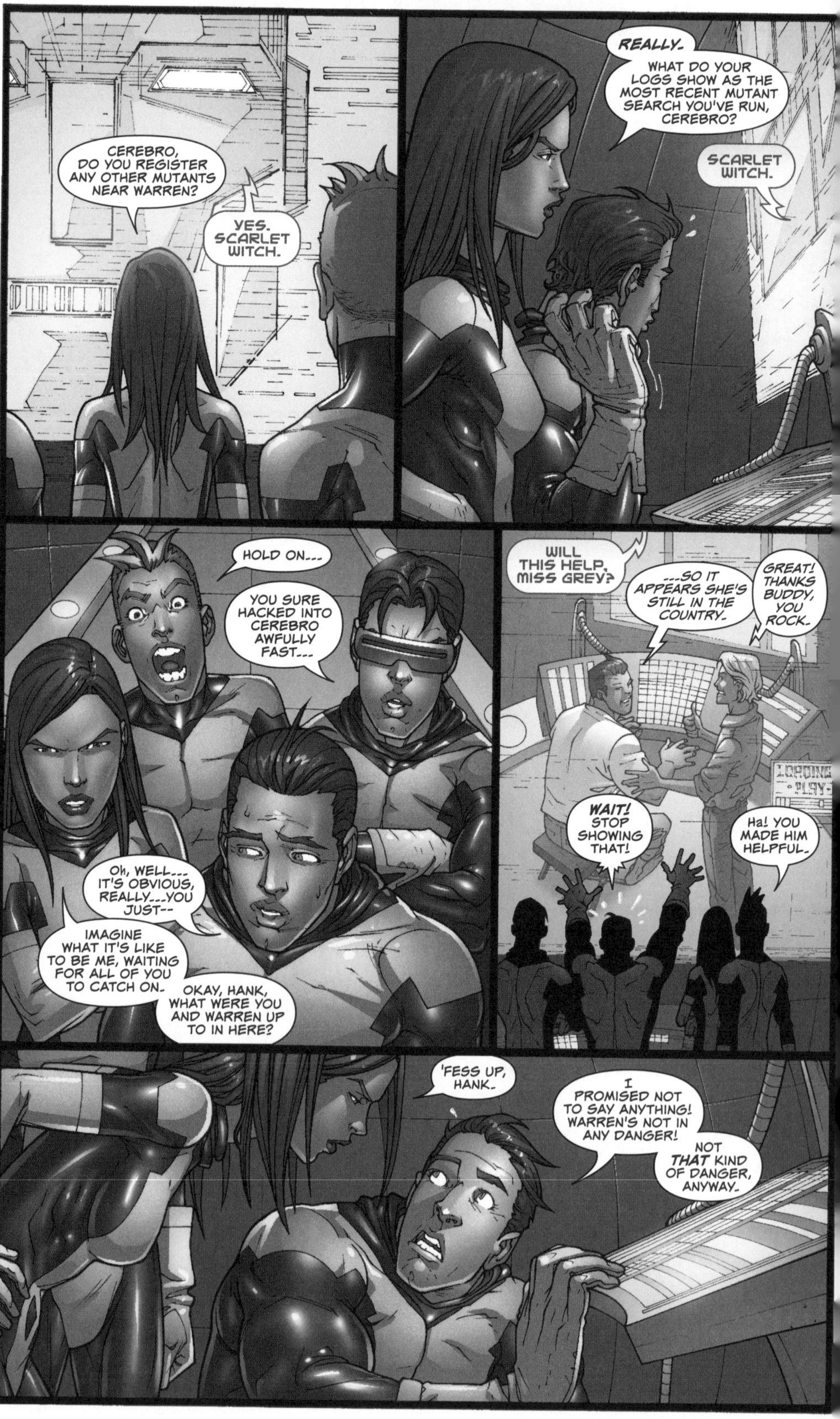
CEREBRO, DO YOU REGISTER ANY OTHER MUTANTS NEAR WARREN?
YES. SCARLET WITCH.
REALLY.
WHAT DO YOUR LOGS SHOW AS THE MOST RECENT MUTANT SEARCH YOU'VE RUN, CEREBRO?
SCARLET WITCH.
HOLD ON...
YOU SURE HACKED INTO CEREBRO AWFULLY FAST...
Oh, WELL... IT'S OBVIOUS, REALLY...YOU JUST--
IMAGINE WHAT IT'S LIKE TO BE ME, WAITING FOR ALL OF YOU TO CATCH ON.
OKAY, HANK, WHAT WERE YOU AND WARREN UP TO IN HERE?
WILL THIS HELP, MISS GREY?
...SO IT APPEARS SHE'S STILL IN THE COUNTRY.
GREAT! THANKS BUDDY, YOU ROCK.
WAIT! STOP SHOWING THAT!
Ha! YOU MADE HIM HELPFUL.
'FESS UP, HANK.
I PROMISED NOT TO SAY ANYTHING! WARREN'S NOT IN ANY DANGER!
NOT THAT KIND OF DANGER, ANYWAY.

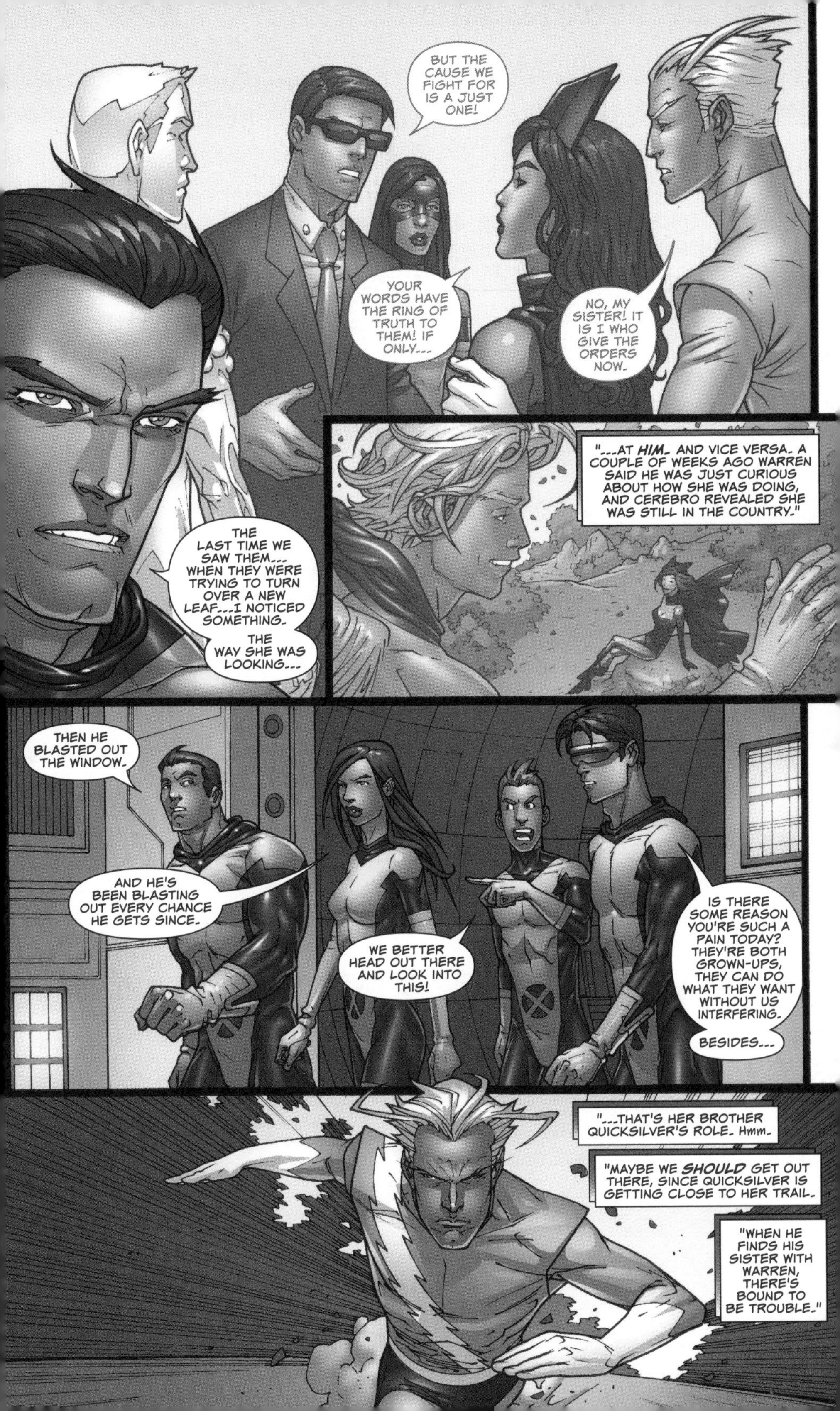
BUT THE CAUSE WE FIGHT FOR IS A JUST ONE!
YOUR WORDS HAVE THE RING OF TRUTH TO THEM! IF ONLY...
NO, MY SISTER! IT IS I WHO GIVE THE ORDERS NOW.
THE LAST TIME WE SAW THEM... WHEN THEY WERE TRYING TO TURN OVER A NEW LEAF...I NOTICED SOMETHING.
THE WAY SHE WAS LOOKING...
"...AT HIM. AND VICE VERSA. A COUPLE OF WEEKS AGO WARREN SAID HE WAS JUST CURIOUS ABOUT HOW SHE WAS DOING, AND CEREBRO REVEALED SHE WAS STILL IN THE COUNTRY."
THEN HE BLASTED OUT THE WINDOW.
AND HE'S BEEN BLASTING OUT EVERY CHANCE HE GETS SINCE.
WE BETTER HEAD OUT THERE AND LOOK INTO THIS!
IS THERE SOME REASON YOU'RE SUCH A PAIN TODAY? THEY'RE BOTH GROWN-UPS, THEY CAN DO WHAT THEY WANT WITHOUT US INTERFERING.
BESIDES...
"...THAT'S HER BROTHER QUICKSILVER'S ROLE. Hmm.
"MAYBE WE SHOULD GET OUT THERE, SINCE QUICKSILVER IS GETTING CLOSE TO HER TRAIL.
"WHEN HE FINDS HIS SISTER WITH WARREN, THERE'S BOUND TO BE TROUBLE."

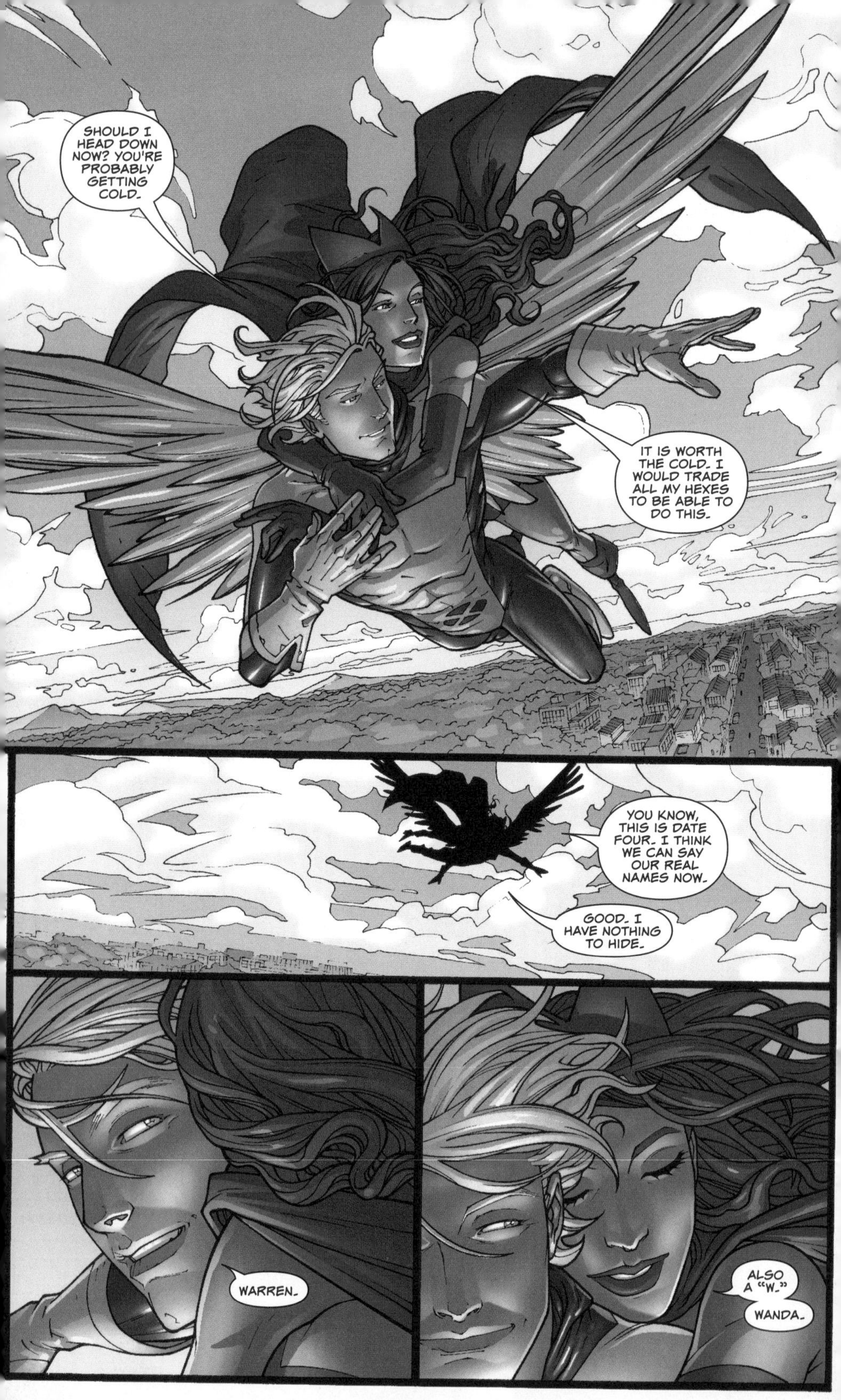
SHOULD I HEAD DOWN NOW? YOU'RE PROBABLY GETTING COLD.
IT IS WORTH THE COLD. I WOULD TRADE ALL MY HEXES TO BE ABLE TO DO THIS.
YOU KNOW, THIS IS DATE FOUR. I THINK WE CAN SAY OUR REAL NAMES NOW.
GOOD. I HAVE NOTHING TO HIDE.
WARREN.
ALSO A "W."
WANDA.

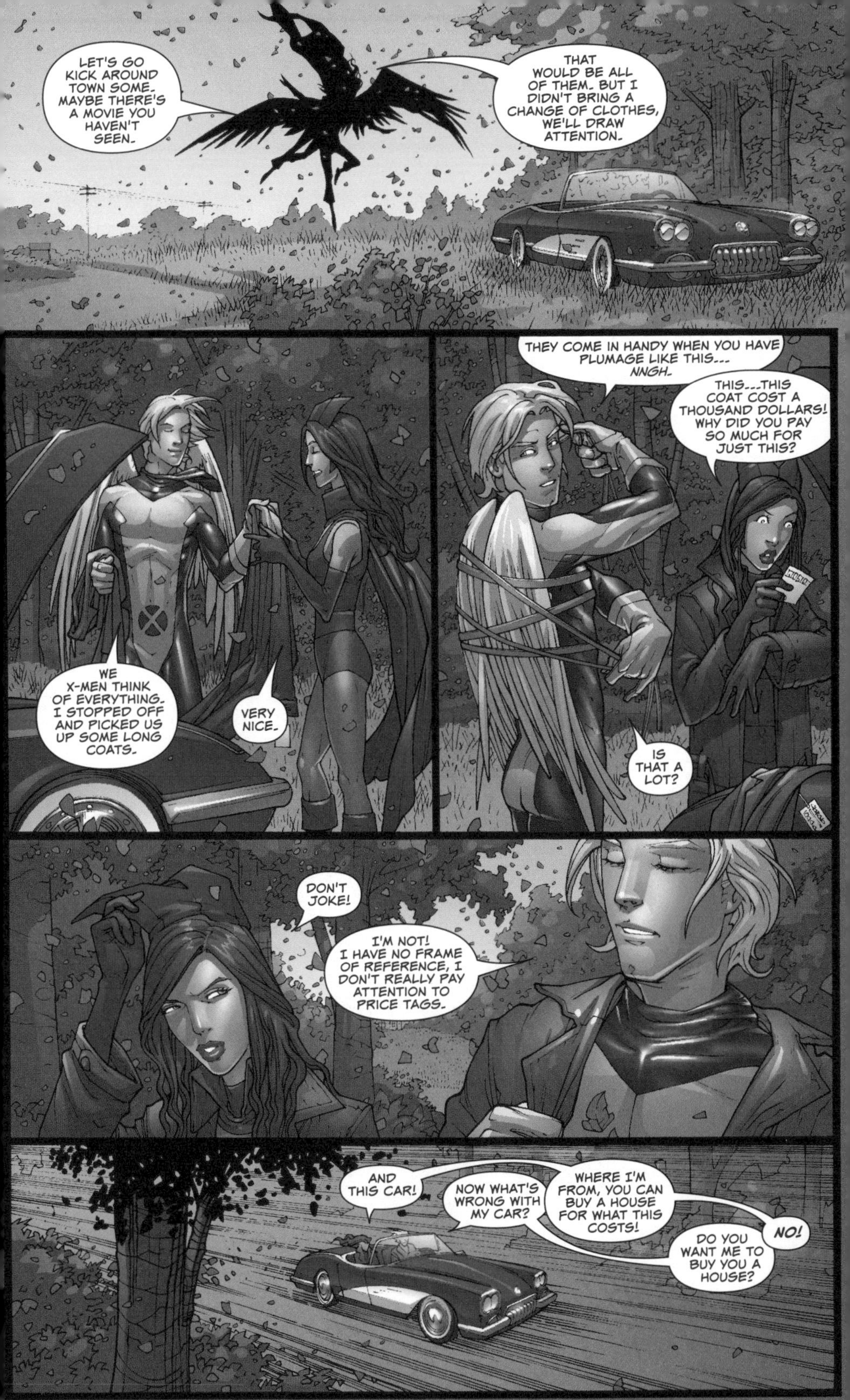
LET'S GO KICK AROUND TOWN SOME. MAYBE THERE'S A MOVIE YOU HAVEN'T SEEN.
THAT WOULD BE ALL OF THEM. BUT I DIDN'T BRING A CHANGE OF CLOTHES, WE'LL DRAW ATTENTION.
WE X-MEN THINK OF EVERYTHING. I STOPPED OFF AND PICKED US UP SOME LONG COATS.
VERY NICE.
THEY COME IN HANDY WHEN YOU HAVE PLUMAGE LIKE THIS... NNGH.
THIS...THIS COAT COST A THOUSAND DOLLARS! WHY DID YOU PAY SO MUCH FOR JUST THIS?
IS THAT A LOT?
DON'T JOKE!
I'M NOT! I HAVE NO FRAME OF REFERENCE, I DON'T REALLY PAY ATTENTION TO PRICE TAGS.
AND THIS CAR!
NOW WHAT'S WRONG WITH MY CAR?
WHERE I'M FROM, YOU CAN BUY A HOUSE FOR WHAT THIS COSTS!
DO YOU WANT ME TO BUY YOU A HOUSE?
NO!

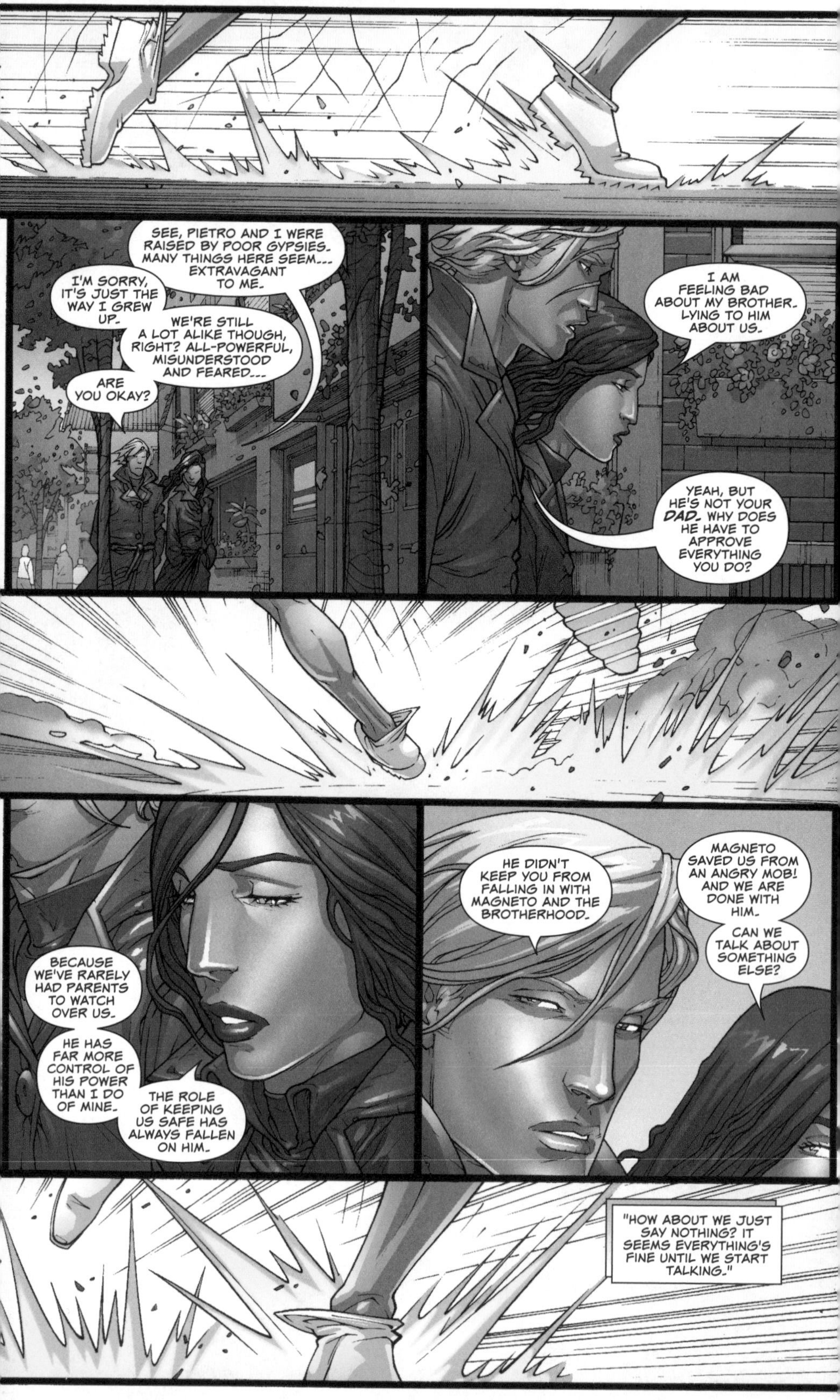
SEE, PIETRO AND I WERE RAISED BY POOR GYPSIES. MANY THINGS HERE SEEM... EXTRAVAGANT TO ME.
I'M SORRY, IT'S JUST THE WAY I GREW UP.
WE'RE STILL A LOT ALIKE THOUGH, RIGHT? ALL-POWERFUL, MISUNDERSTOOD AND FEARED...
ARE YOU OKAY?
I AM FEELING BAD ABOUT MY BROTHER. LYING TO HIM ABOUT US.
YEAH, BUT HE'S NOT YOUR DAD. WHY DOES HE HAVE TO APPROVE EVERYTHING YOU DO?
BECAUSE WE'VE RARELY HAD PARENTS TO WATCH OVER US.
HE HAS FAR MORE CONTROL OF HIS POWER THAN I DO OF MINE.
THE ROLE OF KEEPING US SAFE HAS ALWAYS FALLEN ON HIM.
HE DIDN'T KEEP YOU FROM FALLING IN WITH MAGNETO AND THE BROTHERHOOD.
MAGNETO SAVED US FROM AN ANGRY MOB! AND WE ARE DONE WITH HIM.
CAN WE TALK ABOUT SOMETHING ELSE?
"HOW ABOUT WE JUST SAY NOTHING? IT SEEMS EVERYTHING'S FINE UNTIL WE START TALKING."

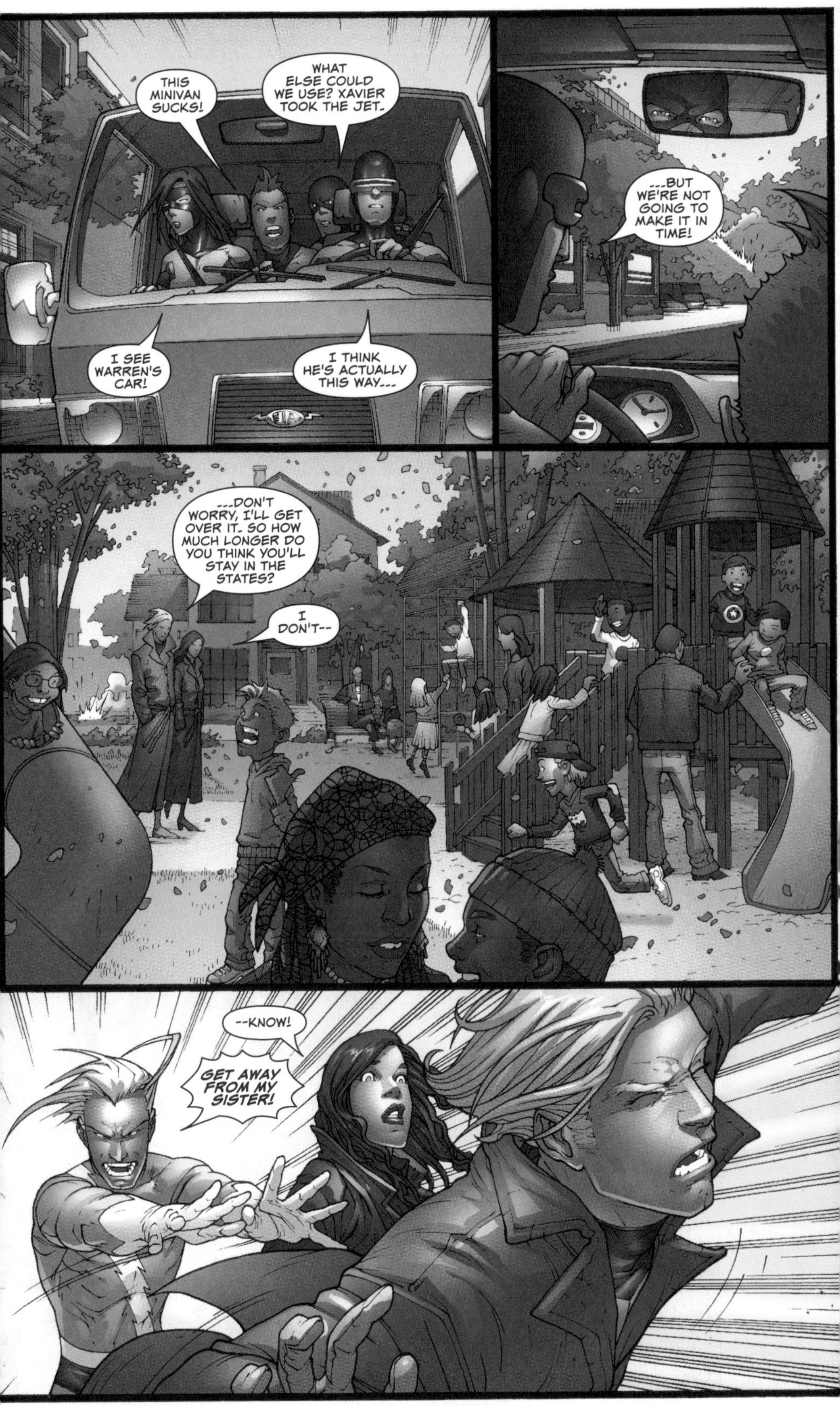
THIS MINIVAN SUCKS!
WHAT ELSE COULD WE USE? XAVIER TOOK THE JET.
I SEE WARREN'S CAR!
I THINK HE'S ACTUALLY THIS WAY...
...BUT WE'RE NOT GOING TO MAKE IT IN TIME!
...DON'T WORRY, I'LL GET OVER IT. SO HOW MUCH LONGER DO YOU THINK YOU'LL STAY IN THE STATES?
I DON'T--
--KNOW!
GET AWAY FROM MY SISTER!

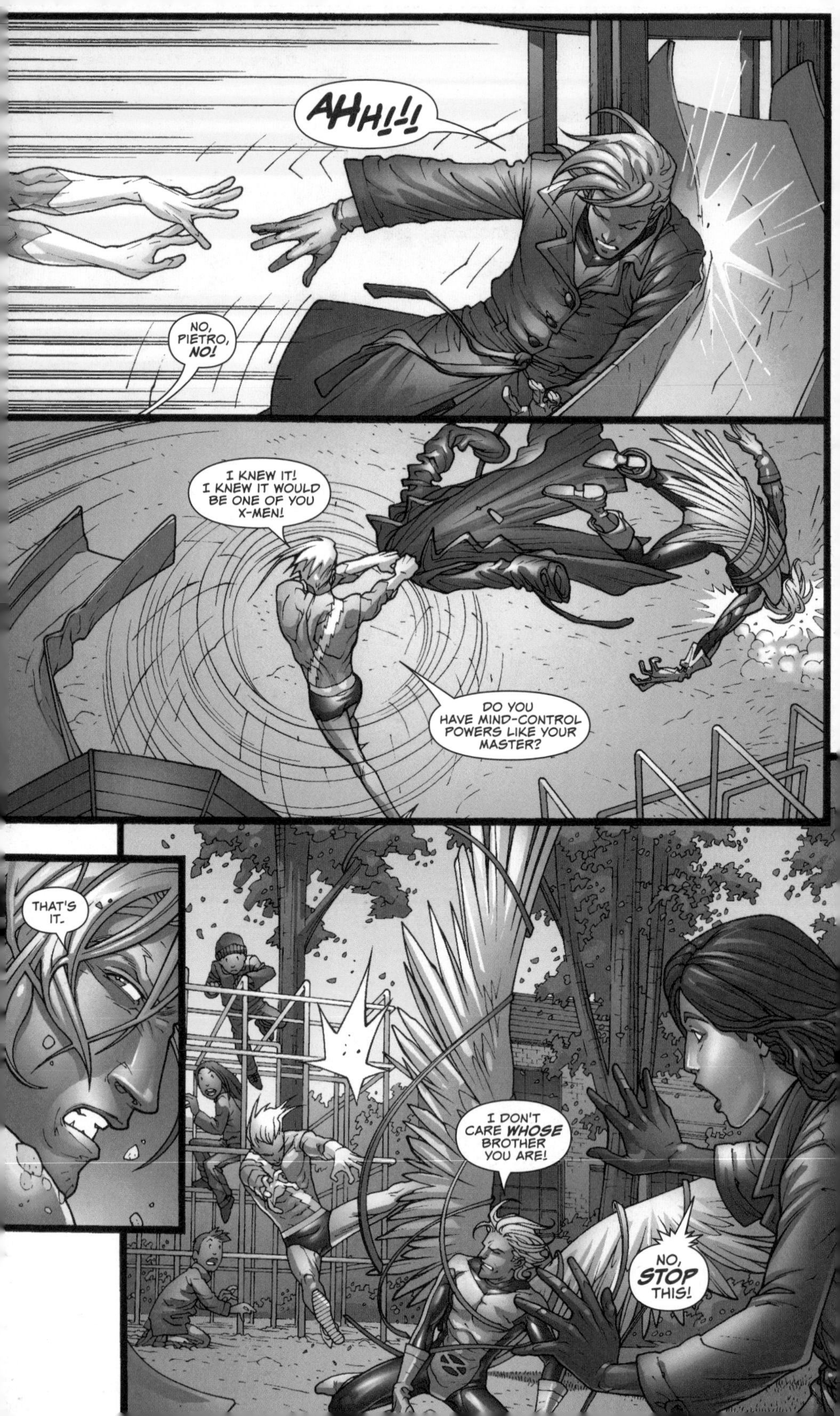
AHH!-!!
NO, PIETRO, NO!
I KNEW IT! I KNEW IT WOULD BE ONE OF YOU X-MEN!
DO YOU HAVE MIND-CONTROL POWERS LIKE YOUR MASTER?
THAT'S IT.
I DON'T CARE WHOSE BROTHER YOU ARE!
NO, STOP THIS!

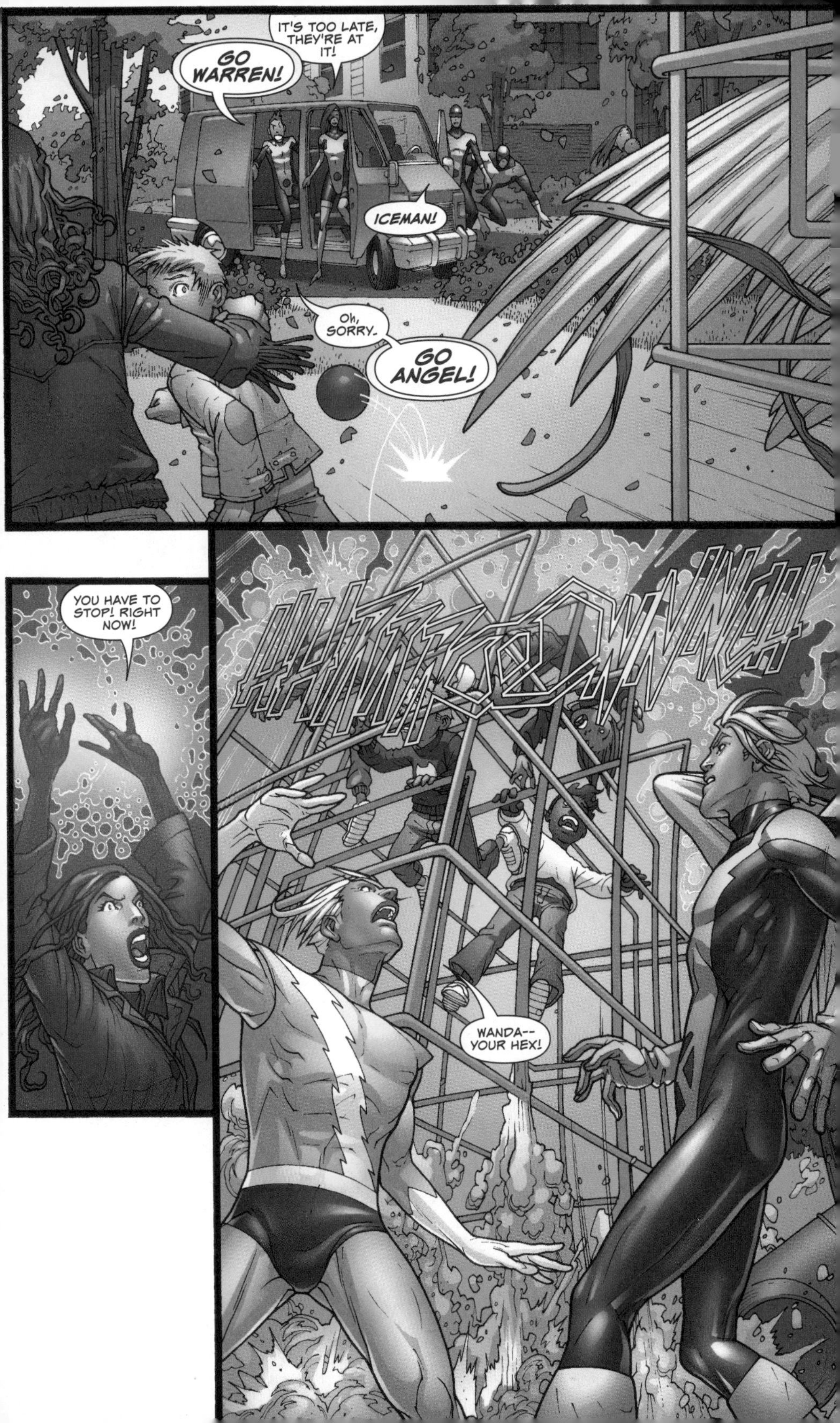
GO WARREN!
IT'S TOO LATE, THEY'RE AT IT!
ICEMAN!
Oh, SORRY-
GO ANGEL!
YOU HAVE TO STOP! RIGHT NOW!
WANDA-- YOUR HEX!

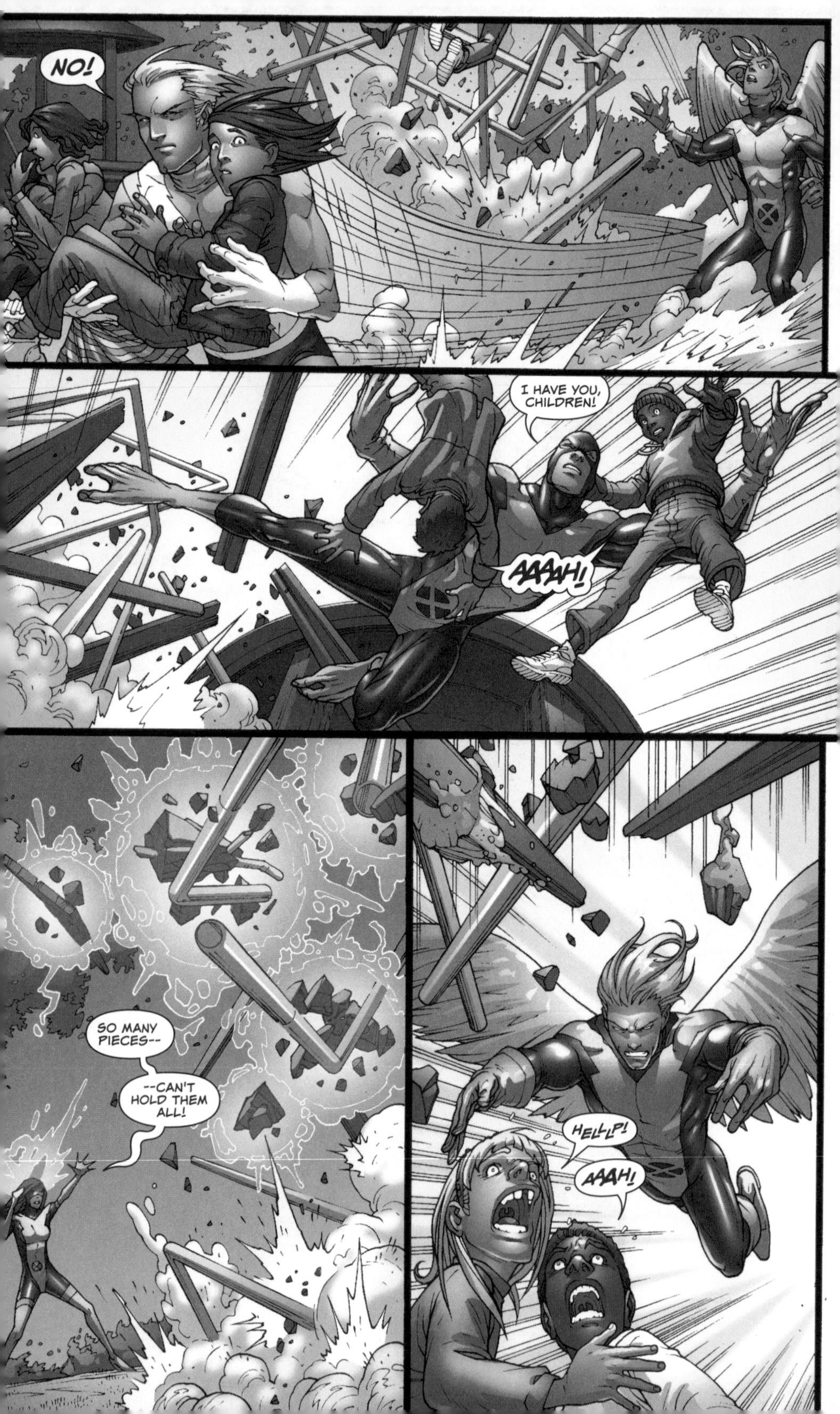
NO!
I HAVE YOU, CHILDREN!
AAAAH!
SO MANY PIECES--
--CAN'T HOLD THEM ALL!
HELLLP!
AAAH!

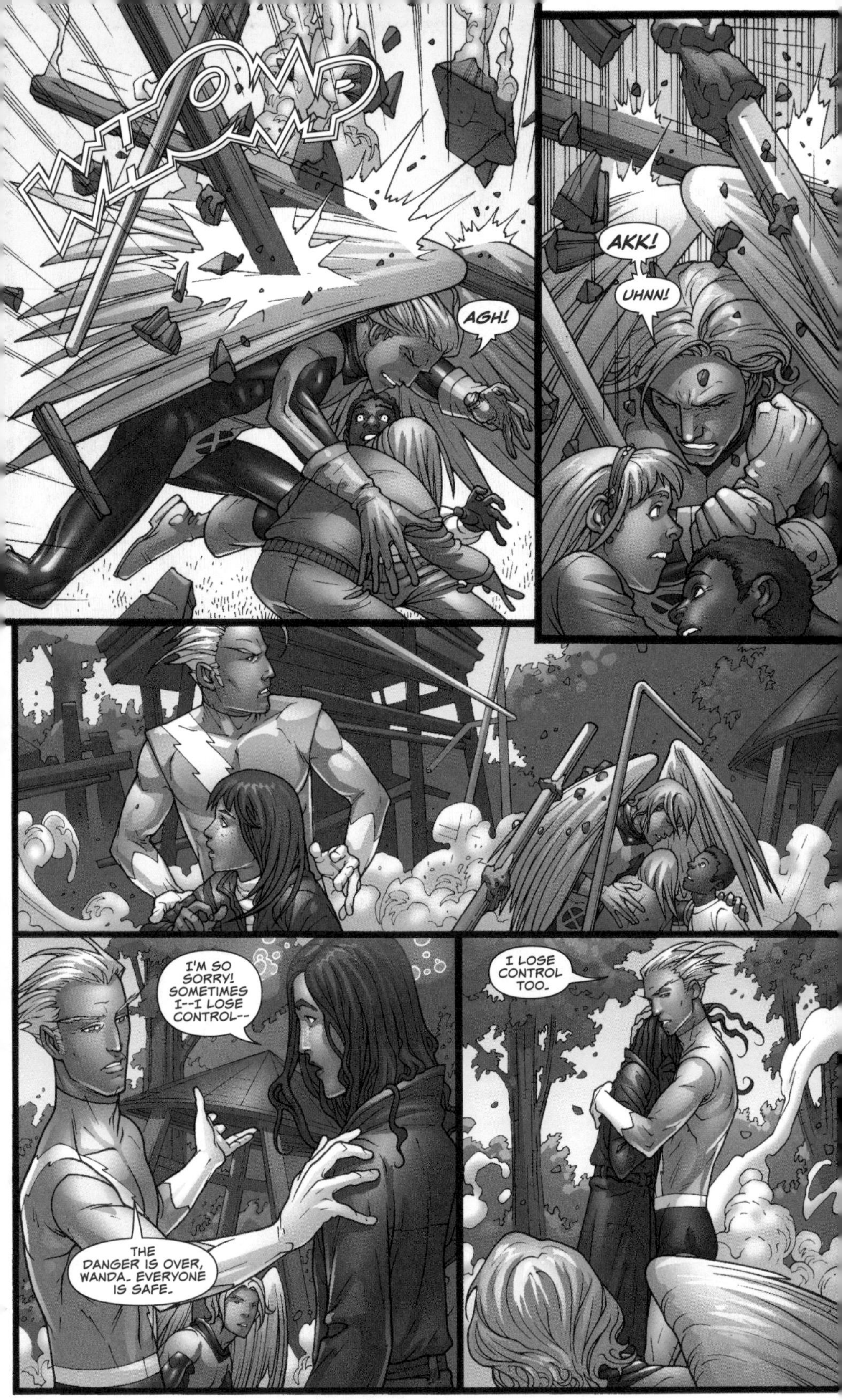
WHOOMP
AGH!
AKK!
UHNN!
I'M SO SORRY! SOMETIMES I--I LOSE CONTROL--
THE DANGER IS OVER, WANDA. EVERYONE IS SAFE.
I LOSE CONTROL TOO.

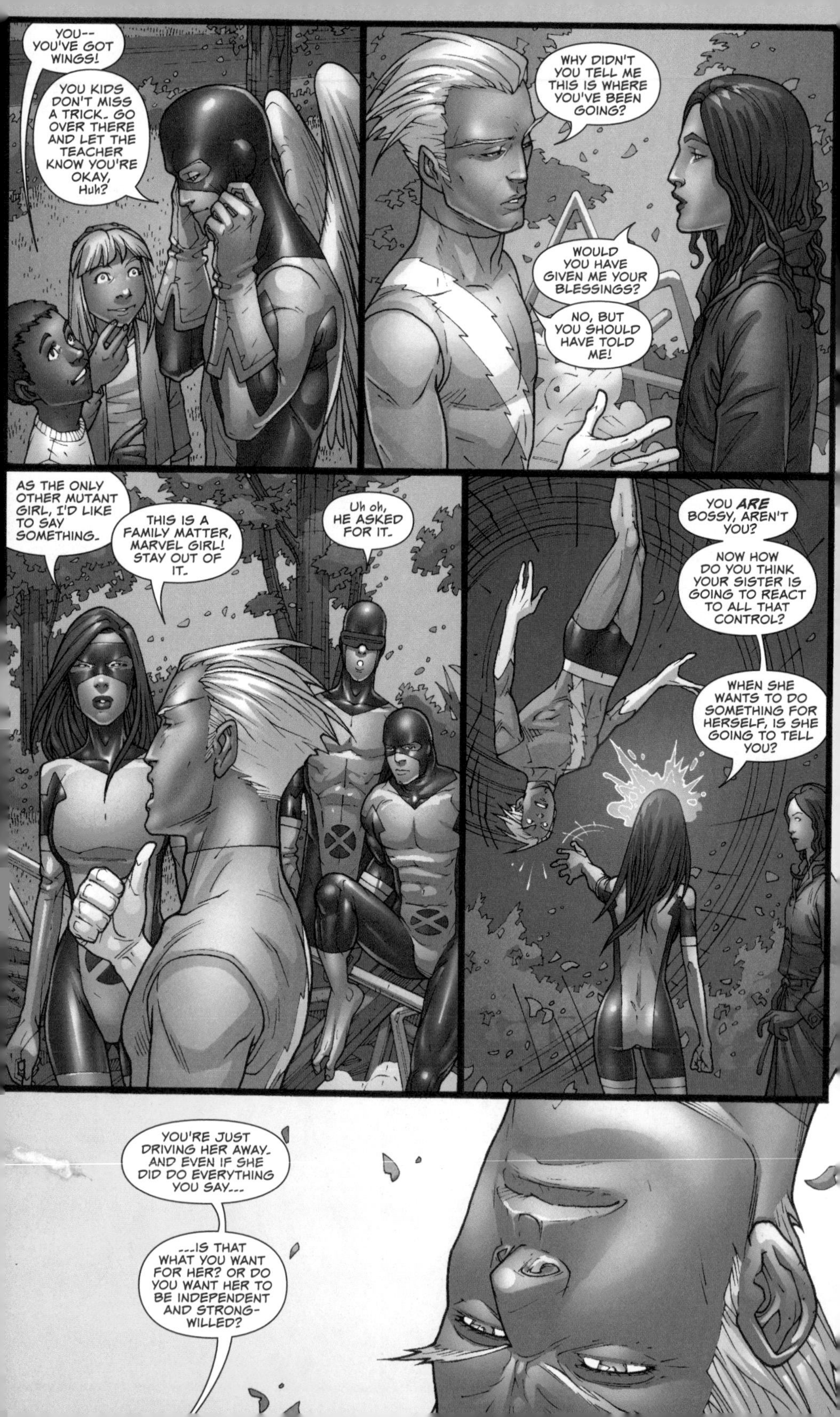
YOU-- YOU'VE GOT WINGS!
YOU KIDS DON'T MISS A TRICK. GO OVER THERE AND LET THE TEACHER KNOW YOU'RE OKAY, Huh?
WHY DIDN'T YOU TELL ME THIS IS WHERE YOU'VE BEEN GOING?
WOULD YOU HAVE GIVEN ME YOUR BLESSINGS?
NO, BUT YOU SHOULD HAVE TOLD ME!
AS THE ONLY OTHER MUTANT GIRL, I'D LIKE TO SAY SOMETHING.
THIS IS A FAMILY MATTER, MARVEL GIRL! STAY OUT OF IT.
Uh oh, HE ASKED FOR IT.
YOU ARE BOSSY, AREN'T YOU?
NOW HOW DO YOU THINK YOUR SISTER IS GOING TO REACT TO ALL THAT CONTROL?
WHEN SHE WANTS TO DO SOMETHING FOR HERSELF, IS SHE GOING TO TELL YOU?
YOU'RE JUST DRIVING HER AWAY. AND EVEN IF SHE DID DO EVERYTHING YOU SAY...
...IS THAT WHAT YOU WANT FOR HER? OR DO YOU WANT HER TO BE INDEPENDENT AND STRONG-WILLED?

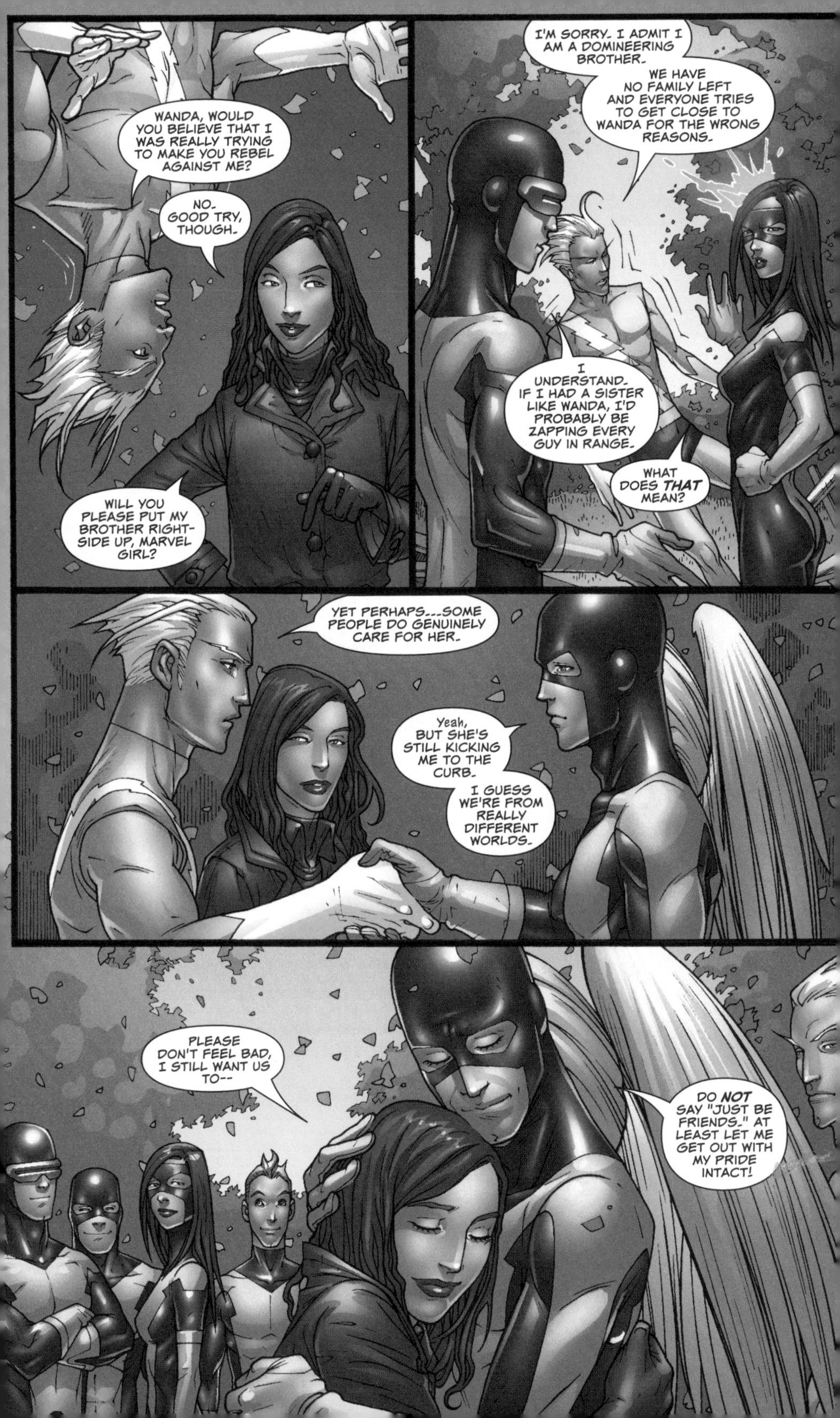
WANDA, WOULD YOU BELIEVE THAT I WAS REALLY TRYING TO MAKE YOU REBEL AGAINST ME?
NO. GOOD TRY, THOUGH.
WILL YOU PLEASE PUT MY BROTHER RIGHT-SIDE UP, MARVEL GIRL?
I'M SORRY. I ADMIT I AM A DOMINEERING BROTHER.
WE HAVE NO FAMILY LEFT AND EVERYONE TRIES TO GET CLOSE TO WANDA FOR THE WRONG REASONS.
I UNDERSTAND. IF I HAD A SISTER LIKE WANDA, I'D PROBABLY BE ZAPPING EVERY GUY IN RANGE.
WHAT DOES **THAT** MEAN?
YET PERHAPS...SOME PEOPLE DO GENUINELY CARE FOR HER.
Yeah, BUT SHE'S STILL KICKING ME TO THE CURB.
I GUESS WE'RE FROM REALLY DIFFERENT WORLDS.
PLEASE DON'T FEEL BAD, I STILL WANT US TO--
DO **NOT** SAY "JUST BE FRIENDS." AT LEAST LET ME GET OUT WITH MY PRIDE INTACT!

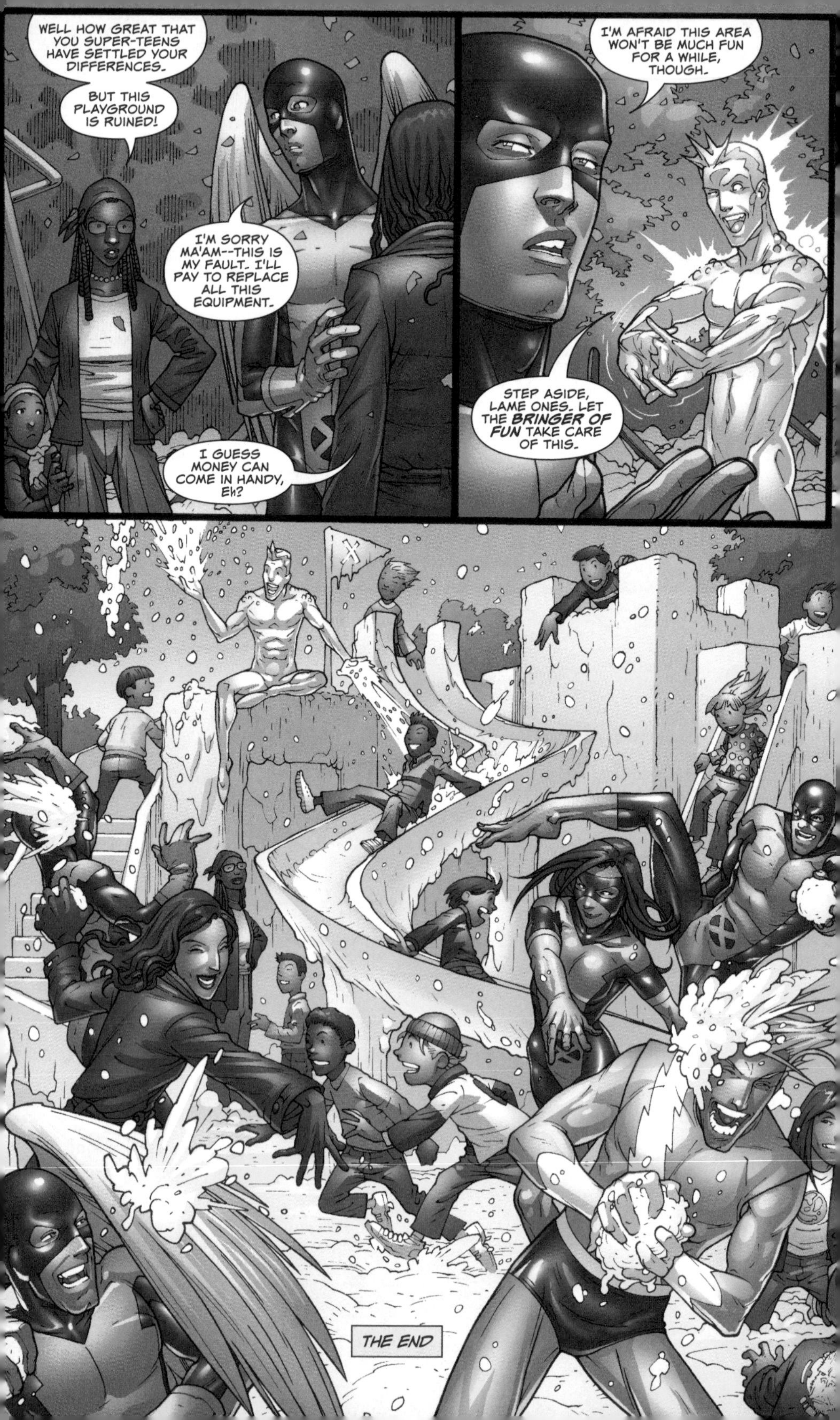
WELL HOW GREAT THAT YOU SUPER-TEENS HAVE SETTLED YOUR DIFFERENCES.
BUT THIS PLAYGROUND IS RUINED!
I'M SORRY MA'AM--THIS IS MY FAULT. I'LL PAY TO REPLACE ALL THIS EQUIPMENT.
I GUESS MONEY CAN COME IN HANDY, Eh?
I'M AFRAID THIS AREA WON'T BE MUCH FUN FOR A WHILE, THOUGH.
STEP ASIDE, LAME ONES. LET THE *BRINGER OF FUN* TAKE CARE OF THIS.
THE END

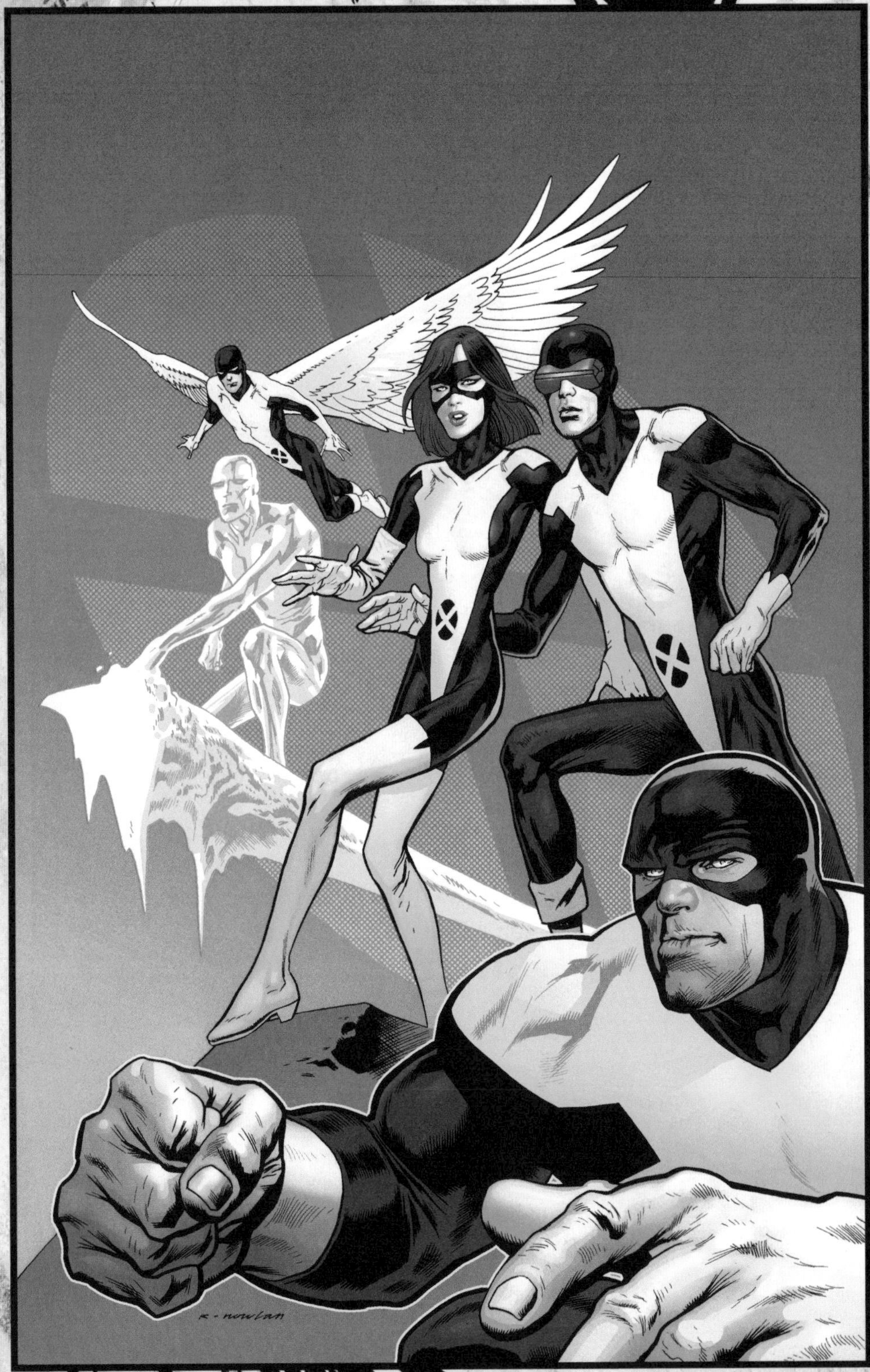
K. Nowlan

X-Men: First Class Special (2007)

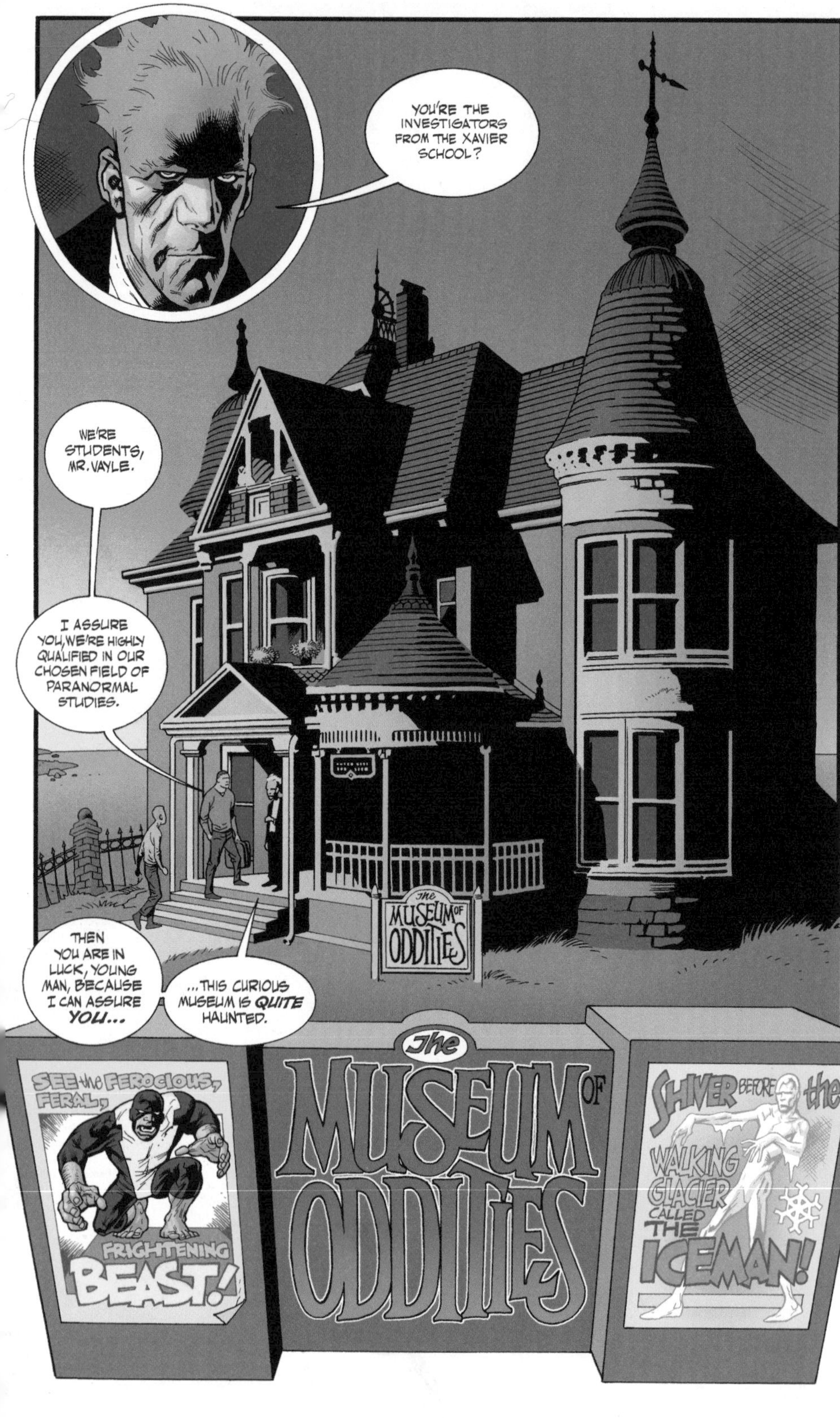
YOU'RE THE INVESTIGATORS FROM THE XAVIER SCHOOL?
WE'RE STUDENTS, MR. VAYLE.
I ASSURE YOU, WE'RE HIGHLY QUALIFIED IN OUR CHOSEN FIELD OF PARANORMAL STUDIES.
THEN YOU ARE IN LUCK, YOUNG MAN, BECAUSE I CAN ASSURE *YOU*...
...THIS CURIOUS MUSEUM IS *QUITE* HAUNTED.
The MUSEUM OF ODDITIES
SEE the FEROCIOUS, FERAL, FRIGHTENING BEAST!
The MUSEUM OF ODDITIES
SHIVER BEFORE the WALKING GLACIER CALLED THE ICEMAN!

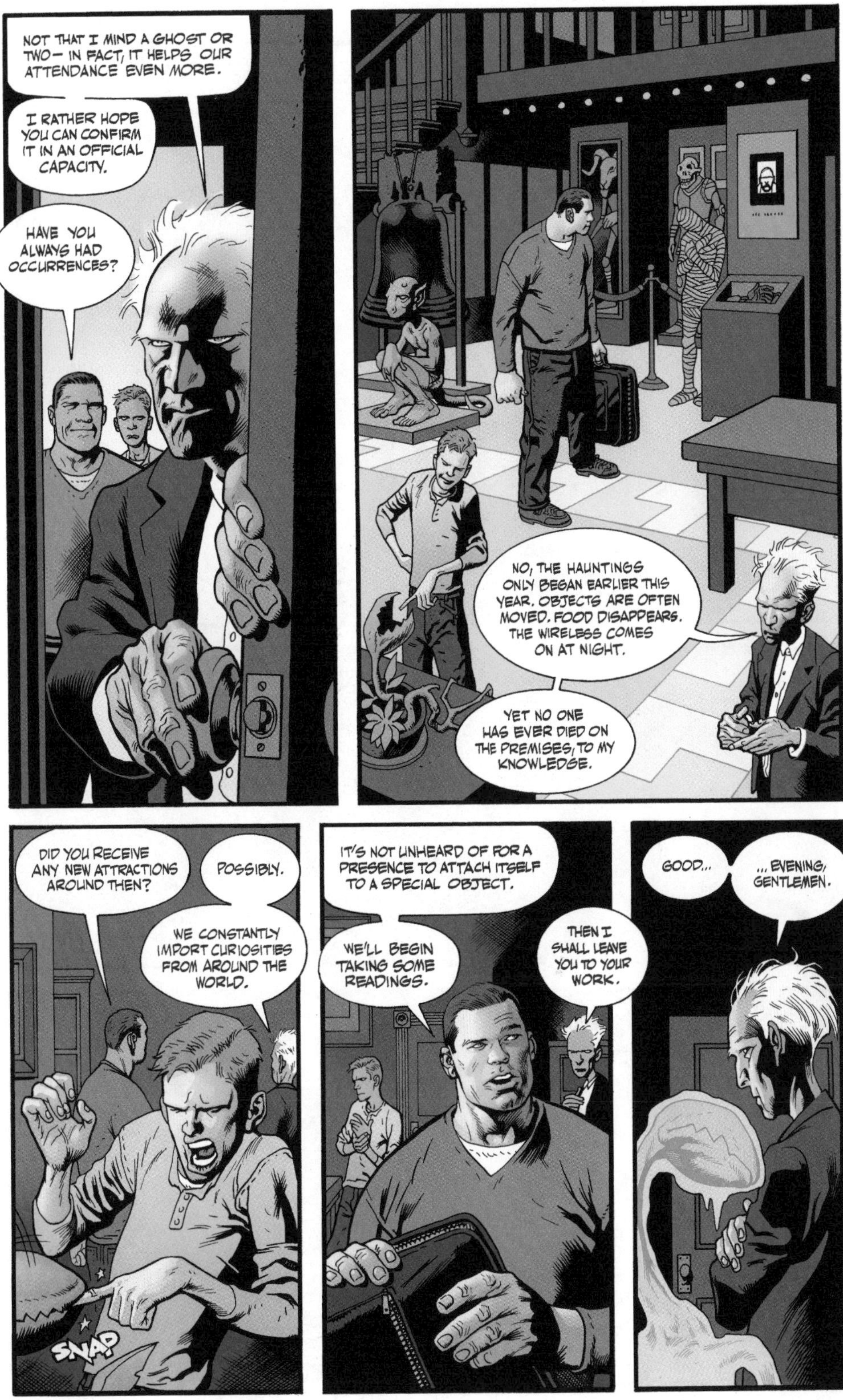
NOT THAT I MIND A GHOST OR TWO— IN FACT, IT HELPS OUR ATTENDANCE EVEN MORE.
I RATHER HOPE YOU CAN CONFIRM IT IN AN OFFICIAL CAPACITY.
HAVE YOU ALWAYS HAD OCCURRENCES?
NO, THE HAUNTINGS ONLY BEGAN EARLIER THIS YEAR. OBJECTS ARE OFTEN MOVED. FOOD DISAPPEARS. THE WIRELESS COMES ON AT NIGHT.
YET NO ONE HAS EVER DIED ON THE PREMISES, TO MY KNOWLEDGE.
DID YOU RECEIVE ANY NEW ATTRACTIONS AROUND THEN?
POSSIBLY.
WE CONSTANTLY IMPORT CURIOSITIES FROM AROUND THE WORLD.
SNAP
IT'S NOT UNHEARD OF FOR A PRESENCE TO ATTACH ITSELF TO A SPECIAL OBJECT.
WE'LL BEGIN TAKING SOME READINGS.
THEN I SHALL LEAVE YOU TO YOUR WORK.
GOOD...
...EVENING, GENTLEMEN.

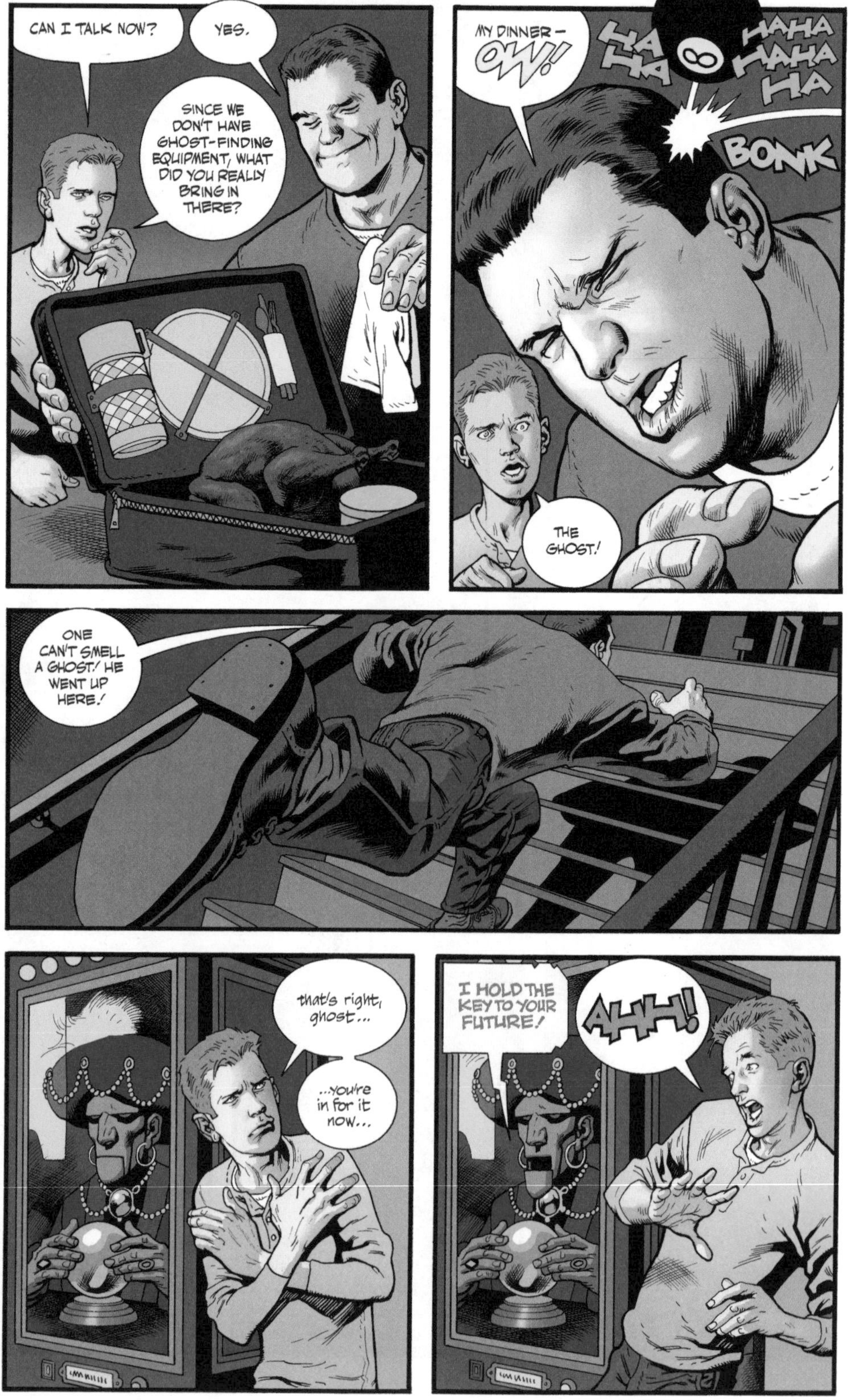
CAN I TALK NOW?
YES.
SINCE WE DON'T HAVE GHOST-FINDING EQUIPMENT, WHAT DID YOU REALLY BRING IN THERE?
MY DINNER— OW!
HA HA
HAHA HAHA HA
BONK
THE GHOST!
ONE CAN'T SMELL A GHOST! HE WENT UP HERE!
that's right, ghost...
...you're in for it now...
I HOLD THE KEY TO YOUR FUTURE!
AHH!

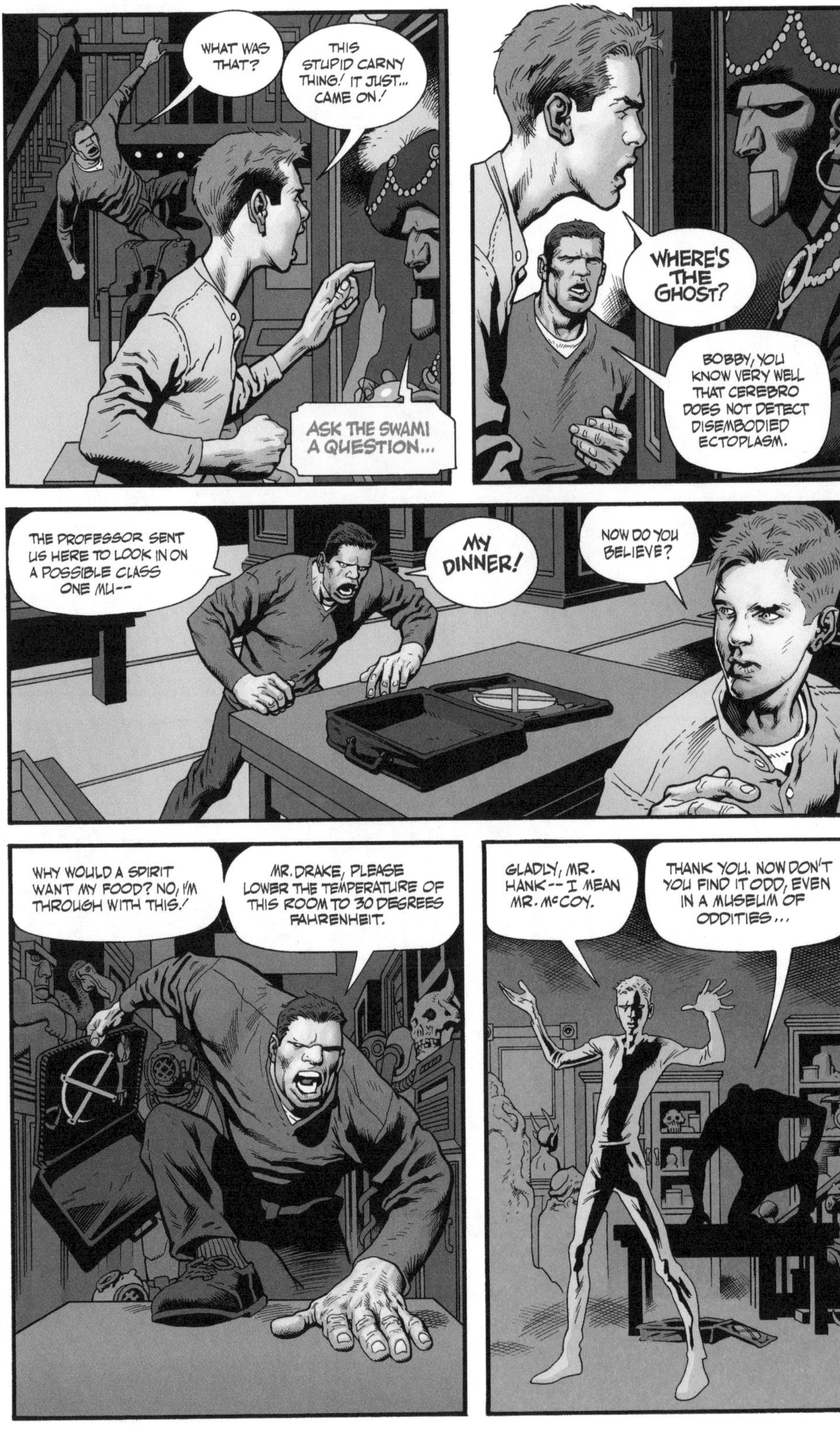
WHAT WAS THAT?
THIS STUPID CARNY THING! IT JUST... CAME ON!
ASK THE SWAMI A QUESTION...
WHERE'S THE GHOST?
BOBBY, YOU KNOW VERY WELL THAT CEREBRO DOES NOT DETECT DISEMBODIED ECTOPLASM.
THE PROFESSOR SENT US HERE TO LOOK IN ON A POSSIBLE CLASS ONE MU--
MY DINNER!
NOW DO YOU BELIEVE?
WHY WOULD A SPIRIT WANT MY FOOD? NO, I'M THROUGH WITH THIS!
MR. DRAKE, PLEASE LOWER THE TEMPERATURE OF THIS ROOM TO 30 DEGREES FAHRENHEIT.
GLADLY, MR. HANK-- I MEAN MR. McCOY.
THANK YOU. NOW DON'T YOU FIND IT ODD, EVEN IN A MUSEUM OF ODDITIES...

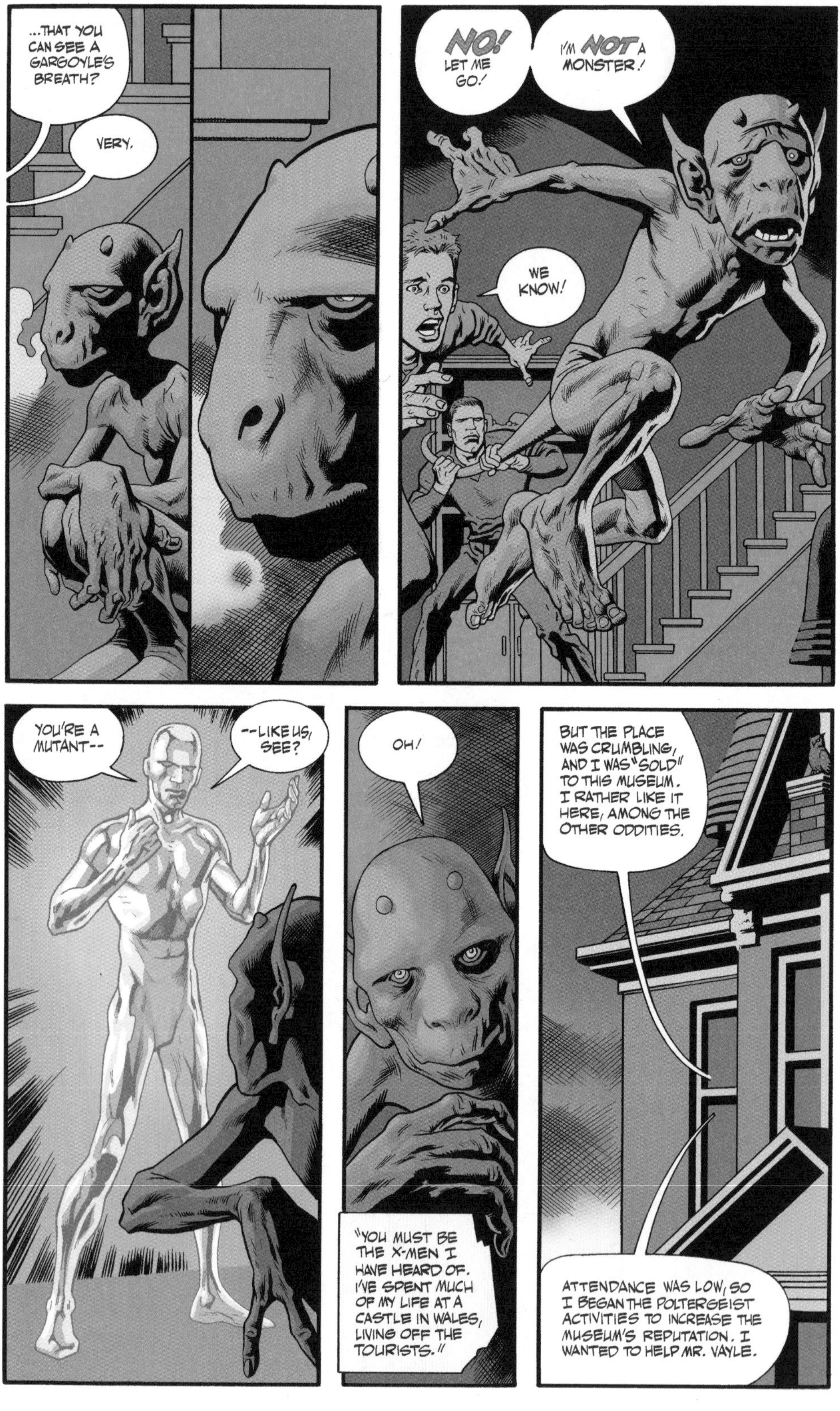
...THAT YOU CAN SEE A GARGOYLE'S BREATH?
VERY.
NO! LET ME GO!
I'M NOT A MONSTER!
WE KNOW!
YOU'RE A MUTANT--
--LIKE US, SEE?
OH!
"YOU MUST BE THE X-MEN I HAVE HEARD OF. I'VE SPENT MUCH OF MY LIFE AT A CASTLE IN WALES, LIVING OFF THE TOURISTS."
BUT THE PLACE WAS CRUMBLING, AND I WAS "SOLD" TO THIS MUSEUM. I RATHER LIKE IT HERE, AMONG THE OTHER ODDITIES.
ATTENDANCE WAS LOW, SO I BEGAN THE POLTERGEIST ACTIVITIES TO INCREASE THE MUSEUM'S REPUTATION. I WANTED TO HELP MR. VAYLE.

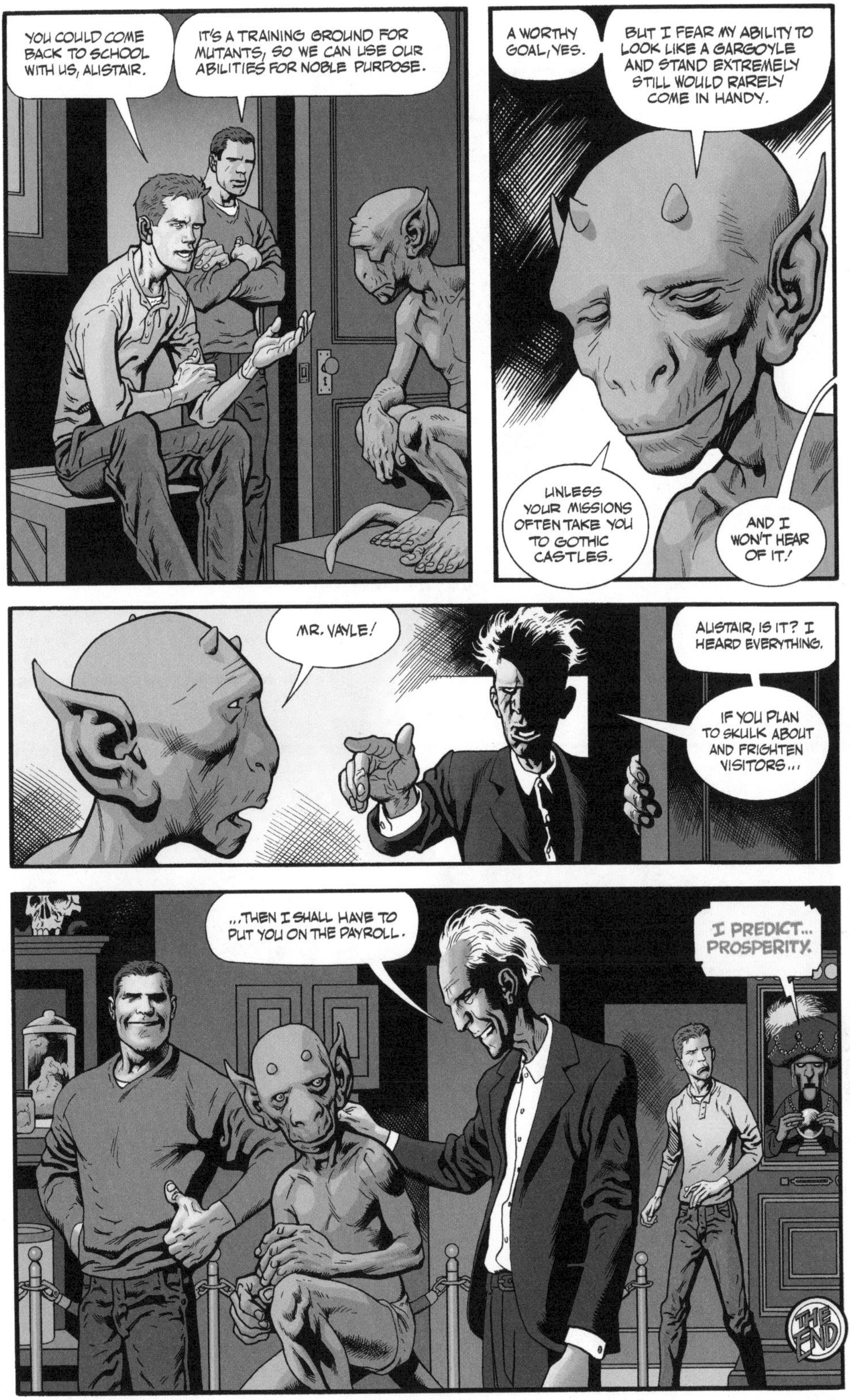
YOU COULD COME BACK TO SCHOOL WITH US, ALISTAIR.
IT'S A TRAINING GROUND FOR MUTANTS, SO WE CAN USE OUR ABILITIES FOR NOBLE PURPOSE.
A WORTHY GOAL, YES.
BUT I FEAR MY ABILITY TO LOOK LIKE A GARGOYLE AND STAND EXTREMELY STILL WOULD RARELY COME IN HANDY.
UNLESS YOUR MISSIONS OFTEN TAKE YOU TO GOTHIC CASTLES.
AND I WON'T HEAR OF IT!
MR. VAYLE!
ALISTAIR, IS IT? I HEARD EVERYTHING.
IF YOU PLAN TO SKULK ABOUT AND FRIGHTEN VISITORS...
...THEN I SHALL HAVE TO PUT YOU ON THE PAYROLL.
I PREDICT... PROSPERITY.
THE END

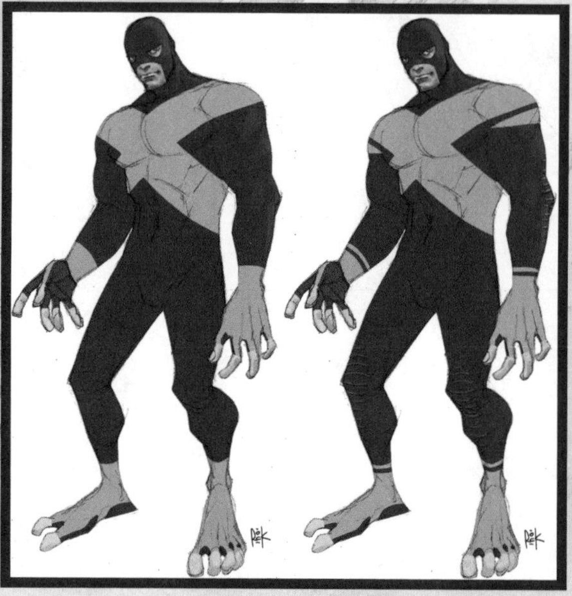

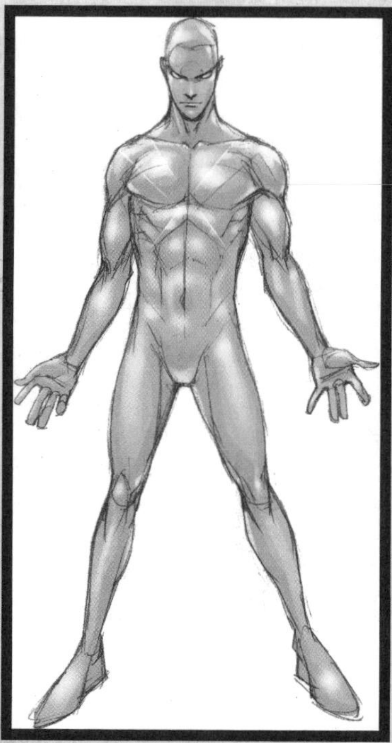

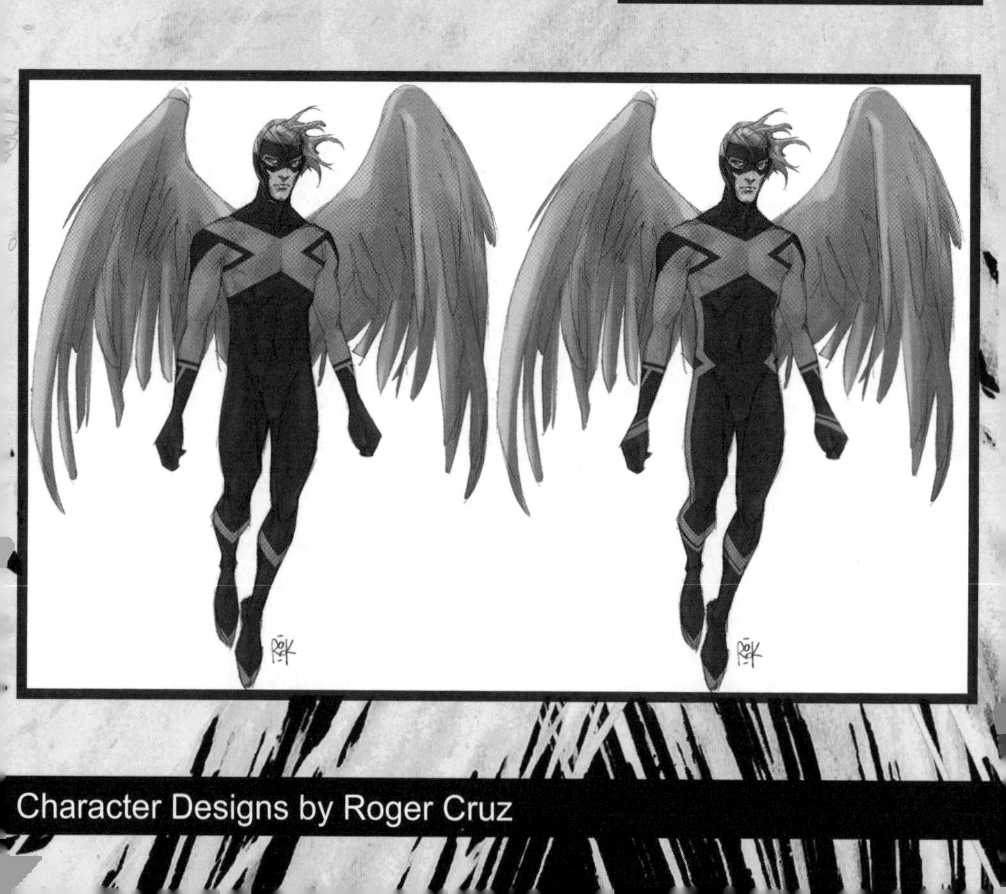

Character Designs by Roger Cruz